# Animals in Person

## Cultural Perspectives on Human–Animal Intimacy

**Edited by**
**John Knight**

*Oxford • New York*

English edition
First published in 2005 by
**Berg**
Editorial offices:
First Floor, Angel Court, 81 St Clements Street, Oxford OX4 1AW, UK
175 Fifth Avenue, New York, NY 10010, USA

Berg is the imprint of Oxford International Publishers Ltd.


**Library of Congress Cataloging-in-Publication Data**
Animals in person : cultural perspectives on animal-human intimacy / edited by
John Knight.— English ed.
　　p. cm.
"Began as a workshop ... which took place at the European Association of
Social Anthropology (EASA) conference held in Krakow, Poland on 27 July
2000"—Pref.
　Includes bibliographical references and index.
　ISBN 1-85973-733-1 (pbk.) — ISBN 1-85973-728-5 (cloth)
　1. Human-animal relationships—Congresses. I. Knight, John, 1960-
　QL85.A562 2005
　590—dc22                                                                2005009761

**British Library Cataloguing-in-Publication Data**
A catalogue record for this book is available from the British Library.


ISBN-13 978 1 85973 728 6 (Cloth)
　　　978 1 85973 733 0 (Paper)

ISBN-10 1 85973 728 5 (Cloth)
　　　1 85973 733 1 (Paper)


Typeset by Avocet Typeset, Chilton, Aylesbury, Bucks
Printed in the United Kingdom by Biddles Ltd, King's Lynn.

**www.bergpublishers.com**

# Contents

# Illustrations

## Figures

## Tables

# Contributors

**Ben Campbell** is a Research Associate at the Department of Social Anthropology, University of Manchester.

**Peter D. Dwyer** is a Research Fellow at the School of Anthropology, Geography and Environmental Studies, The University of Melbourne.

**Birgitta Edelman** is affiliated to the University of Newcastle upon Tyne.

**Michael Emmison** is a Reader in Sociology at the School of Social Science, University of Queensland.

**Candi Forrest** is currently a postgraduate student in the Research School of Pacific and Asian Studies, Australian National University.

**Laurence Goldman** is an adjunct Associate Professor in Anthropology in the School of Social Science, University of Queensland and an anthropological consultant with Oilsearch.

**Lynette A. Hart** is an Associate Professor at the Department of Population Health and Reproduction and is Director of University of California Center for Animal Alternatives, School of Veterinary Medicine, University of California.

**John Knight** is a Lecturer in Social Anthropology at Queen's University Belfast.

**Garry Marvin** is a Reader in Social Anthropology at the School of Business and Social Sciences, Roehampton University.

**Monica Minnegal** is a Senior Lecturer at the School of Anthropology, Geography and Environmental Studies, The University of Melbourne.

**Kay Milton** is a Professor of Social Anthropology at Queen's University Belfast.

**Adrian Peace** is a Reader in Anthropology at the University of Adelaide.

**Véronique Servais** is an Associate Professor in the Department of Arts and Communications Sciences, University of Liège, Belgium.

**Joanna Swabe** is affiliated to the Department of Animals and Society, Faculty of Veterinary Medicine, University of Utrecht.

**Dimitris Theodossopoulos** is a Lecturer in Social Anthropology at the University of Bristol and a senior research fellow at St Peter's College, Oxford.

# Preface

This book began as a workshop entitled 'Are Animals "Good To Love"? Human–Animal Intimacies in Anthropological Perspective', which took place at the European Association of Social Anthropology (EASA) conference held in Kraków, Poland on 27 July 2000. I am grateful to the organizers of this conference for providing the opportunity to hold the workshop, as well as to the many people, in addition to the presenters themselves, who attended and contributed to what turned out to be a lively and stimulating workshop. Finally, I would also like to acknowledge the constructive criticisms and suggestions made by the anonymous readers appointed by the publisher.

JK

# Introduction

## *John Knight*

One of the main anthropological contributions to the field of human–animal relations has been to show that, while are animals are exploited by human societies for
a variety of products and uses, human relations with animals are not simply utilitarian in character but should also be understood in broader symbolic terms. Much
of this work on animal symbolism focuses on animals as symbols of human
society, whereby animals are approached as 'windows' or 'mirrors' that offer the
anthropologist insight into human society or culture (Mullin 1999). These studies
of animal symbols in different cultures have shown that animals inhabit the human
mind or imagination as well as the physical environment, and that human beings
draw on animals to think about themselves. However, these studies are still open
to the objection that they tend to treat animals as passive objects of human activity
rather than as active subjects or agents in their own right. Although anthropology
has effectively countered utilitarian reductionism (reducing animals to their
human-determined uses), arguably it still engages in a symbolic reductionism
(reducing animals to their human-determined meanings).

The point of departure for this book is an interest in animals as *subjects* rather
than *objects*, in animals as *parts* of human society rather than just *symbols* of it, and
in human *interactions and relationships with* animals rather than simply human
*representations of* animals. The contributors to this book recognize the existence of
intimate relations between humans and animals that, in many respects, recall relations among humans themselves. Intimacy is understood as a two-way relationship,
implying a degree of affective mutuality, even if this is unequal and asymmetrical.
The studies contained in this book describe a range of affective interactions
between humans and animals in the context of both functional or working relationships and relationships arising in the domain of leisure. The following chapters
contain discussions of livestock animals and pet animals, as well as wild animals.
Case studies are drawn from different parts of the world, including Australia, New
Guinea, Nepal, India, Japan, Greece, Britain and Holland. Overall, the book is
informed by an anthropological perspective which approaches the study of
human–animal relations in terms of their specific social and cultural contexts.

1

## Animals as Persons

According to the dictionary definition, a 'person' is a 'living soul or self-conscious being', and a 'human being (natural person), or a corporation (artificial person) regarded as having rights and duties under the law'. In this sense, personhood is a legally defined status of moral inclusion. Underlying this notion of the person is the contrast between persons and things or objects. Persons are beings that merit moral concern and legal entitlements, whereas objects are things that merit consideration in terms of their status as the property of legal persons. Human beings have not always been recognized as persons in this way. Slaves were people who were legally assimilated to things – humans reduced to the status of property, a kind of human 'livestock'. But just as people are not always persons, so persons are not always people.

Calls have been made for the kind of moral personhood applied in the first instance to other human beings to be extended to animals. A prime example of this is the Great Ape Project launched in the early 1990s, which argues 'for the extension of the basic ideal of equality to include all the great apes' (chimpanzees, gorillas and orang-utans, as well as humans), and aims to bring about 'a reassessment of the moral status of chimpanzees, gorillas and orang-utans' and promote 'the acceptance of some non-human animals as persons' (Cavalieri and Singer 1993: 2). This attribution of moral status of personhood to animals arises from a recognition that great apes have 'mental capacities and an emotional life sufficient to justify inclusion within the community of equals' and is 'based on scientific evidence about the capacities of chimpanzees, gorillas and orang-utans' (Cavalieri *et al.* 1993: 5). In concrete terms, this would entail a radical revision in the law to bring about the recognition of animals as legal subjects. In this fomulation of animal personhood, animals only qualify for moral inclusion to the extent that they possess certain capacities.

But the issue of animal personhood also arises, less formally, in human interactions with animals. This too presumes certain commensurable capacities on the part of the animals concerned. But it also tends to involve another aspect of personhood – the recognition of the individuality and particularity of the animal interactant. This feature of personhood is of course given in the verb 'personalize' or to make personal – in contrast to generality and abstraction. Human beings become persons to the extent that their irreducible individuality is recognized through, among other things, naming, face recognition and biographical awareness. When we get to know another human being in these ways he or she becomes a 'somebody', but to the extent that such individuality is denied or erased human beings become abstractions and even things.[1] That an animal too can become a *somebody* in this way might seem counter-intuitive at first glance, given that animals have long been understood as substitutable items in a common category. Indeed, animals are often represented as the very image of disindividualized collectivity (as when human beings are likened to bees, ants, sheep, rats, and so on) to the extent that they appear as little more than animate stereotypes that can be consigned to abstract categories. However, people who have direct contact with animals are likely to develop a much more differentiated perspective, according to which individual variations become obvious and meaningful. This personalized knowledge of animals is likely to extend the potential for effective communication and interaction with them.

This book's focus on human–animal *intimacy* concerns human interactions with animals that are informed by – as well generative of – this kind of situated knowledge. The ethnographic study of human interactions with animals *in person* provides an opportunity to advance our understanding of animals *as persons*.

## Intimacy with Prey Animals?

Another part of the background to this book is a shared dissatisfaction among contributors to human–animal dualism and a readiness to look beyond it and address the issue of human–animal commonality and continuity. One influential anthropological challenge to human–animal dualism has come from anthropologists studying hunter-gatherers who argue that hunters have a special relationship with their prey, which is characterized by mutuality and interconnection, in stark contrast to the relationship of hierarchy and domination obtaining between humans and domestic animals. In other words, it is the onset of the domestication of animals that marks the key divide in human–animal relations. Although none of the contributors to this book address the issue of human–animal intimacy in hunter-gatherer societies, the work of these hunter-gatherer specialists has, to a considerable extent, set the terms of debate in anthropology on human–animal relations in general and on animal personhood in particular and is therefore worth examining as a prelude to outlining the specific contributions of the following chapters.

The key figure is the anthropologist Tim Ingold. In one well-known paper Ingold has argued that hunter-gatherers see hunting as non-violent because it takes place in the context of a world-view that emphasizes human–animal connectedness. Prey animals are not

> conceived to be bent on escape, brought down only by the hunter's superior cunning, speed or force. To the contrary, a hunt that is successfully consummated with a kill is taken as proof of amicable relations between the hunter and the animal that has willingly allowed itself to be taken. Hunters are well known for their abhorrence of violence in the context of human relations, and the same goes for their relations with animals: the encounter, at the moment of the kill, is – to them – essentially *non*-violent. (Ingold 1994: 12, original emphasis)

The hunter establishes a relationship of 'mutuality and co-existence' with his prey animals (Ingold 1994: 12). Ingold even suggests that there is a relationship of 'trust' between the hunter and the animals he hunts, one which contrasts with the relationship of domination that supposedly characterizes human relations to domestic animals. This is an elegant, thought-provoking formulation, which mounts a fundamental challenge to our intuitive understanding of hunting as predation. But does it amount to a credible claim for animal personhood in the context of the hunt?

What is missing in Ingold's argument is any mention of the encounter between the individual hunter and the individual animal(s) hunted in a given hunt. He refers not to real hunts but to *generic hunting*, in effect suggesting that prey animals are experienced not as individuals but as types. Presumably, the non-violent character of the hunt is supposed to be understood in this way – that is, in relation to the hunters' symbolic relationship to the animal type, rather than the actual human predation on the prey animal in the hunting ground (which, of course, *is* violent). Actual encounters with prey animals are treated as encompassed by this larger (cosmological) relationship to the animal kind. But to subordinate individual animals to some larger animal category in this way would seem to amount to a denial that individual animals have standing in their own right – that is, that they arouse little or no moral concern *qua* individuals among the people who hunt them. This recalls the population-centred perspective of modern hunters, wildlife managers and conservation biologists for whom the focus is on population aggregates rather than individual animals, thereby rhetorically neutralizing the moral objections levelled by animal welfarists at both recreational hunting and the use of culling in wildlife management and conservation.

This impression is further reinforced when Ingold likens hunters getting to know animals to people getting to know other people:

> To know someone is to be in a position to approach him directly with a fair expectation of the likely response, to be familiar with that person's past history and sensible to his tastes, moods and idiosyncrasies. You get to know other human persons by sharing with them, that is by experiencing their companionship. And if you are a hunter *you get to know animals by hunting.* (Ingold 1994: 16, emphasis added)

Ostensibly, Ingold is suggesting that hunting is a process whereby prey animals come to assume the status of persons in a way similar to that in which other people stand as persons on the basis of a history or shared interaction. But there is, in fact, a crucial slippage here between human and animal referents: hunter-gatherers get to know other people *in particular*, but, it seems, only get to know animals *in general*. The two things – interaction with other people and interaction with prey animals – which are supposed to conform to a common logic of sociality are therefore discrepant. Human sociality is based on a recognition of other human beings as individual persons, whereas hunter sociality with prey seems to be based on a view of empirical animals as substitutable tokens in a class. In other words, Ingold's account of animal personhood in fact suggests a *depersonalized* relationship on the part of hunter-gatherers to the animals they hunt, which contrasts sharply with the personalized relations among hunter-gatherers themselves. Ironically, the argument inadvertently rests on a dualism in the way hunters interact among themselves (as persons) and the way they interact with animals (as kinds).[2]

It might be argued that intimacy is not possible with prey animals anyway – because of their flight behaviour in the presence of humans. Encounters between human hunters and the wild animals they hunt are episodic and unrepeated. Insofar as the hunt is successful, and the prey animal dispatched, the encounter comes to an end there and then. Of course the hunt itself is repeated, but this can only be with *other* prey animals. Relations with prey animals can only at most be *serially repetitive* and cannot usually be repeated with the same individual. By their nature, hunter–prey relations are one-off encounters which are interactively discrete and cannot really become temporally cumulative. In this sense, hunters necessarily lack familiarity with the individual animals they hunt, even if, as they gain experience over time, they acquire a generic familiarity with the patterns of behaviour associated with the kind of animal in question.

By contrast, domestication does provide the temporal and spatial conditions for human–animal intimacy to emerge. In relations with domestic animals, there is often a continuous daily association with individual animals (even if these animals exist in a wider collectivity) that makes possible precisely the kind of relationship that cannot arise in the hunting ground. Rather than one-off encounters, the relationship with domestic animals involves a pattern of interaction that engenders a high level of mutual familiarity. The spatial restriction or enclosure of domestic animals is also conducive to human–animal familiarity – the animals can be encountered in the same place on a regular basis, making for a high level of experiential familiarity.

## Intimacy with Domesticates and Pets

Domestic animals are often seen as the prime manifestation of a subordinate animal status. They tend to appear as animate 'objects' that are exploited by human society as sources of food, hides, draught power, and so on. However, we should be wary of collapsing the two separate dimensions of the human relationship to domestic animals – outcome and process. The preoccupation with the outcome of the relationship (e.g. slaughter for meat) is apt to conceal the protracted relationship of nurturance and care that precedes it. Typically, in this relationship the animal is not reduced to the status of an animate object but may well be conferred with attributes of personhood. Close-up, long-term interaction with animals is likely to generate a clear awareness of individual difference – in terms of appearance, behaviour, temperament, and so on – to the extent that farmers who interact regularly with their animals come to see each animal as unique.

Anthropologists have challenged the view that domestic animals are simply kept for utilitarian reasons. The relationship between livestock farmers and their animals may well be understood in terms of notions of reciprocity according to which the animals are represented as volitional beings. In his chapter on the relationship between farmers and domestic animals on a Greek island, Dimitrios Theodossopoulos (Chapter 1) challenges the characterization of this relationship as simply utilitarian. He argues that while the farmer's relationship to his animals might originate as a utilitarian tie, over time the nature of the relationship changes as the animal becomes a part of the moral sphere of the household. Animals that have given their products and labour to the family come to merit moral consideration among their human keepers, who incur a sense of indebtedness to them. As domestic animals enter the moral economy of the household, what begins as a utilitarian relationship becomes a *utilitarian-plus* relationship. This is not necessarily to deny that domestic animals are exploited but to make the point that in practice this exploitative relationship is mediated by moral sentiments otherwise associated with social relations between people.

If useful animals come to generate human attachment to them, it is also the case that animal attachment to humans can make them all the more useful. In other words, animals are not just exploited as objects but also, in a sense, exploited as subjects. Human intimacy with animals can fulfil an important function in the domesticatory relationship. Much human nurturance of animals serves to instil an attachment to humans for specific purposes. Human nurturance of and sustained contact with young animals creates human-friendly adult animals. Intervention in the early socialization phase can facilitate effective and economical control over the animals. The chapter by Peter Dwyer and Monica Minnegal (Chapter 2) provides a good example of this. It looks at a number of different forms of pig husbandry in New Guinea, focusing on the removal of piglets from their mothers in infancy as a means of creating an emotional attachment on the part of the pigs to their human carers. They show how human nurturance of young pigs, by making them dependent on their carers, ensures human authority and control over them. One important practical benefit this generates is that the pigs do not have to be physically enclosed or confined, but can be allowed to roam and graze freely and relied on to return to their human keepers at the end of the day.

In his chapter on the raising of young foxhounds for the English foxhunt, Garry Marvin (Chapter 3) describes another example of strategic human intervention in the affective socialization of a domesticated animal. This is the practice whereby puppies are removed from their mothers and placed with human families – known as 'puppy-walkers' – who 'foster' the puppies for a number of months (in a relationship that resembles pet-keeping), after which time the young dogs are taken back to kennels and introduced into the foxhound pack. This early experience with human families is an important part of the formation of human-friendly hounds who must function as working animals in human society. Overall, this pattern of dog-rearing, which makes consecutive use of the human family and the dog pack as social environments, would seem to reflect the twin imperatives of ensuring that the dogs are amenable to human control *and* that they become effective members of the foxhound pack.

Ben Campbell's study of Tamang livestock-keeping (Chapter 4) is also concerned with the existence of affective ties between people and domestic animals. Among these Himalayan villagers the relationships with water buffaloes and other animals develop into bonds of intimacy and dependency that resemble those between kinsmen. Campbell explores what he calls 'the ethnographic realities and issues of relationship in interspecies social dwelling' in the context of the villagers' ties to their livestock. In particular, he focuses on the tension that can arise when people are seen to devote themselves to their animals at the expense of fulfilling their responsibilities to care for dependent family members – hence the title of his chapter, 'On "Loving Your Water Buffalo More than Your Own Mother"'. This chapter offers an interesting variant of the kind of moral denunciation of excessive human care of animals at the expense of fellow humans that has often been directed at pet-keeping (Serpell [1986]1996: Ch. 3).

The chapter by Joanna Swabe (Chapter 5) examines the views on pet-keeping of Dutch veterinarians. Against the background of the progressive blurring of boundaries between pets and humans in modern Dutch society, Swabe focuses on the views of these professional mediators of the pet-keeping relationship, including a number of highly controversial issues such as animal euthanasia, chemotherapy as an animal treatment, the use of animal 'wheelchairs', and kidney transplants. The extension of these forms of care and treatment – associated with the human domain – to pet animals is likely to raise precisely the above kind of zero-sum objection that sees them as evidence of extravagance and of misdirected concern in a world where a great many human beings do not have access to them.

In Chapter 6 Birgitta Edelman also addresses the theme of pet-keeping, but her concern is not so much with the issue of pets as breachers of the human–animal boundary than with the issue of how a particular animal species crosses the boundaries between pets and other animal status categories. She analyses the changing status and place of rats in society, tracing their changing identity from 'vermin' to their use in laboratories and their status as pets, pointing out how the rat has been transformed through breeding to fit in with new human uses. She describes the history of rat-breeding and rat-fancying in England by way of background to the increased popularity of rats as pets in recent decades. But she also points out that the status of rats as pets remains a special one – for at least some rat-keepers, it seems, they are, as it were, *outrageous pets*, the appeal of which draws on the old negative image of the 'feared and hated' rat.

Human intimacy with domestic animals does not simply have desirable socialization effects on the animals. Intimate interaction with animals can also have important socialization or educational effects on the humans involved, especially children charged with the care of animals. As an area in which children are given nurturant responsibilities over animals, pet-keeping has often been praised as a means of aiding the personality development of children (Beck and Katcher 1996: 61–2). Children with pets learn what it is to have dependants – and, therefore, to be responsible for others. 'It appears to us that companion animals are our children's children, and the best thing we can do for our children is to help them be better parents' (Beck and Katcher 1996: 62). By assuming pet-keeping duties, children come to be inculcated with a more general sense of responsibility.

We might add, however, that pet-keeping is sometimes condemned for not really representing an authentic human–animal engagement at all, but as being little more than a one-sided human relationship *to* the pet animal rather than a truly *mutual* relationship. One of the most vehement condemnations of pet-keeping has been made by Paul Shepard for whom pets are 'monsters of the order invented by Frankenstein', 'biological slaves who cringe and fawn' and do 'whatever we wish', and 'organic machines conforming to our needs' (Shepard 1996: 151). This same kind of criticism is evident in references to pet-keeping in modern Western society as 'petishism' (i.e. fetishism towards pets) (Szasz 1969) and as 'narcissistic' (Lofgren 1985: 199). Although pets are now commonly referred to as 'companion animals', these sorts of criticisms would seem to reject as a fantasy the very idea of people entering into meaningfully mutual relationships with their pets.

This presence of animals in the lives of children is not limited to real 'flesh and blood' animals such as pets, but extends to the fantasy animals that appear on children's television. Candi Forrest, Laurence Goldman, Michael Emmison (Chapter 7) analyse an example of such televisual fantasy animals popular among young children – British television's *The Sooty Show* that features animal glove puppets. On the one hand, such 'adult-generated representations of animals' for young children would seem to be straightforward examples of anthropomorphic projection onto animal surfaces that have little value in teaching children about real animals in the world, but are basically to do with imparting certain basic forms of cultural knowledge to children, as well as, of course, entertainment. But read in the context of the other chapters in this book that deal with human interactions with actual animals, this careful analysis of the puppet show raises the question of the formative role of early exposure to animal imagery in the development of the human imagination in a mysterious world of similar-but-different animate others.

## Encounters with Animals

Lynette Hart (Chapter 8) looks at the mahout–elephant relationship in South Asia, drawing on data from southern India and Nepal. The mahout's relationship with his elephant is a personal one, based on extensive interaction with the elephant from when it is very young. Hart describes how mahouts control the movements of their elephants by means of a range of commands, but also how they feed the elephants their favourite foods and rub them down at 'bath' time. The larger theme of Hart's chapter is the shifting context of the mahout–elephant relationship – in particular, the emergence of elephants as a tourist attraction in national park tourism. Tourists too now have given the opportunity to engage in intimate interactions with the elephants, such as feeding them and swimming with them, in addition to the thrill of riding them.

It is clear from Hart's chapter that elephants are an awe-inspiring or 'charismatic' presence for the tourists. The theme of encounters with 'charismatic' animals recurs in three other chapters – Adrian Peace's chapter on whale-watching in Australia (Chapter 9), Véronique Servais's chapter on 'enchanted encounters' with dolphins (Chapter 10), and John Knight's chapter on Japanese monkey parks (Chapter 11). The nature of the human–animal encounter varies significantly in these three chapters. Peace's study of whale-watching shows that the tourist relationship with whales can be understood in terms of anthropomorphic projection, albeit one that is strongly mediated by the skipper of the whale-watching boat who acts as 'narrator' for the encounter. In his analysis Peace draws attention to the content of this anthropomorphic discourse, especially its emphasis on what we might call *rhetorical particularity*, according to which specific human qualities are attributed to individual whales through the whale-watching narrative.

In the chapters by Servais and Knight the animals themselves appear much more as active parties to the human encounters with them, such that it becomes meaningful to talk in terms of *mutual interaction*. This impression of mutuality is evident in the accounts of 'enchanted' encounters between people and dolphins offered by Servais in which dolphins are experienced as willing partners. Visitors to the Japanese monkey parks Knight describes are offered the opportunity to 'play' with monkeys by feeding them directly, an interaction interpreted as an act of 'giving' that is consummated by the 'receiving' monkey. This said, in both of these latter cases there are likely to be discrepancies between the way such encounters are experienced as mutual and intimate by the humans involved (which is clearly prone to romanticism) and the reality of a complex cross-species interaction. Such human interpretations of intimacy with these animals may well prove difficult to sustain in the face of behaviour that clearly contradicts it – such as monkey violence towards food-bearing visitors in the monkey parks, which is clearly at odds with the idea of monkey-as-receiver.

Servais makes the point, however, that, notwithstanding the potential pitfalls associated with the human tendency to attribute mutuality in such encounters, we should still be prepared to take seriously their potential intersubjectivity, complex as this is likely to be, rather than simply approach them as instances of unilateral symbolic imposition. This of course raises the issue of the competence of anthropologists and others to really study human–animal interactions in this way, given their species-bound training in methodology and in data collection. To grasp the complex reality of 'interspecies communication' would require the ability to go beyond the human perspective and try and access the perspective of the animal party to the interaction. We can accept that the animals themselves may well see human interactants as conspecifics, but to actually make sense of this 'zoomorphism' as a form of sociality is likely to require expertise beyond anthropology – such as that of primatology in the case of human–animal interactions in the monkey park, or marine ethology in the case of human–dolphin encounters.

## Challenging Anthropomorphism

In Chapter 12 Kay Milton raises objections to the concept of 'anthropomorphism' as a tool for analysing how humans understand animals, suggesting instead an alternative model, which she calls 'egomorphism', that focuses on human *understanding* of animals rather than human *representation* of animals in discourse. Drawing on the Gibson's theory of direct perception, she makes the distinction between perceiving characteristics *in* non-human animals and attributing characteristics *to* them, and suggests that much human interaction with non-human animals should be understood in terms of the former. A key part of her argument – which she has set out in greater length in a recent book (Milton 2002) – is that humans tend to locate personhood in animals that show themselves to be responsive to them. In other words, human engagements with animals begin not from a state of ontological separation but from a state of preexisting interconnection.

This kind of objection to the dualistic basis of anthropomorphism is in fact borne out by many of the intimate human interactions with other mammals mentioned in this book, such as riding, petting and feeding. But perhaps the most striking instance of this is cross-species suckling. Dwyer and Minnegal mention a Melanesian example of women suckling piglets at the outset of their discussion of human–pig attachment in the region, but there are many other reported examples of humans suckling the young of other animals such as dogs, monkeys, deer and bears (Schwartz 1997: 11; Smith and Wiswell 1982: 229; Batchelor 1901: 484). In addition to these examples of humans suckling young animals, there are well-known examples of animals suckling young humans such as among the Nuer where children drink 'straight from the udders' of sheep and goats (Evans-Pritchard [1940]1969: 38).

As Dwyer and Minnegal point out in relation to piglets in New Guinea, cross-species suckling is a practice apt to be sensationalized, as well as exaggerated in terms of the extent of its occurrence. However, the fact that the practice exists at all can be seen as striking evidence of the similarity of the species involved. Although such behaviour might seem shocking and disturbing at first, when viewed in terms of the biological similarity of the two parties (human suckler and suckled animal, or the other way around), it appears an obvious response to a situation where the animal's biological mother is (for one reason or another) not available. It is an axiomatical interaction for the two parties involved on account of the anatomical fit between mammalian lips and mammalian breasts that makes it possible in the first place. Suckling can be considered mammalian behaviour, par excellence – as the etymology of the word 'mammal' (from *mamma* or breast) suggests. Thus, in Milton's terms we could say that when a human mother nurtures a non-human infant, such behaviour should be understood as an instance of the *perception* of familiar interpersonal 'affordances' in a fellow mammal (an implicit recognition of the anatomical compatibility between mammals) rather than the *attribution* of human characteristics to an 'animal'. Strictly speaking, this is not anthropomorphism but intermammalian sociality.

## Delimiting Animal Personhood

This book describes many human–animal interactions that have an intimate, mutualistic, and even intersubjective character that makes it reasonable talk in terms of sociality beyond the species barrier. But in addition to identifying the possibility of such cross-species sociality, it is important to acknowledge its limits. I have already pointed to certain contextual conditions under which animals can become persons, and have suggested that these are found in human relations with domestic animals and not in human relations with prey animals. The foregoing discussion of interaction between mammals also implies that human-centred animal personhood is subject to certain phylogenetic limitations. Interactional intimacy – to the extent it is really mutual – implies a degree of symmetry between the two interactants, which makes phylogenetic 'relatives' such as mammals (and even more so, primates) more credible candidates for intersubjectivity than other animals at a greater evolutionary distance from humans.

In order to make sense of human–animal interactions it is necessary to recognize basic distinctions between different kinds of animals, rather than group different kinds of animals together in an over-inclusive category. This, I would suggest, is in fact the unfinished work of critics of human–animal dualism. The point has often been made that the notion of a human–animal dualism results in a subtracted view of humanity (Man = human – animal) rather than an understanding of human beings in the round. But we must not forget that the criticism of dualism also requires that the notion of 'animal' also be subject to critical scrutiny. As an artefact of dualist thinking, this notion of 'animal' is, of course, open to the objection that it is *too narrow* because of the way that it excludes the human species from it. But there is a second, less obvious objection to the notion of 'animal' deriving from human–animal dualism: that it is *too broad*, including all other animal species together in a generic (non-human) 'animal' category that begs the question of the differences between these species. In short, human–animal dualism is problematic not just because it obscures *human–animal commonality*, but also because it obscures *differences between other animals*. This point applies especially to the topic of human–animal intimacy and mutuality insofar as different animals vary considerably in terms of their capacity to interact with people.

## Notes

1. The sense of individuality is different from that which emerges in theories of individualism. The *individual person* can be understood as socially embedded and relational in character and therefore as different from the *individual* of classical political economy, social contract theory in politics or transactionalism in anthropology. In these latter formulations of individualism the individual is deemed to somehow exist prior to relations with others or to the social order (or economy or polity).
2. One might question the adequacy of this account of hunter–prey relations. Do hunters really manage to depersonalize the animals they hunt? On the basis of accounts of hunting elsewhere, I think this is dubious. It is probably more a reflection of hunter talk (especially to the outside anthropologist seeking to find out about hunting in general) than actual hunting practice.

## References

Batchelor, J. (1901), *The Ainu and Their Folklore*. London: The Religious Tract Society.

Beck, A. and A. Katcher (1996), *Between Pets and People: The Importance of Animal Companionship*. West Lafayette: Purdue University Press.

Cavalieri, P. and P. Singer (1993), 'Preface'. In P. Cavalieri and P. Singer (eds) *The Great Ape Project: Equality Beyond Humanity*. London: Fourth Estate.

Cavalieri, P. *et al.* (1993), 'Declaration'. In P. Cavalieri and P. Singer (eds) *The Great Ape Project: Equality Beyond Humanity*. London: Fourth Estate.

Evans-Pritchard, E. E. ([1940] 1969), *The Nuer: A Description of the Modes of Livelihood and Political Institutions of a Nilotic People*. New York and Oxford: Oxford University Press.

Ingold, T. (1994), 'From Trust to Domination: An Alternative History of Human–Animal Relations'. In A. Manning and J. Serpell (eds) *Animals and Human Society: Changing Perspectives*. London: Routledge.

Lofgren, O. (1985), 'Our Friends in Nature: Class and Animal Symbolism'. *Ethnos* 50 (3–4): 184–213.

Milton, K. (2002), *Loving Nature: Towards an Ecology of Emotion*. London: Routledge.

Mullin, M. (1999), 'Mirrors and Windows: Sociocultural Studies of Human–Animal Relationships'. *Annual Review of Anthropology*, 28: 201–24.

Schwartz, M. (1997), *A History of Dogs in the Early Americas*. New Haven: Yale University Press.

Serpell, J. ([1986] 1996), *In the Company of Animals: A Study of Human–Animal Relationships*. Cambridge: Cambridge University Press.

Shepard, P. (1996), *The Others: How Animals Made Us Human*. Washington, DC: Island Press.

Smith, R. J. and E. L. Wiswell (1982), *The Women of Suye Mura*. Chicago: Chicago University Press.

Szasz, K. (1969), *Petishism: Pets and Their People in the Western World*. New York: Holt, Rinehart and Winston.

# Care, Order and Usefulness: The Context of the Human–Animal Relationship in a Greek Island Community

*Dimitrios Theodossopoulos*

The farmers of a Greek island community discuss their animals and their investment in animal care in terms that emphasize the usefulness of the animals to the rural household. Despite this stress on usefulness, their engagement with small-scale and relatively unprofitable forms of animal husbandry has an intrinsic, non-material value, one however, which is hardly ever offered as a justification for the farmers' involvement with animal care. This chapter traces this non-articulated aspect of the human–animal relationship as it becomes apparent in Vassilikos, a community on the island of Zakynthos in south-west Greece,[1] and places the interaction of the farmers with their animals in its meaningful context: one that involves care, reciprocity and a fundamental conceptualization of the place and purpose of each living organism on the farm.

In the relatively brief anthropological literature that directly focuses on human attitudes to animals, farmers – along with pastoralists and other 'Western' or 'modern' people – are often treated as representative of one over-generalizing category of cultures that share common utilitarian, anthropocentric and hierarchical principles towards the natural world. This generalizing cluster of cultures is contrasted to another, equally generalized but highly idealized, category of pre-modern, non-Western, small-scale societies, associated with an egalitarian, reciprocal, interdependent cultural approach towards the non-human living organisms (Morris 1995; 1998: 2–4). The dualistic and rigid character of such generalizations has been identified by some anthropologists (Willis 1990: 20; Morris 1995: 301–3; 1998: 1–6; Ellen 1996: 103), while others such as Tim Ingold (1980, 1986, 1988, 1994, 1996), although critical of Western dualisms *per se*, present the hunter-gatherer attitudes to animals as the most evident cultural alternative to Western European anthropocentrism and ethnocentrism.[2]

More directly than other authors, Morris has denounced the arbitrary grouping of diverse cultural attitudes towards animals into dualistic categories, such as the pre-literate cluster of societies with the 'egalitarian, sacramental' view of nature, and the Western cultural traditions that are allegedly defined by a mechanistic, dualistic and controlling approach towards the natural environment (1995: 302–3; 1998: 2). 'Many scholars', he argues, 'write as if historically there are only two possible "world-views", the mechanistic (anthropocentric) and the organismic (ecocentric)' (1995: 303; 1998: 2). This kind of theorization based on all-inclusive antinomies obviously underestimates the diversity and changing character of Western traditions – which include a multiplicity of different ontologies and historically specific understandings of nature – and fails to account for particular cultures where those two kinds of contrasting attitudes, the antagonistic and the egalitarian, coexist in complementary opposition (Morris 1995: 301–12; 1998: 2–4).

Following Morris (1995, 1998), I will argue in this chapter that questions regarding the human–animal interaction do not neatly resolve themselves in simplistic utilitarian versus non-utilitarian dichotomies. The meaning of animal usefulness in Vassilikos is directly dependent upon considerations relating to the independence, self-sufficiency and well-being of each farm. Consequently the attitudes of the indigenous actors towards their animals are permeated by strong anthropocentric priorities (see Papagaroufali 1996: 244; Theodossopoulos 1997: 263; 2003: 168–74). Those priorities, however, are not strictly utilitarian: decisions concerning animals on the farm indicate an appreciation of the animals' membership to the domestic economy. The inclusion of animals in the rural household was recognized, for the first time, by du Boulay (1974). This recognition sets the initial parameters for deciphering the expectations individual farmers have of their animals and the meaning they attribute to animal usefulness. Domestic animals, through their inclusion in the household economy, are seen as forming close relationships with their owners. They exist within a clearly defined and reciprocal system of order and care, one which consists of rules, duties and rights.

Starting with these observations, I will now focus on the ways men and women in Vassilikos care for their animals; the ways they punish them or complain about them; and the repetitive, simple but exhausting tasks of their everyday interaction with them. The following section introduces the community, the farmers and the animals in question; that is, the domestic animals 'kept' by the average household in Vassilikos. Some reference is made to the basics of their husbandry, their locally defined usefulness and their place in the order of the farm. Then, in the subsequent section, I proceed to examine the meaning of 'order' (*taksi*) and 'care' (*frondidha*), the two most central concepts pertaining to the relationship between farmers and farm animals. 'Order', in particular, embraces and directs the content of several other concepts examined in this chapter, such as 'care' and 'usefulness'. The final ethnographic section focuses on rare examples of wild animals disrupting the order of the farm or being incorporated by it. The farmers in Vassilikos openly express their grief for the loss of domestic animals to wild predators, revealing their attachment to these animals. They are also prepared to re-examine their confrontational views towards the elements of the wild and grant to some captured wild animals, independently of their usefulness, the privilege of inclusion in the protective environment of the farm.

## Vassilikiots and their Animals

Vassilikiots, the human protagonists of this chapter, enjoy the benefit of a double occupational identity. They are farmers and tourist entrepreneurs. Both farming and tourism in their community are undertaken as small-scale enterprises dependent upon the labour provided by the members of individual household enterprises (see Galani-Moutafi 1993: 250–1; Zarkia 1996: 156). Despite the fact that tourism provides the greater portion of individual incomes, a significant majority of the local men and women proudly declare that they are 'farmers' (*agrotes*). Their persistence to carry on practising farming jobs with limited (in comparison to tourism) economic rewards is part of Vassilikiots' more general economic attitude, according to which 'resources readily available on their farmland should never be wasted' (Theodossopoulos 1999: 613–14). This strategic over-utilization of living and material constituents of individual farms accords to a more widespread cultural ideal focusing on household independence,, referred to in the regional literature as 'self-sufficiency' (see Campbell 1964: 257; du Boulay 1974: 244, 247; Loizos 1975: 44, 50; Kenna 1976: 349–50; 1990: 151–2; 1995: 135, Herzfeld 1985: 270; 1991: 132).

In the context of tourism, and in accordance with Vassilikiots' general attitude towards self-sufficiency, the products of farming and animal husbandry constitute additional resources which are unlikely to be completely ignored or looked down upon. Hence, the introduction of tourism in Vassilikos did not lead to a complete abandonment of farming and agriculture (Theodossopoulos 1997: 253–4; 1999: 612–14; 2002: 247–8; 2003: 49–64). During the tourist season Vassilikiots devote a greater part of their time to the 'care' (*frondidha*) of their tourist enterprises: numerous restaurants or *tavernas*, mini-markets, room, car and motorbike rentals. They do not completely neglect, however, the minimum duties required for the maintenance of their farms and the 'care' (*frondidha*) of the animals living on them. The successful participation of individual households in the economy of tourism depends on the mobilization of all able-bodied household members and all available household resources. Meat from small animals (chickens and rabbits) raised on the local farms is frequently consumed in the Vassilikiot *tavernas* – often the *tavernas* owned by the same households that raised the animals – while locally produced animal products (eggs and cheese) are proudly displayed in Vassilikos's several seasonal mini-markets.

Thus, farming and animal care are not perceived by the inhabitants of Vassilikos as strictly antagonistic to their new involvement in tourism. In their engagement with both tourism and farming, Vassilikiots constantly encounter novel situations and adapt to new economic challenges. Until the early 1990s, the time I completed the fieldwork upon which this analysis is based, new economic strategies were constantly accommodated to complement older cultural ideals. Technical innovations in agriculture or tourism were complemented by the willingness of household members to co-operate, while investments in tourism were often dependent upon the effective maximization of living and non-living household resources. In most cases, Vassilikiots' labour reflected the perpetual struggle of realizing family independence and an economic logic that prioritized the benefit of the household as a whole over particular individual ambitions (Hirschon 1989: 141; Theodossopoulos 1999: 621).

Despite the existence of a clearly defined, ideal code in respect of the gender division of labour in Vassilikos and in several other Greek communities (Friedl 1967: 103–4; Couroucli 1985: 78–9; Hirschon 1989: 99, 104, 143; Greger 1988: 25–6, 34–7; Cowan 1990: 49–51; Gefou-Madianou 1992: 115, 121, 124–7; Hart 1992: 243–6; Galani-Moutafi 1993: 253–4), in practice the labour contributions of Vassilikiot men and women to small-scale, farm-based animal husbandry do not distinctively differ. Men, more often than women, punish animals and take decisions concerning major issues related to animal husbandry and temporary or permanent buildings on the farmland. But women usually are responsible for poultry and smaller animals (see Pina-Cabral 1986: 82–4), and participate in milking and various everyday tasks on the farm. In their husbands' absence or illness, women are capable of undertaking most jobs associated with animal 'care', even those related to the larger animals of the farm, which are locally expected to be a male concern. Consequently, the distinction between male and female spheres of responsibility on the farm represents the ideal of 'order', rather than its actual application. In practice, both men and women farmers take care of animals and are concerned with animals.

In daily conversation Vassilikiots use the term 'animals' (*ta zoa*) to refer to 'their' animals on 'their' farm. 'Wild', undomesticated animals are also entitled to the term 'animal', but Vassilikiots are mainly concerned with their own animals, 'their' farm animals. Similarly, while all animals on the farm are called 'animals', the term is more usually applied to sheep and goats. For example, in the context of any particular discussion, a farmer will refer to chickens and dogs with their generic names – that is, 'chickens' or 'dogs' – and to sheep, goats and occasionally cattle with either their generic name or simply the term 'animals'. Here, the generalizing use of the term 'animals' does not indicate negligence or disregard for the animals in question; on the contrary, it suggests an implicit recognition of their contribution to the well-being of the farm. In this respect, sheep and goats are 'animals' proper.

Sheep and goats are typical examples of what the local farmers consider to be useful farm animals. They are common, present on almost every farm, and comprise an indispensable unit of animal stock held by the average household in the village. While most Vassilikiot families do not maintain 'flocks of animals',[3] the great majority of them 'keep' (*kratoun*) a small number of female goats or sheep, which can be easily watched, grazing on the farmland adjacent to individual households. The adult ones are tethered to an iron stake with a five-metre-long rope. The stake is driven into a different piece of land every day. The young animals, kids or lambs, are left free to gambol and graze around their mothers. This small-scale kind of animal husbandry is not energy intensive and provides Vassilikiots with access to some EU (European Union) benefits and subsidies. To qualify for these subsidies the farmers are expected to keep a minimum of seven or eight sheep or goats on their farmland.

Like other Mediterranean countrymen (see Campbell 1964: 26, 31; Blok 1981: 428–30; Brandes 1980: 77–9; 1981: 221), Vassilikiots openly declare their preference for sheep over goats. They blame goats for 'disobedience' and having an 'untamed' character, while, at the same time, they praise sheep for their submissive and benevolent constitution. 'Sheep are more obedient' and 'more docile (*irema*) animals', Vassilikiots explain, and argue that 'sheep are blessed animals!' (*ine zoa evlogimena*). At the same time, however, the farmers do not hide their secret admiration for the strength and stamina of goats. They perceive goats, and especially kids, as wilder than sheep and argue that 'these animals' are more resistant to disease and harsh environmental conditions. On the other hand, Vassilikiots recognize that goats' milk doesn't produce the same good quality of cheese, and those farmers who are seriously engaged with cheese production always take care to maintain more sheep than goats.

Cattle husbandry was more widespread in the past, and the old, local variety of cows were used in Vassilikos for both milking and ploughing (*gia gala ala kai gia zevgari*). This older variety of cow is described as having greater 'endurance' (*andohi*) or 'strength' (*dinami*), requirements adjusted perfectly well to the local prescriptions of an animal's 'usefulness' and the local ideal of self-sufficiency. Nowadays, the old, local variety of cow has been replaced by a hybrid breed, a mixture of the old local cow with 'improved (*veltiomenes*) cows from abroad'. Endogenous developments in European farming, as van der Ploeg and Long have argued, enhance heterogeneity and contain 'a specific balance of 'internal' and 'external' elements' (1994: 1–4). In fact, Vassilikiots strategically plan crossbreeding, since they believe that it adds to the 'strength' of their animal stock (see Marvin 1988: 88, 92).

In the absence of foxes and large mammal predators on the island, Vassilikiots allow poultry to roam freely in backyards, olive groves and the nearby fields. In the evenings, the birds return to the farm to be sheltered and fed by the farmers. They crowd around their owners, who throw them some corn, wheat or other kinds of grain as a supplement to their diet. The farmers do not worry much about adult birds, but they do devote significant time and concern to 'caring' for new-born chicks. Most hens, for example, lay their eggs unobserved in various hidden places on the farmland, but as soon as the farmers notice their new-born chicks they collect them and put them in cages along with their mothers or foster mothers. There, the chicks are protected and fed well for a couple of weeks until they are old enough to protect themselves from rats and other small predators. Similar protection is devoted to turkey chicks because Vassilikiots do not trust the motherly instinct of adult turkeys. 'Turkeys are clumsy and often destroy their own eggs', Vassilikiots explain, and invest a great deal of care into setting the turkey nests themselves.

In the late autumn months, Vassilikiot olive groves are filled with turkeys, and their characteristic call can be heard everywhere. These birds are raised for the sole purpose of being sold at Christmas, when they bring a significant profit to households. Like turkeys, geese and ducks are only kept for their meat, but unlike turkeys they are rarely found in Vassilikiot farms. Most farmers maintain that geese and ducks are dirty and unruly, while those Vassilikiots who keep them do so either out of habit or because they adhere to the ideal that 'a farm must have all kinds of animals on it'. Unlike turkeys, geese and ducks, chickens are valued for both their meat and eggs, and are consumed throughout the year in tourist establishments owned by the household, at household celebrations, and on those occasions when the household members wish to honour a guest (see Friedl 1962: 31).

Since the introduction of tourism in Vassilikos, pig husbandry has become unpopular. As a Vassilikiot woman explains: 'If you rent rooms and have tourists close to your farm, you can't have many pigs, because these animals smell.' Despite this general avoidance of pigs, some farmers insist on keeping one or two in their farms. They feed them well and plan the occasion of their death – often a religious or other celebration – well in advance. In comparison to pigs, rabbits play a more integral role in the farm's yearly cycle. They are usually reared in cages in large numbers and fed by the farmers with special care. Vassilikiots perceive rabbits as weak animals, susceptible to disease and in need of their caring attention. They are raised for their meat, which is essential for cooking '*stifadho*', a well-known local recipe. During the summer months, rabbits and chickens raised on the local farms are consumed in the local tavernas or restaurants. On several cases, the same individuals that own the tourist enterprises also raise the animals, and subsequently have to kill and cook the animals themselves. In this sense, tourism and farming appear as complementary manifestations of an economy centred around the household (see Theodossopoulos 1997: 253–4; 1999: 612–14; 2003: 49–64).

Dogs, finally, are present on any Vassilikiot farm and make their presence felt with their persistent and monotonous barking. They are straightforwardly

described as 'useful' animals by their owners. 'Dogs do work', Vassilikiots maintain, and acknowledge the conventional role of dogs as guards. But individual dogs
are primarily evaluated in terms of their contribution to hunting, and the special
attention and care devoted to some of them is justified in terms of their performance in hunting (see also Marvin, this volume). According to my observations,
dogs unsuccessful in hunting are relatively neglected: they are only fed, and spend
endless hours tied up. However, the farmers often spare a few sympathetic words
even for these less fortunate animals. This is because a dog, more than any other
animal on the farm, meets the expectations of a farmer in respect of the notion of
'order' (*taksi*). As I will describe in the following section, for the Vassilikiot
farmers, obedience and devotion are not merely stereotypical qualities of canine
behaviour – they represent what one expects from every animal on the farm but
very rarely gets.

## Care and Order

The farmers of Vassilikos usually enjoy showing visitors around their farms.
Talking about the farm while walking around it is a form of conversation with a
distinctive dynamic: the participants communicate about creatures or objects right
in front of their eyes, and the discussion is often stimulated by the physical presence of these objects or creatures. The farmer will discuss vegetable gardens,
animal shelters, and animals of all kinds with the visitor, emphasizing the labour
and 'care' needed for their maintenance. If the visitor has been to the farm many
times before, the farmer will concentrate on recent changes, newly acquired/born
animals, and projects currently being undertaken. The same applies if the visitor is
a neighbour and a fellow farmer; but here the discussion is more likely to focus on
instrumental aspects of animal care or cultivation. Vassilikiots appear eager to
share their knowledge or experience with their neighbours. In fact, any new ideas
related to animal husbandry or cultivation are disseminated around the neighbouring farms with amazing speed and efficiency.

A visiting fellow farmer and the host farmer will almost always exchange some
comments about their animals' behaviour, information about animal diseases, or
ideas about more efficient animal shelter construction. In the context of such a
conversation, the host farmers will straightforwardly demonstrate their pride and
satisfaction in the well-being of the farm. The orderly arrangement of animals and
structures on a farm is understood as the farmer's personal achievement. Visiting
farmers, being in a position to appreciate the host farmer's accomplishments,
express their admiration with praise and recognition. The conversation will eventually concentrate on issues such as the organization of the farm and projects to be
undertaken in the near future. At some stage, farmers are likely to encounter specific problems relating to the practical requirements of running a farm and the

'care' of particular animals. These considerations are expressed in the farmers' words while they are walking around, or working on the farm in the presence of a second person. For the visiting farmers, such conversation is informative and instrumental; for an anthropologist it supplies an abundance of ethnographic insights.

Whenever the farmer is discussing the farm, past experiences and plans for the future are reflected in the present. Narratives focus on earlier stages of the farm's development: what the state of the farmland was when it was bought from the landlord; how and in which order each aspect of the farm was developed; and how much 'struggle' or effort was required for the present ordered state of 'things' to be achieved. But while the present is filled with the satisfaction of achievement – the realization of the farmers' effort – the future is already upon them. The sense of order in the present is intimately linked with future plans for the organization of the farm, new cultivation to be undertaken, and new animals to be 'cared for'. The farmers point to empty plots of land and describe new shelters for animals not yet born, or vegetable gardens that will be better 'fenced and watered' than the present ones.

Safeguarding 'order' on the farm is a constant responsibility for the Vassilikiot farmer. Clearing undesirable vegetation is a preoccupation of this kind, a 'struggle' that never ends due to nature constantly regenerating itself. Cleaning and repairing animal shelters, maintaining the fences of vegetable gardens, repairing all material constructions subjected to animal activity or the weather are, similarly, typical repetitive undertakings for preserving 'order' on the farm. But above all, 'order' on the farm is defended against the chaos of its animal members. The farm animals are considered to be prone to disorder if left unattended. In this sense, domestic animals are treated by the farmer as young children; they are thought to be unable to survive without the farmer's 'caring' presence, intervention and control. They are punished for violating the farm's order, rewarded for complying with it. The following ethnographic examples will illustrate this in detail.

During my days in Vassilikos I was heavily involved in animal care. That was part of my general scheme of helping the local farmers in their daily routine. Every afternoon each farmer had to 'gather' the household's sheep and goats, which were tethered on various parts of their farmland. This job can be particularly tiring – at least for older people – not simply because it is repetitive but because it involves walking across rough ground and pulling the animals along by their tethers. Some animals, especially the younger ones, tend to be disobedient and add some extra difficulty to the job. They might refuse to get in the pen and remain in their appointed 'place' within it. Most of the farmers expect the animals to 'learn' (*na mathoun*) their 'right place' in the pen, and punish those that refuse to stay in it.

Punishment consists of beating and shouting at the animals. 'Why don't you stay in your place', they cry out in anguished exasperation. 'How many times do I have to teach you your right place!' Young animals are expected to disobey and are thus punished more often. 'After some time they learn', the farmers repeatedly explain. 'If you don't beat them they don't learn!' Goats tend to 'disobey' the farmer more often than the sheep, and are, consequently, more frequently punished. While beating their goats, the farmers tend to compare a goat's disobedience with a sheep's submissiveness: 'Look how the ewe knows its place. Goats are not like that. Neither is the ewe-lamb, but it will learn in time.'

Like du Boulay (1974), I did not witness deliberate cruelty in the punishment of animals by their owners. Punishment, in the form of beating and shouting at the animals, always takes place in the context of safeguarding 'order' on the farm. Examples of animal misbehaviour that are most often punished consist of intrusion into forbidden places, such as vegetable gardens or barns, physically harming another animal, or eating its food. The villagers appear particularly distressed when they 'have' (*ehoun*) to punish their animals, and almost always talk to them while they mete out punishment. They explain to them their misdemeanours and scold them as parents do their children: 'I am rearing you! Why don't you listen? Why don't you learn your place.' Some animals often refuse to be confined to their shelters (goats or pigs) or cages (hens with new-born chicks), and the farmers become particularly irritated by the animals' inability to 'understand' that their confinement is aimed primarily at protecting them from predation or bad weather. The words 'I am rearing you' (*ego sas anasteno*), repeatedly shouted by the farmers in Vassilikos, still ring in my ears.

It is a matter of common sense in Vassilikos that all animals on the local farms have 'somewhere' to sleep. Shelters for animals considered to be more vulnerable to disease, such as cows or rabbits, are more carefully designed, while more resilient animals, such as chickens and dogs, are usually sheltered in more temporary or rudimentary structures. Sheltering animals adequately is an important constituent of 'order' on the farm. Farm animals wandering around the farm at night signify disorder, and the farmers become particularly distressed at the sight of domestic animals wandering freely after dark.

Most of the larger mammals on the farm are entitled to some basic form of veterinary care. In cases of serious illness they receive vitamins or antibiotics in the form of injections or capsules mixed with their food. Smaller animals, like chickens or rabbits, suffering from disease or accidents are usually killed. This is understood as a means of relieving those animals of unbearable pain. The farmers claim that they 'know about' (*gnorizoun*) or 'can recognize' (*xehorizoun*) the most frequent or common diseases their animals suffer from, and rarely resort to veterinarians. Although they tackle the most serious animal diseases with medication obtained from the town, in less critical situations they apply traditional remedies handed down from their forefathers. Vassilikiots had little to say about modern medicines, but they were pleased to explain to me the ingredients of the traditional remedies. They used stereotypical phrases like the following: 'camomile and oil make the ewe's stomach move again', or 'ash from reeds mixed with water makes a horse's wound heal'.

Killing animals, like punishment, is a critical point in the relationship between the farmer and the animal members of the household. It is the point when 'order' on the farm dictates the end of a long-established process of 'care'. An animal's death is always discussed in terms of the animal's contribution to the farm's economy and well-being. The farmers are conscious that their animals cannot exist outside the context of security, 'care' and 'order' provided by the farm environment and themselves. In this context, the death of a farm animal is interpreted as a kind of reciprocity on the animal's part for the 'care' received in the past. Du Boulay recognized this kind of reciprocity and described the relationship between animals and animal owners as a 'mutual' or 'reciprocal' one (1974: 86). Extending her work one step further, I understand both 'care for' and 'death of' an animal as different phases of the 'order' on the farm.

The farmers in Vassilikos refer to the emotional stress when killing their own animals as 'sorrow' (*stenohoria*). 'This is not a pleasant job', they say, 'but it is a "necessary" one (*aparetiti*).' They often try to rationalize their feeling of 'sorrow' with jokes and humour. In addition, they hire other villagers to 'do the slaughtering' (*to sfaksimo*) of their 'own animals'. A few men in the village are particularly competent in performing this task. They are locally respected for 'knowing how to kill an animal quickly', that is 'painlessly', and for having the 'skill' (*tehni*) to identify, name and extract particular parts of an animal.[4] However, smaller animals like chickens and rabbits are always killed by the farmers themselves.[5] Both men and women know how to kill animals of this sort, but plucking is done primarily by women, probably because it involves the use of kitchen utensils like casserole dishes. Chickens and rabbits are killed on the spot, at any time their meat is required; this can be an unexpected visit from a friend or a family celebration planned in advance.

'If you have animals, you have to kill them, as well ... There is no other way ... how are you going to get the food to feed the rest of animals?' the farmers in Vassilikos repeatedly argue. Here, the practical necessity – dictating an animal's death – is stated in terms of the mutual interdependence between the farm's constituent parts. From this understanding, the farm appears to operate as a closed system managed by a household-centred economy and the ideal of self-sufficiency. Each farmer, being at the apex of the household's hierarchical organization, is in a position to decide the life-expectancy of particular animals: 'This chicken will die in eight months, this tree in a thousand years', the local people explain, and add, 'There is a time for everything to die.'

## Wild Animals and the Order of the Farm

The relationship of Vassilikiots to wild animals is a one-way relationship. Vassilikiots perceive of non-domesticated animals in terms of their own established presence in the local environment. They refer to wild animals in relation to their own point of view: their position as guardians of welfare and order on their farms. They are concerned about the potential 'harm' (*zimia*) or 'use' (*hrisimotita*) wild animals 'cause' to (*kanoun*) or 'have' for (*ehoun*) their households; that is, themselves and all the domesticated plants and animals on their farm. Their attitudes towards wild animals usually follow three general tendencies: First, lack of benefit or harm done by the wild animal in question results in indifference. Second, the edibility of a wild animal renders it a legitimate target for hunting – a positive characteristic – and justifies its predation. Since hunting is, in general, celebrated in the narratives of the local people, Vassilikiots are eager to talk about the 'huntable' animals and share their knowledge and experience of hunting them. Third, animals locally portrayed as causing 'harm or damage' (*zimia*) are persecuted with anger and resentment. Harmful animals are an obvious threat to the farmer's persistent efforts to establish a form of 'order' in the farm environment.

Since foxes do not exist on the island, the farmers of Vassilikos let poultry, and sometimes rabbits, roam freely around the farmland in search of food. But some smaller mammals attack and prey upon poultry and rabbits. 'Martens and hedgehogs take small chicks from their nests; they cause us damage (*zimia*)', the farmers maintain. But more often than martens or hedgehogs, large rats attack and kill unprotected chicks or rabbits. On several occasions I witnessed discussions between women and men in small groups, sharing their sorrow (*stenohoria*) over losses of their animals due to rats. Here is the content of a typical discussion:

Two women from neighbouring farms have their coffee while chatting in the late afternoon. The husband of the hostess returns home. He immediately complains about the rats, and talks about the young rabbits he found dead in the rabbit cages that morning. His wife adds to his description by noting the grief (*stehohoria*) of the mother rabbit. The other woman and the farmer proceed to make assumptions about where the rats came from. They refer to the nearest wood (*longos*). Both the woman and the farmer share a similar view: they have seen the rats disappearing into the wood. They 'know' (*xeroun*) that 'this is where the rats come from'. The female neighbour proceeds to give a colourful description of recent rat attacks on her own farm. She tells of the day she saw a rat with its frightening teeth, and how she ambushed (*paramonepse*) it and scalded it with a dish full of hot water. Also how her husband 'watched for the rat' (*tou estise karteri*) with his gun, once he had realized that the rat was coming every morning to the same spot and the chickens were disturbed [by the rat's presence]. They all refer to the sorrow or sadness they feel on account of the rat's attacks. 'It is not that I care about the loss of one or two chickens [i.e. their monetary value] but I am upset (*stenohoriemai*) that I lost them', the woman neighbour explained, while the others nodded their heads in agreement.

The grief, claim the farmers of Vassilikos, is not for the monetary value of the lost animals, but mainly over the daily labour they invested in caring for the young chicks or rabbits. This task involves 'caring' and feeding them; special attention is given to ensuring that small chicks are fed, since adult chickens can consume the young chicks' food in seconds. In addition, in the late afternoon, the farmers must collect all their chicks into crates or small cages to protect them from rat attacks. To confine the young and active chicks is not easy, especially for the older farmers. When the rats succeed (and they often do), the Vassilikiots feel very disappointed and are pessimistic about the nature of their work. They think that their labour is not adequately rewarded and express their resentment in comments such as: 'it isn't worth so much hard work' (*dhen aksizi toso kopo*), or 'our work is wasted' (*o kopos mas pige hamenos*).

Vassilikiots talk about their wasted or 'lost' labour and the 'sorrow' for the 'lost' domestic animals. In conversation they do not distinguish between the care and labour spent on their animals and the affection they show for them. For the farmers of Vassilikos, affection is expressed through labour invested in animal care and the constant process of rewarding or punishing their animals. The eventual and inevitable death of a farm animal is understood as part of the greater body of services offered by any member of the farm in the common goal of sustaining and maintaining the farm itself. Far from being an alienating process, the villagers perceive the exchange of animals for money as the ultimate form of service offered by an animal to the farm. This service is interpreted as the animal's contribution to the welfare of the farm, the reciprocation of the care and protection the animal received on the farm.

Conversely, the sudden death of farm animals in unpredictable circumstances, such as from attack by a wild animal or appropriation by a greedy landlord,[6] provokes grief and a general feeling of helplessness and victimization. In this case, the dead animal is considered as being 'lost' (*hameno*) because it dies in inappropriate circumstances. The process of caring for the domestic animal is interrupted, while the death of the animal does not contribute to the welfare of the farm or household in question. The 'loss' of domestic animals entails the loss of all care invested by the farmer through persistent 'labour and toil' (*kopo*).

The process of investing in animal care, however, can take on a very interesting twist in cases where wild animals are allowed to become part of the order of the farm. A farmer's decision concerning the fate of a captured wild animal sometimes shows slight diversions from the one-dimensional utilitarian prescriptions. The farmer may punish, be merciful, and on some occasions even exhibit care, and, through care, affection. Here I present some ethnographic examples that are indicative of this:

> It was one day in early February when I found myself walking in the fields of Vassilikos with Lefteris. We were on our way to collect the scattered 'animals', sheep and goats, and lead them back to the pen. At one stage, Lefteris suddenly told me to 'stand still' (*stasou*). There was a hare looking for cover in the thick grass. Lefteris seized it with his hand! He was holding the hare by the ears, the same way he holds the rabbits, but his face was now shining with the excitement of success. He brought the hare back to the farm and put it in a small cage. Then he announced that if it was a female he would allow it to mate with his rabbits. He explained to me that the wild qualities of the hare could revitalize the bloodstock of his tame but weak rabbits. His wife disagreed and commented that it would be better to eat it. 'Otherwise others will eat it or it will die of sadness', she said. They both regarded the hare with pride and amazement, commenting on its beauty. For the remainder of the afternoon, the hare in the cage became an object of public display.

Lefteris and I kept on retelling the amazing story to everybody we met. 'To catch a hare with one's hand' happens to be a Greek proverb emphasizing one's alertness. The hare was eventually killed, as it turned out to be male. 'It will get an unfriendly reception from the male rabbits of the farm', Lefteris explained. However, as this example illustrates, the human protagonist was charmed by the hare's wild qualities and beauty, and the hare had a good chance of remaining alive as a semi-wild animal on the farm. It is important to notice here, the flexible application of the criteria that emphasize usefulness, as is revealed when the farmer, being reluctant to kill the animal, readily declares an alternative 'use' to account for the hare's right to life. The farmer chooses between a context-specific application of 'use' (the animal's potential 'to mate with the rabbits on the farm') and a more general sense of 'use' relating to the edible and tasty nature of the hare's meat.

Turtle-doves[7] are regarded as the most important game on the island. Although Vassilikiots exhibit exceptional passion and devotion to hunting all birds of this species flying over their land, I noticed a few examples of people keeping turtle-doves in large cages near their houses. The cages were made from thin wire netting fitted on to large concrete bases painted with lime. The captured turtle-doves were birds that had been slightly wounded by hunting guns. Their keepers argued that since the birds fell 'into their hands' (*sta heria tous*) alive and in good condition, yet unable to fly, they let them stay on the farm for decorative purposes (*gia omorfia*). This is how the personal wish of the farmers to keep the wild but beautiful birds alive was paired with a more reasonable 'use or function'. It would have been inappropriate for a farmer and a turtle-dove hunter to declare that he kept turtle-doves alive out of love or appreciation of their right to exist. As the

Vassilikiots put it: 'only a non-farmer or a city dweller would have argued so'. But the farmers adherence to the code of 'usefulness' is flexible enough to allow for shifts in practice and interpretation, and to accommodate alternative forms of 'usefulness'.

The marten[8] is the largest predator on the island and represents a great threat to free-ranging chickens. I was once astonished to see a collection of stuffed martens in the house of an elderly female informant. She explained that her husband, like other men in the village, had persistently hunted martens. 'They do harm to chickens', she said, and continued: 'There was a time, though, that one marten was caught on a snare (*dokano*). We decided to keep it in a cage and it became tame. When we let it free again it used to hang around my yard.' Allowing a marten to prowl among poultry is risky and the story appeared quite implausible, but the Vassilikiot woman insisted that it was so. She rationalized her decision to keep 'a wild animal' in her garden on the grounds of an alternative 'use or function'. 'Martens kill snakes and rats', she explained.

As these examples demonstrate, the relationship of Vassilikiots to wild animals often bypasses the constraints of utilitarian reasoning. Independent of ideal evaluations based on criteria that emphasize usefulness, there exists the potential for a relationship in which the protagonists – the farmer and wild animal – compete and display their individual characteristics. In this relationship the farmer is considered to be the legitimate dominant partner and rarely experiences ambivalence regarding his/her position in respect of the animal or its fate. Human authority over the wild animal is taken for granted, and human superiority is considered to be recognized by the animal itself. The wild animal, however, may possess certain attributes, which could possibly offer it some advantage in its relationship with the human protagonist. This may be its potential to do harm, its ability to deceive or its own beauty.

## Conclusion

The human–animal relationship as manifested in particular cultures is a topic well recorded in anthropological literature, albeit not for its own sake. Most anthropologists record ethnographic information on animals in order to answer questions other than the human–animal relationship *per se* (see also Franklin 1999; Knight 2000: 5). Being concerned with animal categories as reflections of the 'categories among men' (Durkheim and Mauss 1963), or with natural categories as metaphorical statements of the relationships between humans (Lévi-Strauss 1962, 1966),[9] or with animal categories as indicative of ethnobiological classification (Berlin 1992) and human cognition (Atran 1990, 1993), anthropologists have treated the relationship of people to animals as an analytical tool serving more general theoretical preoccupations, not as an end in itself. In this chapter, I have examined the human–animal relationship itself, as this is manifested in the everyday life of the inhabitants of Vassilikos, who – despite their deep involvement with tourism – continue to define themselves as 'farmers' (*agrotes*).

In the rather extensive anthropological work on Greek communities, references to the human–animal relationship are rare, the only exception being sections or isolated paragraphs in broader ethnographic monographs, like the classic examples of Friedl (1962),[10] Campbell (1964)[11] and du Boulay (1974).[12] The latter offers the most significant analysis by recognizing the inclusion or membership of domestic animals in the rural household, and the pragmatic, rather than utilitarian, attitude of their owners towards them. As du Boulay observes: 'Animals are not loved for themselves as members of the animal kingdom with their own beauty and peculiarity, but nor are they thought of in crude terms which involve only total exploitation of their productivity' (1974: 86). My ethnographic account in this chapter further supports du Boulay's observations and justifies my persistence in examining the human–animal relationship in terms of meaningful local concepts such as 'order', 'care' and 'usefulness'. The preoccupation of Vassilikiot farmers with an animal's usefulness can only be understood against the template of care and order in the farm environment. In the ethnographic context of Greek household-based economy, self-interest has familial or household-oriented connotations (du Boulay 1974: 169–70; Loizos 1975: 66, 291; Hirschon 1989: 104, 141, 260), and 'usefulness' is similarly defined in relation to the needs of the household, a unit including both animals and human members.

While engaged in the repetitive, everyday tasks of 'caring' for their animals and 'keeping' their farms in 'order', Vassilikiots feel that they are responsible for the well-being of their animals, and openly express the belief that 'without them' and 'their struggle' everything would collapse into disorder. What I want to emphasize here is that the farmers consciously present themselves as the indispensable, irreplaceable providers of 'care' and guardians of 'order' on their farms. They understand their role in relation to their farms and animals as being that of the constant caring principle, the source of protection and reciprocity (see Palsson 1996: 71). In fact, it is a matter of personal pride or 'a point of honour' – to quote du Boulay (1974: 86) – for all farmers in Vassilikos, male or female, wealthy or poor, 'to care for their animals well' (*na frondizoun ta zoa tous kala*). 'Caring well' means to provide food, shelter and medical care. Absence of adequate animal 'care' is synonymous with disorder. This is because 'caring' for animals 'well' is a further prerequisite for 'order' on the farm. 'Order' (*taksi*) and 'care' (*frondidha*) are concepts intimately linked and often impossible to separate.

Predation by wild animals on domestic animals arouses sentiments of sorrow (*stenohoria*) and anger (*thimos*) in their owners and caretakers. The process of 'caring' is interrupted and a significant amount of effort and labour is 'lost' (*hanete*) along with the dead animals. Predatory attacks by wild animals on domestic animals can be understood as a violation of the established order of the farm, which the farmer tries to maintain through a persistent lifelong effort. The human protagonists defend their domestic animals against wild predators with determination, a task that is locally perceived as a moral duty towards their community as a whole (Knight 2000: 7). Sometimes a 'disproportional amount of time, money, and emotion' is devoted to hunting wild predators, resources that often outweigh the damage caused by the harmful animals in question (Moore 1994: 83). In fact, Vassilikiot farmers are engaged in a constant, persistent 'struggle' (Friedl 1962: 75; du Boulay 1974: 56; Kenna 1990: 149–50; Hart 1992: 65; Dubisch 1995: 215; Theodossopoulos 2003: 58–62, 162) to establish and defend 'order' in the constantly changing, regenerating and often threatening environment that physically surrounds them.

Despite this contesting attitude towards the elements of the natural environment, Vassilikiots do not always apply a strict utilitarian sense of justice towards wild animals. Although they would normally kill 'harmful' (*vlavera*) animals whenever possible, I recorded several cases in which the farmers kept wild animals in captivity and/or allowed them to remain alive. In those cases, the characteristics of wild animals, rather than their practical 'use', such as their beauty or their friendly behaviour, provided the rationale for keeping them alive. Vassilikiots never justify their protectionist attitudes towards them in terms of affection. A wild animal is not introduced into the context of everyday 'care', which justifies feelings of this kind. Instead, the villagers would think of alternative forms of 'use' to rationalize their non-utilitarian decisions concerning wild animals. Rationalizations of this kind reflect the people's concern to be consistent with household-centred strategies and priorities, but at the same time indicate their personal freedom to negotiate their relationship with wild animals and apply their personal decisions at a practical level.

Thus, despite their frequently articulated emphasis on animal usefulness, Vassilikiot farmers clearly express in conversation the expectations they have of their animals, and often talk to the animals themselves, despite their confident assertion that animals do not possess reason. In this respect, I can safely argue that it is not only hunter-gatherers or other pre-modern, non-Western people who –to use a phrase by Ingold (1994: 11)– 'keep up a dialogue' with the non-human living beings of their immediate environment. Vassilikiots constantly address their domestic animals in an effort to explain to them the order of everyday activities, even the fact that their confinement within this order is for their own benefit. Vassilikiots maintain that animals 'learn' (*mathenoun*), through repetition and punishment, their expected place in space and time, and from my own observations most animals do 'learn'!

With these final observations, I do not wish to undermine the practical, pragmatically oriented attitude of the people I studied; rather, I have attempted to

locate their relationship with animals in the context of daily strategies and practice: one that emphasizes household priorities over self-centred, individualistic
aspirations. In the narratives of the Vassilikiot farmers, the 'usefulness' or 'harm-
fulness' of animals are not mere reflections of a positive or negative utility, but
expected and, in some cases, realized outcomes of a dynamic interrelationship
between human and animal members of individual households. Although
Vassilikiot attitudes towards animals are clearly anthropocentric – or to use a better
term, 'human-household-centred' – they are not strictly utilitarian and exploitative.
As Morris has argued, anthropocentrism does not always imply an ethic of domination (1998: 6). The intentions of the human protagonists of this chapter can only
become meaningful if understood in terms of their everyday investments in caring
for animals and the broader context of care and order that defines the
human–animal relationship in Vassilikos.

## Notes

1.  Vassilikos is the name for both an administrative community (*koinotita*) of
    approximately 600 registered inhabitants and a small peninsula that stretches
    from the south-west of the island of Zakynthos. The fieldwork upon which
    this article is based was conducted in 1992 and 1993 in Vassilikos.
2.  Gisli Palsson, referring to the human–environmental relationship, invents a
    third generalizing category, one that he calls 'paternalism' and which involves
    the recognition of human supremacy combined with some reciprocity and
    responsibility (1996: 66, 69–72, 76).
3.  For information on those Vassilikiots who keep 'flocks of animals', and the
    particular care this form of animal husbandry entails, see Theodossopoulos
    (2002).
4.  Vassilikiots appear to be particularly interested in dead animals' anatomy.
    They carefully observe, and compare each animals' internal condition. Once,
    while I was participating in the killing and skinning of two rabbits, a male and
    a female, I recorded the farmer saying: 'Look at the fatness of the female. The
    male one, although of the same age, is thinner. This is because it mates all the
    time (*giati vatevi sinehia*)!'
5.  Every time Vassilikiots kill a rabbit, they hit the animal twice on the shoulder
    with the handle of their knife, 'in order to anaesthetize it (*gia na
    narkothoun*)'. But this technique 'does not work all the time', they observe.
6.  The traditional system of rights and duties in respect of animal husbandry
    between a landlord and a labourer (κοπιαστή) – a system practised in the
    village until the 1960s – included the following obligation: the labourer would
    be credited with a specific number of animals to 'care' for each season. The
    landlord would attribute the loss of animals as a result of illness or accident

to the labourer's inadequate 'care' for the animals. The labourer would then be expected to replace the value of the lost animals at his own expense.

7.  Turtle-dove (*Streptopelia turtur*).

8.  Beach marten (*Martes foina*).

9.  See also the classic accounts by Edmund Leach (1964) and Mary Douglas (1975).

10. Ernestine Friedl seems to underestimate the relationship rural Greeks have with their animals: 'The villagers do not give their animals individual names', she argues, 'they take no particular care to keep them physically comfortable' (1962: 30). Friedl refers to the 'beating' and 'kicking' of animals at work and the children's 'teasing' of them. She recognizes that dogs and other animals 'are not considered pets' and describes her informants' attitude towards them as being 'completely utilitarian' (ibid.: 32).

11. Unlike Friedl, Campbell, in his well-known study of the Sarakatsani shepherds, acknowledges the importance of the human–animal relationship, which according to his view 'must be seen not only in terms of utilitarian satisfaction or social function' (1964: 34). Campbell explains that the main concerns in the life of the Sarakatsani are 'sheep, children and honour', and underlines the identification of the shepherds with their sheep, the latter being 'a prerequisite of prestige' (ibid.: 19, 30–1, 35). For the Sarakatsani, 'shepherding has intrinsic value', Campbell finally remarks; their conception of time and the organization of their lives revolve around the movements and needs of their flocks.

12. As I have already mentioned in the introduction to this chapter, du Boulay recognizes animals as lower members of the rural household, subjected, like human members, to obligations and privileges of 'total loyalty and mutual support', superimposed by a household-centred organization of the village economy (1974: 16, 18, 86–9). She makes clear that animals 'occupy the lowest position … in the order of things', and in times of hardship are often expected to suffer more than, or at least as much as, the humans do, being the first to become sacrificed for the benefit of the household to which they are attached and bound by links or 'reciprocal obligation' (ibid.: 86–9). Du Boulay further explains that animals are not loved for their 'sheer utility' but because they are 'useful' members of the rural household. And the rural household rarely includes 'non-working' members. Thus animals, by means of their inclusion or membership into the household, enter a relationship of 'mutual' or 'reciprocal obligation', according to which, like any other household member, they are expected to contribute to its welfare, being entitled in turn to the necessary care needed for their maintenance (ibid.: 86–9).

# References

Atran, S. (1990), *Cognitive Foundations of Natural History*. Cambridge: Cambridge University Press.

Atran, S. (1993), 'Whither "Ethnoscience"?' In P. Boyer (ed.), *Cognitive Aspects of Religious Symbolism*. Cambridge: Cambridge University Press.

Berlin, B. (1992), *Ethnobiological Classification: Principles of Categorization of Plants and Animals in Traditional Societies*. Princeton: Princeton University Press.

Blok, A. (1981), 'Rams and Billy-Goats: a Key to the Mediterranean Code of Honour'. *Man* 16(3): 427–40.

Brandes, S. (1980), *Metaphors of Masculinity: Sex and Status in Andalusian Folklore*. Pennsylvania: University of Pennsylvania Press.

Brandes, S. (1981), 'Like Wounded Stags: Male Sexual Ideology in an Andalusian Town', in S. Ortner and H. Whitehead (eds), *Sexual Meanings: The Cultural Construction of Gender and Sexuality*. Cambridge: Cambridge University Press.

Campbell, J. K. (1964), *Honour, Family and Patronage: A Study of the Institutions and Moral Values in a Greek Mountain Community*. Oxford: Oxford University Press.

Couroucli, M. (1985), *Les oliviers du lignage: une Grece de tradition Venitienne*. Paris: Maisonneuve et Larose.

Cowan, J. K. (1990), *Dance and the Body Politic in Northern Greece*. Princeton: Princeton University Press.

Douglas, M. (1975), *Implicit Meanings: Essays in Anthropology*. London: Routledge.

Du Boulay, J. (1974), *Portrait of a Greek Mountain Village*. Oxford: Clarendon Press.

Dubisch, J. (1995), *In a Different Place: Pilgrimage, Gender, and Politics of a Greek Island Shrine*. Princeton: Princeton University Press.

Durkheim, E. and M. Mauss (1963), *Primitive Classification*. London: Cohen and West.

Ellen, R. (1996), 'The Cognitive Geometry of Nature: A Contextual Approach', in P. Descola and G. Palsson (eds), *Nature and Society: Anthropological Perspectives*. London: Routledge.

Franklin, A. (1999), *Animals and Modern Cultures: A Sociology of Human–Animal Relations in Modernity*. London: Sage.

Friedl, E. (1962), *Vassilika: A Village in Modern Greece*. New York: Holt, Rinehart and Winston.

Friedl, E. (1967), 'The Position of Women: Appearance and Reality'. *Anthropological Quarterly* 40(3), 97–108.

Galani-Moutafi, V. (1993), 'From Agriculture to Tourism: Property, Labour, Gender and Kinship in a Greek Island Village (Part One)'. *Journal of Modern Greek Studies* 11, 241–70.

Gefou-Madianou, D. (1992), 'Exclusion and Unity, Retsina and Sweet Wine: Commensality and Gender in a Greek Agrotown', in D. Gefou-Madianou (ed.), *Alcohol, Gender And Culture*. London: Routledge.

Greger, S. (1988), *Village on the Plateau: Magoulas: A Mountain Village in Crete*. Studley, Warwickshire: Brewin Books.

Hart, L. K. (1992), *Time, Religion, and Social Experience in Rural Greece*. Lanham: Rowman and Littlefield Publishers.

Herzfeld, M. (1985), *The Poetics of Manhood: Contest and Identity in a Cretan Mountain Village*. Princeton: Princeton University Press.

Herzfeld, M. (1991), *A Place in History: Social and Monumental Time in a Cretan Town*. Princeton: Princeton University Press.

Hirschon, R. (1989), *Heirs of the Greek Catastrophe: The Social Life of Asia Minor Refugees in Piraeus*. Oxford: Clarendon Press.

Ingold, T. (1980), *Hunters, Pastoralists and Ranchers*. Cambridge: Cambridge University Press.

Ingold, T. (1986), *The Appropriation of Nature: Essays on Human Ecology and Social Relations*. Manchester: Manchester University Press.

Ingold, T. (1988), 'Introduction', in T. Ingold (ed.), *What is an Animal?* London: Unwin Hyman. (Republished Routledge, 1994, with a new preface.)

Ingold, T. (1994), 'From Trust to Domination: An Alternative History of Human–Animal Relations', in A. Manning and J. Serpell (eds), *Animals and Human Society*. London: Routledge.

Ingold, T. (1996), 'Hunting and Gathering as Ways of Perceiving the Environment', in R. Ellen and K. Fukui (eds), *Redefining Nature: Ecology, Culture and Domestication*. Oxford: Berg.

Kenna, M. E. (1976), 'The Idiom of Family', in J. G. Peristiany (ed.), *Mediterranean Family Structures*. Cambridge: Cambridge University Press.

Kenna, M. E. (1990), 'Family, Economy and Community on a Greek Island', in C. C. Harris (ed.), *Family, Economy And Community*. Cardiff: University of Wales Press.

Kenna, M. E. (1995), 'Saying "No" in Greece: Some Preliminary Thoughts on Hospitality, Gender and the Evil Eye', In *Les Amis et Les Autres: Melanges en l'honneur de John Peristiany / Brothers and Others: Essays in Honour of John Peristiany*. Athens: Greek National Centre of Social Research (EKKE).

Knight, J. (2000), 'Introduction', in J. Knight (ed.), *Natural Enemies: People–Wildlife Conflict in Anthropological Perspective*. London: Routledge.

Leach, E. (1964), 'Animal Categories and Verbal Abuse', in E. H. Lenneberg (ed.), *New Directions in the Study of Language*. Cambridge, MA: MIT Press.

Lévi-Strauss, C. (1962), *Totemism*. London: Merlin Press.

Lévi-Strauss, C. (1966), *The Savage Mind*. London: Weidenfeld and Nicolson.

Loizos, P. (1975), *The Greek Gift: Politics in a Greek Cypriot Village*. Oxford: Basil Blackwell.

Marvin, G. (1988), *Bullfight*. Urbana: University of Illinois Press.

Moore, R. S. (1994), 'Metaphors of Encroachment: Hunting for Wolves on a Central Greek Mountain'. *Anthropological Quarterly* 67: 81–8.

Morris, B. (1995), 'Woodland and Village: Reflections on the "Animal Estate" in Rural Malawi'. *Journal of the Royal Anthropological Institute* (N.S.) 1, 301–15.

Morris, B. (1998), *The Power of Animals: An Ethnography*. Oxford: Berg.

Palsson, G. (1996), 'Constructing Natures: Symbolic Ecology and Social Practice', in P. Descola and G. Palsson (eds), *Nature and Society: Anthropological Perspectives*. London: Routledge.

Papagaroufali, E. (1996), 'Xenotransplantation and Transgenesis: Im-moral Stories about Human–Animal Relations in the West', in P. Descola and G. Palsson (eds), *Nature and Society: Anthropological Perspectives*. London: Routledge.

Pina-Cabral, J. (1986), *Sons of Adam, Daughters of Eve: The Peasant Worldview of the Alto Minho*. Oxford: Clarendon Press.

Theodossopoulos, D. (1997), 'Turtles, Farmers and "Ecologists": The Cultural Reason Behind a Community's Resistance to Environmental Conservation'. *Journal of Mediterranean Studies* 7(2): 250–67.

Theodossopoulos, D. (1999), 'The Pace of the Work and the Logic of the Harvest: Women, Labour and the Olive Harvest in a Greek Island Community' *Journal of the Royal Anthropological Institute* (N.S.) 5: 611–26.

Theodossopoulos, D. (2002), 'Environmental Conservation and Indigenous Culture in a Greek Island Community: the Dispute over the Sea Turtles', in D. Chatty and M. Colchester (eds), *Conservation and Mobile Indigenous Peoples: Displacement, Forced Settlement and Sustainable Development*. Oxford: Berghahn.

Theodossopoulos, D. (2003), *Troubles with Turtles: Cultural Understandings of the Environment on a Greek Island*. Oxford: Berghahn.

Van der Ploeg, J. D. and A. Long (1994), *Born from Within: Practice and Perspective of Endogenous Rural Development*. Van Gorum: cip-data kononklijke bibliotheek.

Willis, R. (1990), 'Introduction', in R. Willis (ed.), *Signifying Animals*. London: Unwin Hyman.

Zarkia, C. 1996. '*Philoxenia* Receiving Tourists – but not Guests – on a Greek Island', in J. Boissevain (ed.), *Coping with Tourists*. Oxford: Berghahn.

# –2–

# Person, Place or Pig: Animal Attachments and Human Transactions in New Guinea

*Peter D. Dwyer and Monica Minnegal*

## Introduction

A recurring image in the literature from New Guinea is of a woman suckling her piglet (e.g. Brown 1978: 90; Brutti and Boissière 2002: 147, phot. 2; Goodale 1995: 83; Hallpike 1977: 71; Jolly 1984: 82; Meggitt 1965, pl. 10; Schoorl 1993: 75; Simoons and Baldwin 1982; Sorenson 1976: 54–6). That image is iconic, on the one hand, of Melanesia and, on the other, of the bond which people may establish with domestic animals. It may be imagined to capture that state of 'total community' between people and pigs which Marvin Harris (1975: 39) called 'pig love'. We ourselves have doubts about the image. Though certainly widespread, we doubt it is, or was, a common practice and suspect the survival prospects of the piglets concerned may be low (see Meggitt 1958: 291; Baldwin 1982: 36). It is true, however, that throughout Melanesia the attachment of pig-carers to their pigs is very strong. Many authors have regarded the domestic pig as being 'incorporated into the ... world of the household' (Macintyre 1984: 110). As Rappaport (1968: 58–9) wrote: 'it is hardly facetious to say that the pig through its early socialization becomes a member of a Maring family', it is 'petted, talked to and fed choice morsels. It shares the living quarters of the woman's house'. It is groomed and deloused, is usually named, may be addressed as 'my child' and may be publically mourned at the time it is dispatched and butchered (e.g. Baldwin 1982: 36; Oosterwal 1961: 70–1; Reay 1959: 13; Sorenson 1976: 55). For that is the eventual fate of domestic pigs. As Harris remarked, pig love 'includes obligatory sacrificing and eating of pigs on special occasions'.

Young (1984: 124) wrote of the 'pig-infatuated peoples of Vanuatu and the New Guinea Highlands', while Jolly (1984), in an essay on 'the anatomy of pig love', directed attention to connections between ways in which domestic pigs are managed and the place of pigs in the socio-economic and cultural systems of Melanesian societies. Their importance on the latter counts is indisputable. Whatever their contribution to diet and the nutritional status of people, pigs commonly play a crucial role in ceremonial and spiritual life: in bride wealth and affinal exchanges, in initiation, curing and mortuary rituals, in establishing prestige, and in major regional exchange networks such as *moka* and *tee* of the New Guinea highlands (e.g. Godelier and Strathern 1991; Lemmonier 1993; Meggitt 1974; Rubel and Rosman 1978). They are central to analyses of the evolution of agricultural intensification and socio-cultural complexity within New Guinea (e.g. Bayliss-Smith and Golson 1992; Feil 1987; Kelly 1988). And they mediate relations between men and women where, as in some societies, they serve as substitutes for women at the time of marriage and, as in many, the burden of care falls to women while the ultimate payoffs of wealth and prestige accrue to men (e.g. Jolly 1984; Kahn 1986; Meggitt 1958; Modjeska 1982; A. J. Strathern 1982).[1]

In this chapter we take Jolly's insights as a starting point. We direct attention to differences across societies of New Guinea in the ways in which people manage young pigs and to the implications this has for the kinds of attachments established by pigs. We then show that the strategies of management are themselves correlated with other aspects of human ecology – with mobility, settlement pattern and sub-sistence – and argue that they have consequences for social life in either limiting or facilitating, on the one hand, relations between men and women and, on the other, the possibility that large pigs may be exchanged as live animals (see Kelly 1988).

In this discussion we draw on our own understandings of the Kubo people of the interior lowlands of western Papua New Guinea (Dwyer 1993; Minnegal and Dwyer 1997). The ways in which these people manage young pigs differ greatly from patterns described from elsewhere in the country. Agricultural practices among the lowland Kubo are non-intensified, both hunting and gathering con-tribute much to subsistence, and social structure – which is characterized by the importance of immediate exchange – lacks the complex forms seen among 'Big Man' societies of the highlands (Minnegal and Dwyer 1998). It might be expected, therefore, that these people would keep few pigs and would invest little time or labour in their maintenance (e.g. Feil 1987; Morren 1977). But that is not the case. Among Kubo the investment of time, at least, is very great and the attachment of each domestic pig to a particular carer is exceptionally strong. The outcomes are that here, more than elsewhere, it is difficult to exchange mature pigs as live animals and difficult for men to usurp the rights of women at the times the animals are killed, butchered and distributed. The Kubo case has encouraged us to think again about common understandings of the attachments established between pigs and people in New Guinea.

## The Kubo Case: Attachment to Person

The Kubo form a small, dispersed population living in a region of lowland and foothill rainforest and back swamps in which *Metroxylon* sago palms, an important staple, are abundant. Wild pigs are common here and, together with fish, provide most of the animal protein eaten by the people (Dwyer and Minnegal 1991). But despite the abundance of wild pigs Kubo do keep domestic animals. In 1986 and 1987 the ratio of domestic pigs to people was as high as 0.5: higher, in fact, than is usually observed among other New Guinean populations with easy access to wild pigs. Since that time the ratio of pigs to people has increased and, in parallel, management practices have altered (Minnegal and Dwyer 1997). Here, we describe practices that obtained in the earlier period.

Among Kubo all pigs in the care of people are the offspring of wild boars. This is usual in areas of New Guinea where there are populations of wild pigs. It reflects the substantial costs entailed in maintaining intact boars and is ensured by castrating all males recruited to the domestic population (Dwyer 1996). But, although all Kubo pigs have wild fathers, the mothers of most are domestic; about one-third have dual wild parentage.

Women are the primary carers of domestic pigs. They may receive some assistance from husbands and older daughters, but the identification of particular pigs with particular carers is seldom ambiguous. For the first 18 months of its life the pig and its carer are seldom apart. Beyond that age, however, the pig is encouraged to remain in the forest, often several kilometres from the village, when its carer returns home at night.

Domestic pigs which range free in the forest are monitored closely. As the time approaches when a sow will give birth the rate of visits by its carer increases and, sometimes, because the animal chooses a well-concealed birthing site, it is necessary to search for the animal. When the piglets are about two weeks old they are removed from their mother; in exceptional cases they may be as much as four weeks old. This is well before the time when they would be naturally weaned and, preferably, just before the time that the sow, with her piglets, would abandon use of the birthing site (Boyd 1984: 29; Clutton-Brock 1987: 73; Giffin 1978: 44).

The removal of piglets from a sow is achieved by ambush, preferably at the birthing nest, and often at first light in the morning. The carer, as the only person who can approach the sow, leads the ambush but commonly invites a few others, either male or female. When the sow and her piglets are disturbed by this group they scatter and it is usual that the person who captures a piglet is, henceforth, its owner. Thus the carer, who may not be the owner of the sow, has considerable control over future ownership of piglets produced by that sow. Men or youths who have captured a piglet deliver it to a woman who agrees to act as carer. Thereafter, the animal has no further contact with its mother.

The care of very young piglets, which under natural conditions would suckle for up to four months, is demanding (Hughes and Varley 1980: 136, Špinka 1998: 273). The young animals are kept in string bags, they are petted, carried about, tethered by a leg rope, taught to walk and run while on a leash and fed pre-masticated bananas and other soft, easily digestible foods. Despite this attention, they grow slowly. Relative to the size of occasional same-litter piglets which are left with the sow, either deliberately because it is planned to eat them as young animals or accidentally because they escaped capture, those which are taken into care appear initially to be stunted. Piglets that do escape capture are, if they do not die, fated to be killed and eaten. No piglets in the care of people have been allowed to remain with the sow to the time of natural weaning. Piglets born to wild sows are also only tamed if captured when very young.

For three to four months after capture a domestic piglet is effectively isolated from other pigs, sleeping in the house of its carer. Even well beyond that time its contact with other pigs is very limited. It may be tethered beneath the house at night, but is not in physical contact with other pigs. And because Kubo are mobile on a day-to-day basis, shifting between locations within a 50 square kilometre subsistence zone and visiting other communities up to two days' walk away (Minnegal and Dwyer 2000a), piglets do not become familiar with particular areas of forest. Rather, they learn the routines of their carer. Deprived of association with other pigs, even its mother, from such an early age, the primary attachment formed is to the woman who acts as its carer. The strength of that attachment shapes the future behaviour of domestic pigs and, as discussed later, influences the role of female carers at the time the pig is killed, cooked and distributed.

Close attachment of pig to carer is sustained for about 18 months. Through this period a pig usually accompanies its carer when she leaves the village or bushhouse to attend to subsistence tasks. If she is working at a garden the pig may be tethered nearby, though the tether site is shifted several times through the day. If she is processing sago then the pig wanders freely, feeding at piles of waste pith. If she visits a neighbouring community then, for the early months, when the piglet needs regular attention, she takes it with her. On days when this is inconvenient the animal remains tethered in or near the village, and when she returns it is fed, groomed and petted. As the animal ages, has learned to forage, and its attachment to carer reduces the likelihood that it will run wild, it is granted more freedom. Sometimes a carer will spend the day walking through the forest, with her pig or pigs running free, visiting places which provide attractive foraging prospects for the animals. On other occasions she may release her pigs outside the village with the expectation that they will return to her in the evening. Often, it is necessary to call the animals or instigate an evening search, but it is rare that a pig fails to return. When that does occur it is assumed that the animal is lost or has died, and several days may be spent looking for it.

One consequence of these early management practices is that the attachments pigs form are to particular carers, and not to people in general. Larger domestic pigs may, in fact, be dangerous to people other than their carer and immediate members of her family. The latter are likely to be safe simply because, among

Kubo, members of a family are often together through the day and the pig becomes familiar with them. But other people are not safe. It is for this reason that pigs are usually on a leash when they are taken from, or brought back to, the village. When a pig is older, and forages alone through the day, it is expected that its carer will watch for the evening return, go to meet the pig, attach the leash and, with the animal secured, bring it to her house. If she fails to do this people call that the pig has come; if she does not respond they are wary and may retreat to the security of their own houses. No one other than the carer will attempt to restrain the pig.

As noted, when a domestic pig is about 18 months old its carer attempts to relocate it to a favourable foraging site, usually, though not invariably, in the back swamps. Though not essential, relocation facilitates access to domestic sows by wild boars. Relocation is desirable also because large pigs, whether sows or barrows, become increasingly burdensome if based at the village. They are a nuisance, may be dangerous to other people, and are more difficult to keep out of gardens which, for preference, Kubo people do not fence. Relocation is achieved by remaining with the pig at a bush-house for as much as a week, familiarizing it with the area surrounding that house, supplying it with easy access to very large quantities of attractive food by felling a sago palm and exposing the pith and, thereafter, making regular visits. In effect, it is necessary to establish and then maintain, for the pig, an association between that place and its carer. This phase of management is enormously time consuming. Pigs often abandon the forest location and return to the village so that it is necessary to recommence the process of relocation. We know of domestic pigs swimming the 80- to 100-metre-wide Strickland River, where the current is fast, to return to their carer. Sometimes the attachment of pig to carer is so entrenched that relocation fails and a pregnant sow builds a birthing nest near the village and, soon after farrowing, brings her litter to her carer. In one case, when this scenario prevailed, both the piglets and the sow were judged to be worthless. The former were killed by the carer when they appeared in the village and the latter dispatched soon after by fabricating a need to give gifts of pork.

## Attachment to Place and to Pigs

Knowledge of the ways in which New Guineans incorporate piglets into local populations of domestic animals is, by and large, anecdotal. The earliest phase of rearing has seldom been described in detail. However, the Kubo case directs attention to three dimensions of management which have important implications for the kinds of attachments formed by pigs. These are the usual age of piglets at the time they are removed from their mothers, the duration and intensity of close association between a domestic pig and its carer or carers, and the degree to which, early in their lives, domestic pigs closely associate with other pigs. Across New Guinea there is much inter-societal variation on each of these dimensions, and none is ultimately constrained by the others. There is also intra-societal variation which arises, for example, when young pigs are acquired by trade and, initially, are managed in ways that differ from the treatment accorded to piglets born to local sows. Here we discuss two configurations of management which differ from that found among Kubo but recur, with minor variants, in many societies of New Guinea.

In the first of these alternatives, piglets are typically separated from sows when they are a month or two old – later than among Kubo but still well before they would be naturally weaned. Their period of close association with a human carer is usually only 2–3 months, not the 18 months typical for Kubo pigs. After this time, the pigs are familiarized with particular food-rich areas where they are expected to forage, but there is little attempt to create an association for the pig between these places and their carers.

In the second alternative, most piglets are allowed to wean naturally; at no time are they fully alienated from other pigs. Their attachment to carers is established by regular handling, including petting and grooming, usually while in the company of other pigs. This is reinforced by daily feeding at the place where the animals sleep and, perhaps, by being herded to, though often abandoned at, places where they forage through the day, again usually in the company of other pigs.

Following Kelly (1988), these alternatives may be illustrated, respectively, by the Etoro of the middle altitudes (700–1,100 metres above sea level) and by numerous societies of Highland New Guinea. Population density is about two per square kilometre for Etoro and, in the highlands, usually in the range of 50–150 per square kilometre. Of the former people, Kelly wrote that early management ensured that pigs 'become familiar with the territory that will later become their home range' (1988: 116); they become attached to place. With regard to the latter we argue that the primary attachments formed by pigs are, in fact, to other pigs.

## The Etoro Case

At lower altitudes of Etoro territory domestic sows are sired by wild boars, give birth in the forest, and capture of the piglets is by ambush. Separation from mothers probably does not occur until the piglets are at least a month old, by which age they are able to eat a variety of foods without need for special preparation. This time corresponds to common practice in modern commercial piggeries (Špinka 1998: 273; J. Blackshaw pers. comm.). At higher altitudes, where wild pigs are very rare, domestic sows are sired by domestic boars (Dwyer 1990: 58).[2] Here, before a sow gives birth, her carers – these tasks are often shared by wife and husband – build a secure shelter which they provision with food. The sow is encouraged to sleep here and the shelter is designed such that, though the sow may step in or out, her piglets are held captive. For some weeks she has to return to the shelter to suckle her piglets, though later, with the shelter established as a night-time retreat, the barrier is removed and the piglets accompany their mother during the day. Piglets are handled by the carers from soon after birth, and closely monitored when they begin to wander with the sow.

At one to two months of age the piglets are removed from their mothers and each is in the care of a particular woman. Thereafter, for six or more weeks, they ride in string bags, wander in gardens, or [are] hurried along tracks with a rope tied to one leg (Dwyer 1990: 57). They are fed and fondled and learn to associate their carer, and members of her family, with the promise of food. When they are older they spend less time with carers and, at an age of between three and six months, are encouraged to forage alone. At higher altitudes the animals are placed in an abandoned but securely fenced garden or allowed to forage with other pigs. At first, they might be retrieved in the evening and returned to the village. Eventually they are given greater freedom and forage alone through areas of regrowth. They are visited often, provided with small portions of food, and groomed. Most, in fact, live near the cluster of longhouses that comprise the village and, in the evening, come when called. They are no longer always restrained by fences. Among lower-altitude Etoro it seems that separation of pig and carer is achieved by training the pig to remain at a place where there is abundant forage. Usually, however, because patterns of day-to-day movement among these people are more tightly constrained than among Kubo, the pigs are familiar with these areas before they are abandoned (Kelly 1988: 116). Throughout Etoro territory, free-ranging domestic pigs establish familiarity with a home range which may drift in size and location through time but usually ensures that they can be readily located if wanted. Because the densities both of pigs and people are low – around two people per square kilometre – the animals have relatively few opportunities to establish strong attachments to other pigs.

Relative to the Kubo case, Etoro pigs spend a longer period with their mothers and a much shorter period in close association with a human carer. They interact with more people than do Kubo pigs. The outcome is that the animals are docile. They are not dangerous to people other than their carers. They are easy to approach and content to accept food and a scratch from nearly anyone.

## The Highlands Case

The management of pigs among highland societies differs from that of both Kubo and Etoro on three counts. First, most piglets born to local sows associate with and nurse from their mothers until the time when they are naturally weaned.[3] Second, these piglets generally do not experience a phase of intense association with a human carer during which they are likely to accompany her wherever she goes in the daytime. And, third, from the time of birth and throughout their lives pigs are likely to be associated with other pigs, though not necessarily the same pigs, and are free to initiate physical contact with those pigs.

The highlanders live beyond the range of populations of wild pigs, and all piglets are the progeny of domestic sows and domestic boars. It is usual that relatively few intact boars are kept, perhaps one boar to about twenty sows (Hide 1981: 449), and, in some societies, after they have bred a few times, these are either castrated or killed to minimize costs associated with the care of large intact males (e.g. A. Strathern 1984: 76). The management of older domestic pigs entails either one or both of two systems. Among Sinasina, for example, the animals may be housed at the village and, by day, kept penned or, more often, either 'led to, and tethered at, specific foraging sites' or released at the village perimeter to 'forage freely' (Hide: 1981: 328). Alternatively, they may be kept at pig houses outside the village, and sometimes distant from it, where foraging opportunities are 'unrestricted except for fences protecting cultivation' (ibid.). Under both systems the pigs are usually fed at least once a day by their carers. Similar systems elsewhere in the highlands may be combined with herding wherein the animals are taken to selected foraging areas and may be guarded, perhaps by children, while they forage (e.g. Waddell 1972). Management of intact boars often entails more restriction than management of barrows and sows, with the animals sometimes penned. The extra costs incurred are acknowledged in that owners of boars receive payment – as money, piglets or meat – when a sow is serviced (e.g. Meggitt 1958: 290; Sillitoe 1979: 147; A. Strathern 1984: 76).

When a sow is ready to give birth she is usually given enough freedom to avoid other pigs and make a nest (e.g. Hide 1981: 460–1). For several days after farrowing she is unlikely to be approached by anyone other than her carer. Later she is encouraged to return to the pig house and, with her piglets, is fed at this place. The piglets themselves are picked up, petted, groomed and talked too. They are taught to accept being tethered. But, unless they are orphaned or sick, it is unlikely that they will be removed permanently from their mother. Rather, they accompany the sow when she is released to forage and are weaned at a time when she and they choose. In the highlands, at least locally born pigs are reared in such a way that, though familiar with people, their primary associations are with an often-changing population of other pigs; often-changing, because people regularly exchange live pigs (e.g. Boyd 1985; Feil 1987; Meggitt 1958). But, of course, growing piglets are of intense interest to both their carers and other people. In most parts of highland New Guinea they are given personal names (see Meggitt 1958: 287). Their health and size are often discussed. Through this engagement with their animals, carers develop close attachment to them. It is unlikely, however, that this is reciprocated. The pigs learn to associate people in general, and their carers in particular, with a regular source of good-quality food; they are tame and usually easy to approach and handle, but to the extent that they form strong attachments they do so with other pigs. Perhaps paradoxically, within New Guinea the domestic pigs which are most removed from contact with populations of wild animals are the ones whose contacts with other pigs are most like that of wild animals.

## The Biology of Attachment

It is important to comment, though briefly, on the problematic nature of attachment. Our argument that the management of domestic pigs variously promotes attachment by those pigs to persons, places or other pigs should not be taken as an assertion that 'attachment' is a unitary phenomenon. Far from it. Different, perhaps multiple, biological processes are likely to be operating. But these processes are little understood.

Morren (1986: 88) considered that Miyanmin piglets, which like those of Kubo are removed from sows when they are very young and are initially fed pre-masticated food, 'must become imprinted on the woman caring for them rather than on a sow in order to be well domesticated' (see also Baldwin 1982: 36; Hughes 1970: 276). This had been our own impression in the Kubo case. But, in fact, imprinting in piglets appears to occur gradually through the first few days after birth (J. Blackshaw pers. comm.) and, hence, the extremely close and sustained attachment of pig to person observed in some New Guinean societies must arise from subsequent conditioning that is rewarded, primarily, through the provision of food, shelter and physical contact (see Signoret *et al*. 1975: 300).

Attachments to place by domestic pigs might be understood as implicating home range or territorial behaviour. Certainly it would be inadvisable to attribute this to imprinting, though we note that some authors have treated such attachment as a form of 'social bonding' (Fraser 1985). Different authors vary with respect to the existence or otherwise of well-defined home ranges in wild pigs, but, as with many mammals, this behaviour may vary according to local conditions (e.g. Nowak 1999: 1054–8). In rainforest habitats, where food supply is favourable, particular pigs may well establish relatively long-term associations with particular places. When this behaviour is reinforced because food supply at those places is regularly supplemented by human carers, as with Etoro, home range behaviour may be even more likely. Certainly, from New Guinea, there are reports of pigs which have returned considerable distances to favoured foraging places after being moved elsewhere by their owners. In fact, while Kubo sometimes have difficulty training older pigs to remain at foraging sites in the forest and not seek their carer at the village, Etoro sometimes have difficulty keeping a pig at or close to the village, away from its usual haunts, in readiness for a feast.

Finally, attachment to other pigs, as seen in highland New Guinea, is perhaps most easily accepted as relatively unaltered biologically based behaviour. Where piglets are not separated from their mothers until the time of natural weaning, are allowed relatively free access to other pigs, and roam or are herded with those pigs, then the extent and nature of interactions between pigs is likely to influence their behaviour to a greater extent than the contacts they have with people. Indeed, their association with people is itself most likely a conditioned response to the combination of keeping company with previously trained pigs, the daily provision of high-quality food and, given that nights can be cold in highland New Guinea, the provision of a shelter which may be warmed by fire. In these circumstances, more than in either the Kubo or Etoro cases, pigs can most readily satisfy their attraction to maintaining physical contact with other pigs. As Signoret *et al.* (1975: 317; see also Hemworth 1982) wrote: 'tactile stimuli are important to pigs'. In the highlands the animals often maintain bodily contact while resting or sleeping.

These observations support an argument that patterns of attachment are labile, and can be manipulated by controlling the early developmental experiences of pigs. But this alone does not explain why management practices differ between societies; indeed, as we show later, the diversity of practices is greater than our three key examples suggest. To understand that variation requires that we consider ecological correlates of attachment which, on the one hand, may constrain rearing practices and, on the other, encourage manipulations that yield desired outcomes.

## Ecological Correlates of Attachment

Attachment of pigs to people, place or other pigs affects the ease with which those pigs can be moved, either with their carers or between carers. This returns us to a primary theme in discussions of the place of pigs in New Guinea societies – the ways in which transaction of pigs, as live animals or as pork, mediate social relationships. An earlier argument that live exchange of mature pigs and high pig-to-people ratios invariably co-occurred in New Guinea was challenged by Kelly (1988) on the basis of Etoro data.

Etoro keep relatively large numbers of pigs – approximating a ratio of one pig per person – but do not exchange live pigs; rather, the animals are killed and the meat exchanged. Kelly (ibid.) considered their failure to exchange live pigs to be a correlate of the way in which they managed pigs. His argument had two parts. Mature pigs were difficult to transact live because they were strongly attached to particular places and obtained most of their food as forage rather than, as in highland systems, as fodder. We acknowledge the importance of the first factor, though we think this would make live exchange difficult rather than impossible. But we doubt the generality of the second; we think that discussion of the role of forage versus fodder in New Guinean systems of pig husbandry has conflated the differing perspectives of people and pigs.

Useful quantitative data on pig holdings, garden labour and the proportion of garden produce that is fed to pigs are available for Miyanmin, Tsembaga Maring and Raipu Enga (Morren 1977; see also Rappaport 1968; Waddell 1972). These data are summarized in the first three columns of Table 2.1; the figures for per-person labour at gardens are standardized against the Miyanmin value.

**Table 2.1** Pigs and Gardening Effort in Three New Guinean Societies

| Society | Basic statistics | | | Labour input to pigs | |
|---|---|---|---|---|---|
| | Pigs/person | Garden labour/ person | Garden produce to pigs (%) | Per person | Per pig |
| Miyanmin | 0.10 | 1.00 | 16 | 1.00 | 1.00 |
| Tsembaga Maring | 0.56 | 1.45 | 27 | 2.45 | 0.44 |
| Raiapu Enga | 2.30 | 2.30 | 65 | 9.34 | 0.41 |

*Note*: Values shown under labour input to pigs for Tsembaga Maring and Raipu Enga were standardized against values for Miyanmin. Thus, for Tsembaga Maring, the value of labour input per person was calculated as $(1.45 \times 0.27)/(1.00 \times 0.16) = 2.45$ and the value of labour input per pig was calculated as $(2.45/0.56)/(1.0/0.1) = 0.44$.

The basic statistics in the table support conventional understandings that these societies represent differing levels of intensification of pig management and that an increase in the number of pigs per person is matched by an increase in the labour required at gardens to produce food for those pigs. But the values may be read in another way by converting them to labour inputs to pigs; that is, to the gardening effort per person that is directed to pigs and, as a guide to what pigs themselves actually receive from this work, the gardening effort devoted to each pig. The adjusted figures are shown in the last two columns of the table where, again, they are standardized against the Miyanmin values. Taken at face value they suggest that Tsembaga Maring and Raipu Enga people, respectively, may be working at gardens 2.45 and 9.34 times as hard as Miyanmin to provide each pig with less than half as much fodder. Of course, this model assumes that both effort and value per unit of fodder is constant across societies. But despite simplifying assumptions the strong suggestion is that, from the perspective of a pig, the proportion of its food provided by carers is notably less in the highland system of Raipu Enga than in the seemingly less intensified system of Miyanmin, a system of management which, in its primary features, is more like that of Etoro. As A. J. Strathern (1988: 198–9) suggested, there are places in the highlands where 'the availability of pig pasture areas is a significant factor' in the provision of domestic animals with food.[4]

These observations reinforce our interpretations of attachment in two ways. First, they reflect the fact that, in the highlands, the women who are acknowledged as pig carers are, in fact, very often apart from their pigs. They are at sweet potato gardens producing food for their families and their pigs; at gardens which are usually off-limits to pigs because the primary crop grown there is such an attractive pig food.[5] Sweet potato gardens, indeed gardens in general, occupy much less of the time of women from non-highland societies of mainland New Guinea. Second, they remind us that opportunities for domestic pigs to associate with other pigs is not a function of the ratio of pigs to people *per se* but, rather, of human population density and the size of local communities. It is these latter variables, in combination with ratios of pigs per person, which dictate local densities of domestic pigs and influence the extent of contact between pigs. Through most of highland New Guinea, where both human population densities and ratios of pigs to people are relatively high, there is seldom opportunity for a pig to be closely associated with a person to the degree or for the duration observed among Kubo. Because the people who care for pigs must spend much of their time apart from those pigs the time spent by pigs in the company of people is much less than the time spent in the company of other pigs.

It is clear, therefore, that the ways in which people manage pigs are connected to other components of their lives. These ecological correlates concern mobility, community size and settlement pattern, and subsistence mode. They intersect with constraints imposed by people's access to, or preference for, piglets born to wild or domestic sows and the ways in which large and mature pigs have been incorporated into exchange networks.

Kubo are a mobile people. Traditionally, settlements relocated every three to four years and intra-community disputes were resolved by one party to the dispute – an individual or family – moving to live elsewhere (Dwyer and Minnegal 1992). Very early separation of piglets from sows, combined with a long period of association with a single carer, facilitates both strong attachment of pig to carer and, as necessary, the movement of domesticated pigs from one place of residence to another. But, simultaneously, these factors make it exceptionally difficult to exchange live animals; exchanges here, as among Etoro, are of pork, not pigs. Further, because wild pigs are much more common than domestic pigs in Kubo territory, the alienation of piglets from others of their species reduces the chance that they will join the wild population when left to forage alone. And, finally, the diversity of subsistence modes, the limited emphasis on gardening, and the fact that bananas – plants of little interest to pigs as food – are the dominant crop, have the outcome that Kubo carers are able to combine many daytime activities with tending their pigs. The intense and continuous interaction necessary to induce in pigs an attachment to a particular person is possible here as it is not in many other societies.

The contrast between Kubo and highland societies is striking. In the latter, three constraints shape systems of pig management. First, frequent exchange of live pigs (notably of mature pigs) between people of different settlements is an important part of social life. The people themselves are far less mobile than their pigs. It is necessary, therefore, that pigs are managed so that they do not become closely attached to particular carers and are amenable to association with other pigs. Second, because wild pigs are absent the many pigs that a particular animal may encounter are all domestic animals. And, third, sweet potato is the staple food of people. Women, who do much of the cultivation, spend a great deal of time in gardens which are fenced to exclude pigs; gardening and close interaction with pigs are often separated in time and space. In the highlands, a strategy whereby young animals are able to learn through association with their mothers, and are never excluded from contact with other pigs, may best satisfy both the constraints on a carer's time and the demands of exchanging live pigs.

With respect to both mobility and subsistence Etoro are intermediate between Kubo and societies of the highlands. Like the former, but unlike the latter, Etoro do not exchange live mature pigs though, like most New Guineans, they may trade young animals. The likelihood that Etoro pig carers will change residence within the life of a pig is relatively low, but those people are often working at gardens from which it is desirable to exclude pigs. In addition, Etoro communities are small and separated by large tracts of forest. A management strategy that familiarizes young pigs first with their carers, training the animals to an expectation that these people will provide food, and subsequently with particular foraging areas, accommodates the separation of pigs from carers necessitated by gardening and provides some guarantee that the pigs will remain accessible to people.

The strategies employed by Kubo, Etoro and highland societies are not the only configurations of pig management in New Guinea. There are multiple ways in which the dimensions of early management – the extent of association of a pig with its mother, its carer or other pigs – may intersect. Some of this variation is illustrated by the husbandry practices of Bedamuni, Gogodala, Miyanmin and Wopkaimin and, indeed, by recent changes observed among Kubo (Baldwin 1982; van Beek 1987; Hyndman 1979; Minnegal and Dwyer 1997; Morren 1977, 1986). In each of these cases the differences may be traced in part to the sorts of ecological factors considered above.

Bedamuni live east of Kubo and west of Etoro at altitudes intermediate between the two. Population density is higher than that of either Kubo or Etoro (seven people per square kilometre as against 0.5 and two), but the people keep relatively few pigs (i.e. 0.2–0.3 pigs per person: van Beek 1987: 25; Minnegal and Dwyer 2000b: 506–7). People shift residence infrequently, women spend much time in fenced tuber gardens, and mature pigs are not exchanged live. Here, as in the highlands, piglets are not usually separated from their mothers and, though regularly handled and fed, spend little time in the exclusive company of people. In contrast to the highlands, however, mature animals do not routinely associate with many other pigs; neither domestic nor wild pigs are common. Among Bedamuni, the primary management strategy is to condition pigs to expect food at the village and, thereby, voluntarily limit the distance they travel during day-time foraging. They are in effect reared to become relatively independent central place foragers (e.g. Kaplan and Hill 1992: 184–6). The outcome is that demands on the time of their carers are not great, releasing those people to attend to other necessary tasks.

Most of the pigs reared by Miyanmin of the middle altitudes, and virtually all reared by Gogodala of the lowlands, are the progeny of wild parents. In both places, the density of wild pigs is high, and the ratio of domestic pigs per person is very low (about 0.1). In neither society are mature pigs exchanged live. These people combine very early separation of piglet from sow, as seen among Kubo, with sepa-ration of pig from carer when the latter is only a few months old, as seen among Etoro (Baldwin 1982; Morren 1986). The former strategy serves to alienate piglets from their wild conspecifics, while the latter reflects the fact that mobility of people is comparatively low. There is little need to bond pigs to their carers, so that they can be moved when residential affiliations change. Wopkaimin, like Miyanmin, are a mid-altitude Mountain Ok society who, again, keep few pigs. Details of the early management of piglets are not known, but once old enough to forage for themselves they are kept together at a pig house some distance from the hamlet (Hyndman 1979: 212–13). The women who live here act as carers on behalf of different owners, who thus are free to move while their pigs stay in place. Actual control over pigs is 'very casual; they are allowed to spend a considerable amount of time for-aging' in forest (ibid.). Here, therefore, it is difficult to assert that the animals form more than a weak association with people or place, an association maintained only by the regularity with which they are fed by people at that place. Indeed, in some societies attachment to place is facilitated in recalcitrant animals by blinding them, either 'by slashing or searing their eyeballs' (e.g. Boyd 1984: 35).

The relatively casual management strategies seen in these latter societies – strategies, it seems, which often result in loss of pigs – accommodate limited though important demands for prestations of pork to local patterns of gardening and mobility. Another strategy for minimizing costs associated with pig manage-ment in circumstances of relatively low demand for domestic pork was described by Hughes (1970). He reported that Daribi 'maintain domesticated pigs on a per-manent basis in areas remote from human settlement' by locating them in places where they are enclosed by natural physical barriers and, at intervals, supplied with sago which had been planted nearby; here, there is no necessity to constrain pigs by ensuring attachment to people, place or other pigs. But, perhaps, within New Guinea, the extreme case of the alienated pig is found among Keraki of savanna and riverine forest habitats of the Western Province. As depicted by Williams (1936: 18–19, 224–5), these people captured piglets born to wild parents and housed and fed them separately in pens until each had grown to 'an almost incred-ible fatness'.

In the years from 1986 to 1999 the Kubo people with whom we have lived have established more permanent and larger communities and have increased their holdings of pigs (Minnegal and Dwyer 1997). They thought that more pigs would facilitate access to money. With more pigs in the care of one person it became impossible to give piglets the individual attention, or to monitor free-ranging pigs with the dedication we had seen earlier.[6] Nor, since the likelihood of settlement shifts had been reduced, was there the same impetus to establish close attachment of pig to carer. More large pigs were kept at the village but, again, they could not all be taken to the forest each day; rather, they had to be tethered and fed. The demands on each carer's time and effort increased enormously and the period and intensity of close association with young animals was reduced. In response to these complications people experimented with new ways of managing pigs and even attempted to acquire young pigs of highland stock – pigs whose pedigree included animals of modern commercial breeds. They considered these to be easier to tame than their own animals. On several occasions they adopted a Wopkaimin-like system in which pigs belonging to a number of different people were housed together, far from the village and under the care of a married couple who had volunteered for the task. These experiments were never a success. The animals were either so attached to a particular carer as a consequence of long association early in their lives that they returned to the village in search of her, or were released with other pigs before they had been adequately tamed and were prone to run wild. The changes which have occurred among Kubo show that, first, management options are flexible – there is nothing inherent in pigs which dictates the strategies adopted by people – and, second, people choose strategies within the constraints of other demands on their time and their perceived need for domestic pigs.

## Social Consequences of Attachment

To this point we have emphasized the kinds of attachments which may be established by domestic pigs as a consequence of the ways in which they are managed. In concluding this article we now turn the tables and comment on the attachments people have to their pigs and the consequences of attachment to the social life of people.

Conventional understandings of the extent of 'pig love' in New Guinea are influenced primarily by knowledge of the place of pigs in societies of the highlands. It is here, in particular, that women are reported to protest and weep when the pigs they have cared for are killed or given away. Tales are told of women who cut off a finger, as a public act of mourning, when their pigs died or were slaughtered, of children who are severely punished because they were lax in the care they provided to pigs, and of men who declare 'pigs are our hearts' (e.g. Hide 1981: 483; Meggitt 1958: 286, 1974; Reay 1959: 13; M. Strathern 1988: 163). Without prejudice to the feelings which people have for their pigs we assert that public demonstrations of 'pig love' have less to do with pigs as pigs than with the value of pigs and the place of women in the societies in question. In general, we think that in New Guinea the less the attachment of pigs to people the greater the likelihood that people will proclaim their attachment to pigs through public displays of emotion. Some examples will illustrate our argument.

The Keraki case illustrated an extreme instance of the alienation of domestic pigs from people, places where they are free to forage, and other pigs. These people, who are not highlanders, keep each pig individually caged and feed it untill it 'has sunk down in its fatness and is unable to rise' (Williams 1936: 19). The animals have few opportunities to establish significant attachments of any sort. Yet, as Williams wrote, the people themselves manifest strong attachment to the animals:

> The owner takes an unaffected pride in the large pig with which he has been so long associated, and visitors will gasp and whistle in admiration of the truly portentous creature that has collapsed upon the floor of its sty, often to remain there from sheer inability to rise. It is fondled about the ears by the woman who feeds it, and she will weep inconsolably when it is killed; nor could its owner ever be expected to kill the animal, even if etiquette allowed, for sorrow, I was told, would make his arm too weak to draw the bow. To the owner and his wife, then, the pig becomes the object not only of pride but even of a strong sentimental attachment. (Williams 1936: 225)

At the other extreme are Kubo where each pig spends the first 18 months of its life closely associated with a particular female, foraging near her as she completes a variety of subsistence tasks. Yet Kubo women do not cry at the time a pig with which they have been so intimately associated is killed. They bring it to the village and hand-feed it for a week before the time of slaughter. They are present at the death. They tether the animal to a post, calm it, and stand beside it as men shoot it with arrows (Dwyer 1993: 139). They may be sad, withdrawing from other people for a moment as the animal contorts in death throes, but they soon return to the butchering site to issue directions concerning the distribution of portions of the carcass both before and after cooking. Later they will recall the pig by name and with affection.

Given the vast difference in the engagement of a carer with her pig it is difficult to imagine that Keraki women feel more for their pigs than do Kubo women. Appearances can deceive and public protestations of grief can convey other messages. As Macintyre noted, writing of the Tubetube people of Milne Bay Province, when the time comes that a pig must be killed 'pragmatism and exchange obligations' usually prevail (1984: 112–13). She reported that owners and carers 'confessed to some feelings of remorse when they parted with a pet pig' and sometimes 'removed themselves from the scene when their pig was trussed to a pole before being speared'. They displayed indifference so that the superiority achieved through 'the customary mode of disguising emotion [enhanced] the force of the gift'.

Tubetube are a matrilineal society where patterns of inheritance accord status to women in ways that are largely unavailable among highland societies. In the latter societies gender inequalities are and must be addressed in more subtle ways (e.g. M. Strathern 1988). When highlander women proclaim their loss at the time a pig is killed by men they are making a public statement about the usurpation of the product of their sustained labour. Indeed, the pigs they weep for may well be ones which they themselves did not feed as young animals. Live exchanges are common and a pig, during its lifetime, may be cared for by several women. It is their contribution of labour to pigs in general and not to particular pigs which is of concern to women. When they weep, they are proclaiming their role in exchanges which seem, on the surface, to be the concerns of men. In highland New Guinea to weep for your pig, whatever your feelings for that particular beast, is publically to assert your engagement, and hence the engagement of all women, in the reproduction and creation of the social forms that are made possible through your efforts.

The experience of Kubo women is quite different to the foregoing account. By New Guinea standards, Kubo and their immediate neighbours are egalitarian (Dwyer and Minnegal 1992). Gender relations are relaxed. Husbands and wives frequently work together in gardens, wives accompany husbands on hunting excursions where they may process sago or fish; couples seldom fight and are often affectionate in public. Exclusion of women from participation in public events is not pronounced. They sing at all-night dances and attend curing ceremonies; though, to protect young children and young pigs from potentially dangerous spirit beings, they usually depart in the closing stages of these events and do not attend seances. And their presence and participation at the time a pig is killed is expected. Kelly (1988) argued, with reference to Etoro and highlanders, that the alienation of women who had cared for pigs occurred at the closing phase of the animals' lives when the emphasis was shifted from processes of production, within which women participated, to those of consumption and exchange, which were the proper concern of men. This does not happen with Kubo. Here, the presence of women who cared for pigs is judged to be necessary when the pig is killed and, irrespective of any claim to ownership of the pig, their rights to a say in the subsequent distribution are not in question. That judgement is warranted. The attachment of the pig to its carer is so great that no one else would be able to bring it in for slaughter; without the agreement and complicity of the woman the transaction could not take place.

Indeed, we have argued elsewhere that recent changes in the ways that Kubo manage pigs are resulting in the disempowerment of women (Minnegal and Dwyer 1997). A reduction in the strength and exclusivity of the attachment of pigs to their carer, and the increasing ease with which others can handle pigs as the relationship to people becomes generalized, means that women have less control both over the recruitment of piglets born to the sows they care for, and over the killing of the pig and disposal of its meat in social exchanges. As the need for their co-operation declines, it may soon be necessary for Kubo women, too, to find other ways to publically assert their contribution to the gift.

If the management practices of Kubo and highland societies are taken as well-separated states in a universe of possibilities then it is apparent that, in the first case, the extremely close attachment of pig to carer means that mature pigs are nearly impossible to transact live and that women have strong rights over the distribution of piglets and meat from pigs; in the second, the extremely limited attachment of pig to carer means that mature pigs are relatively easy to transact live and that women have limited control over the distribution of pigs as live animals or as meat. But we insist that the expressions of pig management and sociality which we have recognized as concordant must be understood as mutually constituted; neither dimension can be accorded causal priority. At most, it is likely that, within New Guinea, processes entailed in the domestication of pigs and the intensification of management were characterized by an initial phase in which the animals were bonded to people and alienated from other pigs and a subsequent phase in which they were increasingly alienated from people and permitted to bond with other pigs.[7] At all times and all places, however, the attachment of people to their pigs is not in doubt.

## Acknowledgements

Our own work in Papua New Guinea has been facilitated by periods of leave awarded by the University of Queensland and the University of Melbourne, affiliation with the University of Papua New Guinea and the Papua New Guinea National Museum and Art Gallery, research visas awarded by the Government of Papua New Guinea, administrative assistance from the Papua New Guinea National Research Institute and, between 1995 and 1998, research grants from the Papua New Guinea Biological Foundation and the Australian Research Council. We thank the Bedamuni, Etoro and Kubo people, and Judith Blackshaw and Robin Hide who, in different ways, have contributed much to our understanding of pigs.

## Notes

1. Groves (1981, 1984) considered that both the wild and domestic pigs of pre-colonial New Guinea were derived from a cross between the Sulawesi warty pig, *Sus celebensis*, and the banded pig, *Sus scrofa vittatus*. Since that time, in

more densely populated areas of New Guinea, endemic stock have been crossed with a variety of commercial breeds (e.g. Baldwin 1982: 39; Malynicz 1970: 204).

2. Dwyer (1990) spelled 'Etoro' as 'Etolo'.

3. Our assertion that in the highlands piglets are preferentially left with their mothers to the time of natural weaning was, initially, based on negative data. The ethnographic literature is silent on this point. However, had piglets invariably been separated from sows when very young, and spent several months in the company of a carer, then we think this would have been reported. In the course of preparing the present chapter some information has become available. Watt *et al.* (1975) commented on 'traditional' pig husbandry practices near Mount Hagen. They wrote that 'weaning occurred mostly naturally [i.e. at about four months] not separating the sow from the litter. Sometimes the sows were tied up when the litter was three months old and separated from the litter' (see also Freund, 1968, who stated that, among Enga, weaning 'did not occur before the piglets were anything up to 6 months old by which time the sow was so emaciated that it would take several months before she would breed again'). In addition to drawing these references to our attention, Robin Hide has generously provided unpublished information on litters from sixteen Sinasina sows. These sows produced eighty-two piglets, twenty-three of which died or were culled, usually when less than a month old. Eighteen piglets, from nine sows, were removed from their mothers before they would have been naturally weaned. The approximate age of separation is known for fourteen of these piglets; two at 69 days when the sow died, another from the same sow at about 28 days, six at about 56 days when the sow was in poor condition, three at 46 days and two at 12 days. In the last case the piglets survived, though they were given much special care. For forty-one piglets from thirteen sows the last documented records were at ages of 24 days (4), 41–60 days (11), 61–90 days (14) and 110–150 days (12); all these piglets were still with their mothers and may have been weaned naturally. Though the data are incomplete, the implication is that piglets are unlikely to be separated from their mothers unless their condition or that of the sow is poor. Perhaps the most convincing evidence in Hide's data set comes from four cases where sow and litter – a total of thirteen piglets – were transferred together from one carer to another who lived elsewhere. The sets of piglets were, respectively, 42, 49, 69 and 76 days old; as old or older than the age at which they may be removed from their mother without notable risk to their prospects for survival. Here, it seems, people demonstrated a preference for maintaining the association of piglets with sows for as long as possible.

4. The importance of fodder to domestic pigs in the highlands will vary between households, communities, societies and across time. Recent estimates from

Huli of the contribution of sweet potato to pigs are 2,064 kcal/pig/day among Wenani people (ninety-three people per square kilometre, 1.9 pigs/person) and 1,545 kcal/pig/day among Heli (thirty-seven people per square kilometre, 0.6 pigs/person; Umezaki *et al.* 2000). Hide's (1981: 361–72) estimates from Sinasina (140 people per square kilometre, 1.80 pigs/person in sampled group, 0.72 pigs/person overall) suggest a *per diem* ration of sweet potato equivalent to about 1,155 kcal/pig. All these values are less than the 2,500–4,000 kcal/day that might be consumed by a pig in the weight range 40–50 kg. They hint, however, that Wenani pigs receive most of their food as fodder and that Sinasina pigs receive less than half of their food as fodder.

5. Hide (1981: 260) estimated that pig husbandry and gardening, respectively, occupied Sinasina women for about 2.9 and 19.5 hours per week. These women spend relatively few daylight hours in the company of their pigs, though, sometimes, as elsewhere in the highlands, they tether a pig within a garden where they work and may spend as many as 45 per cent of their nights sleeping at the same house as their pigs.

6. Between 1986 and 1996 the average number of village-based pigs in the care of each Kubo woman increased from 0.7 to three. In the earlier period, only women without young children were likely to care for more than one village-based pig at the same time and, when this occurred, those pigs were of distinctly different ages. In one case, for a brief period only, one woman had three village-based pigs in her care because the largest of the three resisted relocation to the back swamps. In the later period, some women cared for as many as six village-based pigs which varied in weight from 4 to 80 kg, and several cared for two piglets simultaneously. In highland New Guinea married women regularly care for four or more pigs at the same time; often they may care for more than eight animals (Hide 1981: 319–27).

7. Simoons and Baldwin (1982) suggested that human suckling of the young of animals such as dogs and pigs may have contributed to their full domestication. We think it is more likely that this behaviour appeared after animals had attained an important place in the economic or emotional lives of the peoples concerned. We note that among Kubo of Papua New Guinea women attempt to minimize engagement with pigs during late pregnancy and at least the first six months of lactation, and are careful to keep infants away from pigs so that the latter have no access to the urine or faeces of the former (Dwyer 1993).

# References

Baldwin, J. A. (1982), 'Pig Rearing and the Domestication Process in New Guinea and the Torres Strait Region'. *National Geographic Society Research Reports* 14: 31–43.

Bayliss-Smith, T. and J. Golson (1992), 'A Colocasian Revolution in the New Guinea Highlands? Insights from Phase 4 at Kuk'. *Archaeology in Oceania* 27: 1–21.

Beek, A. G. van (1987), 'The Way of All Flesh: Hunting and Ideology of the Bedamuni of the Great Papuan Plateau (Papua New Guinea)', Ph.D., University of Leiden, Leiden.

Boyd, D. J. (1984), 'The Production and Management of Pigs: Husbandry Option and Demographic Patterns in an Eastern Highlands Herd'. *Oceania* 55: 27–49.

Boyd, D. J. (1985), '"We must Follow the Fore": Pig Husbandry Intensification and Ritual Diffusion among the Irakia Awa, Papua New Guinea'. *American Ethnologist* 12: 119–36.

Brown, P. (1978), *Highland Peoples of New Guinea*. Cambridge: Cambridge University Press.

Brutti, L. and M. Boissière (2002), 'Le Donneur, le Receveur et la Sage Femme, Échanges de Cochons à Oksapmin (PNG)'. *Journal de la Société des Océanistes* 114–15: 141–57.

Clutton-Brock, J. (1987), *A Natural History of Domesticated Mammals*. British Museum (Natural History). Cambridge: Cambridge University Press.

Dwyer, P. D. (1990), *The Pigs that Ate the Garden: A Human Ecology from Papua New Guinea*. Ann Arbor: University of Michigan Press.

Dwyer, P. D. (1993), 'The Production and Disposal of Pigs by Kubo People of Papua New Guinea'. *Memoirs of the Queensland Museum* 33: 123–42.

Dwyer, P. D. (1996), 'Boars, Barrows and Breeders: The Reproductive Status of Domestic Pig Populations in Mainland New Guinea'. *Journal of Anthropological Research* 52: 481–500.

Dwyer, P. D. and M. Minnegal (1991), 'Hunting in Lowland Tropical Rainforest: Towards a Model of Non-agricultural Subsistence'. *Human Ecology* 19: 187–212.

Dwyer, P. D. and M. Minnegal (1992), 'Ecology and Community Dynamics of Kubo People in the Tropical Lowlands of Papua New Guinea'. *Human Ecology* 20: 21–55.

Feil, D. K. (1987), *The Evolution of Highland Papua New Guinea Societies*. Cambridge: Cambridge University Press.

Fraser, A. F. (1985), *Ethology of Farm Animals: A Comprehensive Study of the Behavioural Features of the Common Farm Animals*. Amsterdam: Elsevier.

Freund, R. (1968), 'Agriculture Then and Now', Anthropological Study Conference, pp. 1–13, Amapyaka, Western Highlands District, New Guinea.

Giffin, J. (1978), *Ecology of the Feral Pig on the Island of Hawaii*. Department of Land and Natural Resources, Division of Fish and Game, State of Hawaii.

Godelier, M. and M. Strathern (ed.) (1991), *Big Men and Great Men: Personifications of Power in Melanesia*. Cambridge: Cambridge University Press.

Goodale, J. C. (1995), *To Sing with Pigs is Human: The Concept of Person in Papua New Guinea*. Seattle: University of Washington Press.

Groves, C. P. (1981), *Ancestors for the Pigs: Taxonomy and Phylogeny of the Genus Sus*. Canberra: Australian National University.

Groves, C. P. (1984), 'Of Mice and Men and Pigs in the Indo-Australian Archipelago'. *Canberra Anthropology* 7: 1–19.

Hallpike, C. R. (1977), *Bloodshed and Vengeance in the Papuan Mountains: The Generation of Conflict in Tauade Society*. Oxford: Clarendon Press.

Harris, M. (1975), *Cows, Pigs, Wars and Witches: The Riddles of Culture*. London: Hutchinson.

Hemworth, P. H. (1982), 'Social Environment and Reproduction', in D. J. A. Cole and G. R. Foxcroft (eds), *Control of Pig Reproduction*. London: Butterworth Scientific.

Hide, R. L. (1981), 'Aspects of Pig Production and Use in Colonial Sinasina, Papua New Guinea', Ph.D., Columbia University.

Hughes, I. (1970), 'Pigs, Sago, and Limestone: The Adaptive Use of Natural Enclosures and Planted Sago in Pig Management'. *Mankind* 7: 272–8.

Hughes, P. E. and M. A. Varley (1980), *Reproduction in the Pig*. London: Butterworths.

Hyndman, D. C. (1979), 'Wopkaimin Subsistence: Cultural Ecology in the New Guinea Highland Fringe', Ph.D., University of Queensland.

Jolly, M. (1984), 'The Anatomy of Pig Love: Substance, Spirit and Gender in South Pentecost, Vanuatu'. *Canberra Anthropology* 7: 78–108.

Kahn, M. (1986), *Always Hungry, Never Greedy: Food and the Expression of Gender in a Melanesian Society*. Cambridge: Cambridge University Press.

Kaplan, H. and K. Hill (1992), 'The Evolutionary Ecology of Food Acquisition', in E. A. Smith and B. Winterhalder (eds), *Evolutionary Ecology and Human Behaviour*. New York: Aldine de Gruyter.

Kelly, R. C. (1988), 'Etoro Suidology: A Reassessment of the Pig's Role in the Prehistory and Comparative Ethnology of New Guinea', in J. F. Weiner (ed.), *Mountain Papuans: Historical and Comparative Perspectives from New Guinea Fringe Highlands Societies*. Ann Arbor: University of Michigan Press.

Lemmonier, P. (1993). 'Pigs as Ordinary Wealth: Technical Logic, Exchange, and Leadership in New Guinea', in P. Lemmonier (ed.), *Transformation in Material Cultures since the Neolithic*. London: Routledge.

Macintyre, M. (1984), 'The Problem of the Semi-alienable Pig'. *Canberra Anthropology* 7: 109–22.

Malynicz, G. L. (1970), 'Pig Keeping by the Subsistence Agriculturalist of the New Guinea Highlands'. *Search* 1: 201–4.

Meggitt, M. J. (1958), 'The Enga of the New Guinea Highlands'. *Oceania* 28: 253–330.

Meggitt, M. J. (1965), *The Lineage System of the Mae-Enga of New Guinea*. Edinburgh: Oliver and Boyd.

Meggitt, M. J. (1974), '"Pigs Are Our Hearts!": The *Te* Exchange Cycle Among the Mae Enga of New Guinea'. *Oceania* 44: 165–203.

Minnegal, M. and P. D. Dwyer (1997), 'Women, Pigs, God and Evolution: Social and Economic Change among Kubo People of Papua New Guinea'. *Oceania* 68: 47–60.

Minnegal, M. and P. D. Dwyer (1998), 'Intensification and Social Complexity in the Interior Lowlands of Papua New Guinea: A Comparison of Bedamuni and Kubo'. *Journal of Anthropological Archaeology* 17: 375–400.

Minnegal, M. and P. D. Dwyer (2000a), 'A Sense of Community: Sedentary Nomads of the Interior Lowlands of Papua New Guinea'. *People and Culture in Oceania* 16: 43–65.

Minnegal, M. and P. D. Dwyer (2000b), 'Responses to a Drought in the Interior Lowlands of Papua New Guinea; A Comparison of Bedamuni and Kubo-Konai'. *Human Ecology* 28: 493–526.

Modjeska, N. (1982), 'Production and Inequality: Perspectives from Central New Guinea', in A. J. Strathern (ed.), *Inequality in New Guinea Highlands Societies*. Cambridge: Cambridge University Press.

Morren, G. E. B. (1977), 'From Hunting to Herding: Pigs and the Control of Energy in Montane New Guinea', in T. P. Bayliss-Smith and R. G. Feachem (eds), *Subsistence and Survival: Rural Ecology in the Pacific*. London: Academic Press.

Morren, G. E. B. (1986), *The Miyanmin: Human Ecology of a Papua New Guinea Society*. Ames: Iowa State University Press.

Nowak, R. M. (1999), *Walker's Mammals of the World*, 6th edition, Vol. II, Baltimore: Johns Hopkins University Press.

Oosterwal, G. (1961), *People of the Tor: A Cultural-anthropological Study on the Tribes of the Tor Territory (Northern Netherlands New-Guinea)*. Assen (Netherlands): Royal Van Gorcum Ltd.

Rappaport, R. A. (1968), *Pigs for the Ancestors: Ritual in the Ecology of a New Guinea People*. New Haven: Yale University Press.

Reay, M. (1959), *The Kuma: Freedom and Conformity in the New Guinea Highlands*. Melbourne: Melbourne University Press.

Rubel, P. G. and A. Rosman (1978), *Your Own Pigs You May Not Eat: A Comparative Study of New Guinea Societies*. Canberra: Australian National University Press.

Schoorl, J. W. (1993), *Culture and Change among the Muyu*. Leiden: KITLV Press.

Signoret, J. P., B. A. Baldwin, D. Fraser and E. S. E. Hafez (1975), 'The Behaviour of Swine', in E. S. E. Hafez (ed.), *The Behaviour of Domestic Animals*. London: Baillière Tindall.

Sillitoe, P. (1979), *Give and Take: Exchange in Wola Society*. Canberra: Australian National University Press.

Simoons, F. J. and J. A. Baldwin (1982), 'Breast-feeding of Animals by Women: Its Socio-cultural Context and Geographic Occurrence'. *Anthropos* 77: 421–48.

Sorenson, E. R. (1976), *The Edge of the Forest: Land, Childhood and Change in a New Guinea Protoagricultural Society*. Washington, DC: Smithsonian Institution Press.

Špinka, M. (1998), 'Pigs', in M. Bekoff and C. A. Meaney (eds), *Encyclopaedia of Animal Rights and Animal Welfare*. Westport, Connecticut: Greenwood Press.

Strathern, A. J. (ed.) (1982), *Inequality in New Guinea Highland Societies*. Cambridge: Cambridge University Press.

Strathern, A. J. (1984), *A Line of Power*. London: Tavistock Publications.

Strathern, A. J. (1988), 'Conclusions: Looking at the Edge of the New Guinea Highlands from the Center', in J. F. Weiner (ed.), *Mountain Papuans: Historical and Comparative Perspectives from New Guinea Fringe Highlands Societies*. Ann Arbor: University of Michigan Press.

Strathern, M. (1988), *The Gender of the Gift: Problems with Women and Problems with Society in Melanesia*. Los Angeles: University of California Press.

Umezaki, M., Y. Kuchikura, T. Yamauchi and R. Ohtsuka (2000), 'Impact of Population Pressure on Food Production: An Analysis of Land Use Change and Subsistence Pattern in the Tari Basin in Papua New Guinea Highlands'. *Human Ecology* 28: 359–81.

Waddell, E. (1972), *The Mound Builders: Agricultural Practices, Environment, and Society in the Central Highlands of New Guinea*. Seattle: University of Washington Press.

Watt, I. R., R. F. McKillop, P. J. Penson and N. A. Robinson (1975), *Pig Handbook*. Port Moresby: Department of Primary Industry.

Williams, F. E. (1936), *Papuans of the Trans-Fly*. Oxford: Clarendon Press.

Young, M. W. (1984), 'The Hunting of the Snark in Nidula: Ruminations on Pig Love'. *Canberra Anthropology* 7: 123–44.

# –3–

# Disciplined Affections: The Making of an English Pack of Foxhounds

## *Garry Marvin*

Dogs have a thousand countries and each is in character what his country makes him.
Gratius, *Cynegetica*

## Introduction

At the core of foxhunting in England are a series of complex relationships between humans and animals – particularly between humans, horses, hounds and foxes. Of these the most elaborate (because it is through them that the actual hunting of foxes takes place) are the relationships between the huntsman and the animals that comprise the pack of hounds. This chapter explores the nature and structure of the relationships that allow the huntsman to shape the behaviours of scores of individual animals into a harmonious unity as a free-ranging but disciplined collectivity, the pack, such that they can perform their task of hunting foxes across the countryside. In the context of animal-keeping in England, foxhounds constitute an unusual group. They are domesticated animals but are expected to enact some of the characteristics of a pack of wild dogs. Although they live together in large numbers in rural spaces, they are different from other groupings of livestock. They are known and recognized as individuals but, unlike most dogs, they are collectively owned. They are working animals but, unlike other working dogs, they work together, physically unrestrained, in large numbers under the guidance of a single person.

This chapter touches on only some aspects of the practice of foxhunting. It might, therefore, be useful to give a thumbnail sketch of its central features. Foxhunting centres on the activities of the huntsman and his pack of hounds who are followed and observed by horse-mounted or foot followers. At the beginning of a day's hunting all the participants come together for a short social gathering – the 'meet'. When the process of hunting begins the mounted huntsman leads the pack away from the followers, who are thus separated from the huntsman and hounds for the rest of the day. They may follow the huntsman but they must not interfere with him and the hounds during the actual pursuit. At the point where he has decided to begin hunting, the huntsman encourages his hounds to begin searching for a fox. This is done by scent rather than by sight. The pack splits up and if one or a group of them find a scent they begin crying in a way which draws the other hounds to them. They all then attempt to pick up and follow this scent. Ideally this will lead them to the fox which left the scent; but this is not a simple chase. The fox realizes that it is the focus of attention and will attempt to flee in such a way as to disguise its scent or, if possible, to escape somewhere where it is difficult for the hounds (being much larger than the fox) to follow. The hounds must 'work' with the scent. They must attempt to discover what has happened if the scent disappears or becomes faint or confused. They must try to work out what the fox has done. Often the huntsman has to help them by suggesting or demanding that they move in a particular direction, but the ideal of hunting is for the hounds to work this out for themselves. When they are successful they slowly close in on their prey until they finally see it and, in a burst of speed, surge forward to catch and kill it. This process can take over an hour and is enacted over several miles of countryside. It is rare for any hunt to develop in this simple form – often there is no scent at all and the hounds are moved to another place, often they find the scent only to lose it again after a short while, and often they hunt the scent for some time but then become distracted, confused or lose their fox at the very last moment. Some people participate because of the opportunity presented by the hunt for an exciting ride across the countryside, while others come mainly to see how a pack of hounds resolve the problems of finding and hunting foxes and to observe the style in which they do so. Many come for a mixture of these reasons or to participate in an important social event in their local community.

## Marking and Making Foxhounds

Foxhounds are owned by the registered foxhunt organizations that breed them.[1] They are a unique dog breed in England because they are working dogs which are owned collectively and bred for only one purpose. If we look only at foxhunting (despite the name 'foxhounds', these hounds are also used to hunt stag, mink and hare) there are some 200 registered hunts with their associated packs, and (at a rough estimate) there are perhaps only 12,000 working foxhounds in the country. Given that in each hunt only two or three people have a close working relationship with them, and only one or two are directly responsible for decisions about their breeding, then overall the number of people with an immediate relationship with the breed amounts to only a few hundred people.

**Figure 3.1** The English Fox Hunt.

Many breeds of dog are used for working purposes – such as sheep herding, as gun (retriever) dogs, for flushing out game, for guarding, as guide dogs for the blind, for military, police and customs work, and in search and rescue operations. But while particular breeds might be associated with particular work practices, they are not associated exclusively and uniquely with these tasks. Spaniels might be bred as gun dogs, but they are also used as drug-scenting dogs; German shepherds are favoured as control dogs by the police, but they are also used as guide dogs. Most breeds of dog are multipurpose, used for specific purposes *and* widely found as household pets. They are all dogs. This is not the case with the foxhound: it is bred, kept and used for the sole purpose of hunting, and individuals from the working stock do not transfer into the general English dog-keeping culture – they do not become pets. Other pedigree breeds can be purchased and owned, but no one may buy into the stock of foxhounds – they are never offered for sale. All foxhounds have a recognized and recorded pedigree, but the attribution of this pedigree identity is exclusively related to being working animals and having been sired by working animals. This identity is clearly set out in the requirements for eligibility for inclusion in *The Foxhound Kennel Stud Book*:

> To be eligible for entry in the Stud Book, Hounds must have been bred, 'entered' and worked in the Kennels of a Recognized Hunt; besides which their sires and dams must also have been so bred, 'entered' and worked and must have been registered in the Stud

Book, or both their grand-sires and both their grand-dams must have been registered in the Stud Book. (Masters of Foxhounds Association 1999).

The breed (along with the animals that comprise it) is set apart from other dogs. This is not simply because they are working dogs but because of their particular role – as hunting hounds. The association of hunting hounds with monarchs, emperors, the aristocracy, the nobility and the gentry has a long history in Europe, and hounds have been praised, lauded and celebrated in a range of European literature (see, for example, Ahl 1989; Cummins 1988; De Quoy 1971; Longrigg 1977; Phœbus 1984). Hounds have been marked as elite dogs because of their central place in the sport of hunting – itself traditionally an elite event. The special quality of the foxhound continues to be marked in present-day foxhunting through the linguistic device of always referring to the animal as a *hound* and never, ever, as a *dog*.[2] The quickest way for an outsider to show their ignorance of the event or to denigrate it, is to ask about or talk about 'the dogs'. This key distinction between hounds and other dogs is given added weight within the world of hunting by reference to hounds and *cur dogs*. In this context a *cur dog* is any dog, however illustrious its pedigree, that is not a foxhound. Such usage is not a disparaging one, despite the term *cur*, and it is not that the user despises other dogs (indeed, most people involved in hunting are the loving owners of pet dogs); rather, it is a way of clearly marking and distinguishing 'hounds'.

The distinction between foxhounds and other dogs is further marked by the system of naming individual animals. Each hound has an individual name, but these are unlike those given to other domesticated dogs in England[3] and form a system which is unique to these animals and to their social and cultural identities and status. Names such as Brampton, Cider, Safeguard, Foxham, Gaffer, Gameboy, Sandford and Gunshot (to take a selection of names for doghounds which have recently won prizes at premier hound shows) or Brazen, Honour, Chorus, Hopeful, Statue, Patience and Grapeshot (prize-winning bitches) are peculiar to foxhounds. Such names individuate but they are not descriptive of physical qualities, nor are they associated with character (while patience is indeed a quality, the newly born hound would not have been named for any such potential quality). In most cases it is impossible to tell dogs from bitches in names such as Ptarmigan, Cherish, Ballard and Famine, although names such as Norseman, Governor, Fairy and Garland do perhaps suggest gender. The name of each hound in a particular litter must normally begin with the same letter as the first letter of the name of either the sire or the dam. Although this initial letter or letters of the name denotes a linkage of pedigree there is rarely a connection of any other sort. For example, Foxham is a male offspring of Forelock, and Burglar the male offspring of Broadcast; Claret is the mother of Clever, and Famine that of Fairy. Hounds may not be given names of one syllable (a regulation of the Masters of Foxhounds Association), and most huntsmen comment that they chose names which simply sound attractive and which carry well when they are shouted out on the hunting field. Many actually prefer names with three syllables because they feel that they are able to more subtly or emphatically modulate the intonation when they call them across the countryside.[4]

Those involved with foxhounds have a highly developed sense of the breed, and each person responsible for the breeding policy of the hunt will have an extremely complex set of views and opinions of what and how a hound ought to be. There is no space here to go into the technical details of the pedigree breeding involved. Nevertheless it is important to point out that the creation of the foxhound, as with the creation of any domestic animal, is a triumph of cultural ideas in combination with a natural form. There is an appreciation of, an interest in, and perhaps a love of this particular animal form and a desire and dedication to mould, shape, maintain and even improve it. The aim of the breeders is to create an 'ideal' foxhound[5] – an ideal which, of course, is held in their minds and imagination. Scrupulous attention is paid to the breeding of each hound in order to achieve a particular body form that appeals aesthetically. The physical form, the basis of the animal's athletic quality (its speed, drive and stamina), is a fundamental concern because these are working animals which will have to hunt and run perhaps forty or fifty miles a day, twice a week, during the hunting season. Although it is impossible to separate the efficient hound body from that of its aesthetic representation, most breeders comment that one should pay primary attention to this athletic quality. In the words of advice given to an old huntsman when handing over the responsibility of the pack to his son, 'Breed them for work, and get them as good looking as you can' (in Lady Apsley 1949: 179).

Not only are breeders seeking to produce hounds physically robust enough for the rigours of hunting, they are also seeking other important, although less tangible, qualities of which the most important are 'nose', 'voice' and 'fox sense'. These animals hunt by scent, and 'nose', the scenting ability of hounds, is fundamental. All hounds should have this, but some will be able to exercise it in very difficult conditions (when, for example, there is little scent because of the local weather conditions or because it is difficult to follow the scent across particular land surfaces) and are thus regarded as exceptional animals. Each hound must be able to communicate to its fellows that, during the initial search for the scent, it has picked up the traces of a fox. When it does so it emits a 'squeaking' or 'yipping' sound which, when it becomes more convinced of what it has found, develops into a fuller 'baying' that draws other hounds to it. This is its 'voice'. A hound should never silently set off on its own in pursuit of a fox – this should be a collective venture and hounds should communicate with each other and work together. Ideally there should be a harmonization between 'nose' and 'voice' – finding the scent should trigger the sound, and a hound should not use its 'voice' if it is not fully engaged with the scent of a fox. The quality and 'trueness' of 'voice' is highly prized by huntsmen because it indicates the relationship between his hounds and the potential fox. Huntsmen listen intently to the voices – some individuals are always to be trusted, others are less reliable, they may be 'guessing' or only imitating other hounds – he needs to know which to believe in and encourage and which to ignore. The huntsman must be a skilled interpreter of the developing soundscapes of his hounds. Once again, though, this is not a purely practical issue (i.e. of communication), it is also an aesthetic concern. Many huntsmen comment that they like to have a range of voices in the pack – soprano, tenor and bass – to create a melodious and tuneful ensemble. This 'music of hounds' is highly appreciated by the participants and followers of hunting.

The final quality is that of 'fox sense'. The foxhound should only seek out and take notice of the scent of a fox – which it must be able to distinguish from all the other scents around it. But this scent does not come easily to the hound. Perhaps there is no scent at a particular location, perhaps there is the hint of a scent which is quickly dispersing or evaporating. Even if a hound does manage to pick up the scent of a fox which has not long departed, this will not be easy to follow. The fox, once it realizes that it is the object of attention, will attempt to flee in such a way as to disguise its scent; or the hounds might simply lose the scent because of a manoeuvre by the fox. This is when 'fox sense' enters – the ability of the hound to puzzle out where the fox might have gone and where it might regain the scent. The foxhunt is not an immediate or direct pursuit of a fox across the countryside. For much of the hunt the fox is not present and the hounds will only be following the traces of where it has been. The hounds need the speed and stamina to pursue these traces; but at the centre of the hunt is interpretation. Hounds must interpret what the changing scent or line of the fox indicates about the whereabouts of the animal, and the huntsman must interpret what the behaviour of his hounds indicates about their relationship with the fox. These relationships of communication, interpretation and understanding come through the enduring relationships between the human and the hound, relationships that centre on a core purpose, and it is this that will be explored in the following sections.

## Life Cycle: From Individual to Pack

It has already been suggested that the foxhound is an unusual breed in terms of dog-keeping in England. It is clearly a domesticated animal but it is kept with large numbers of others as a pack animal and, unlike pet dogs, it is not associated with, or incorporated into, human domestic space or family relationships. The hounds live in large, purpose-built kennels with the females in one section and the males in another, and they only come together for exercise or when hunting. Although many members of the pack will be closely related, there are no family groupings, and no social or other hierarchies are allowed to develop as they would with wild canines. As has been discussed, hounds are also selectively bred and there is no resorting to natural selection for the maintenance and recreation of the pack. Huntsmen will certainly use the term 'pack' to refer to the collectivity of their hounds, but it is perhaps better to understand this as a group of related animals which only fully become a pack when they are actually hunting.

Although each hound lives its adult life as a working animal in a large group, it begins its life as something much more akin, in terms of its physical location, treatment and relationships with humans, to a pet. When a bitch chosen for breeding comes on heat she will be removed from the pack, a selected doghound will be encouraged to impregnate her, and the puppies are born in isolation from the pack. Each of the puppies will be named and their pedigree recorded. The young hounds are not immediately incorporated into life in the kennels. Instead, the normal procedure is for the huntsman to place them with families or individuals who are associated with the hunt. Those who volunteer for this task are referred to as 'puppy walkers'. In terms of the life cycle of the foxhound this is the only time it will be anything like a pet animal at the centre of structures of affections associated with that sort of human–animal relationship. Significantly though, because the animal will not spend the majority of its life in an anthropomorphized pet relationship, this period is strictly limited and bounded. In a sense this is a 'liminal' period for the animal – a period of separation, of freedom and playfulness – prior to its 'initiation' into the disciplined, social, everyday, working world of the pack. Although it is born a foxhound and has the physical characteristics of a foxhound it has not acquired its full character as a foxhound. During this 'liminal' period (lasting for several months) the foxhound puppy is incorporated into a human domestic world and mixes with other pet animals which form part of that world. Exactly how it is treated and incorporated will vary from family to family and according to what the huntsman requires of them. Some puppy walkers may keep them in kennels outdoors, but most seem to welcome them into the house; during this time they are largely indistinguishable from other pet dogs. The puppy walkers feed them and take them out for exercise – probably the only time they are ever attached to a collar and leash, the restraining devices used to control most dogs. The puppy is subject to some limited discipline, essential to its socialization as a foxhound, to learn that it must not chase or attack other animals and to accustom it to being with people – something that will always be part of its life when away from the kennels. Huntsmen seem not to be too concerned about the type of attention, affection and anthropomorphic treatment lavished on the puppies during this period. They know that after this period they will still be able to mould them into a working animal.

Although the puppies stay with human families for several months, it is known by both human parties that this is a finite period and that the structures of affections developed between the family members and the puppy will be curtailed. The images of the human social process of the short-term fostering of children compared with life-long adoption provides an analogy for, and gives a sense of, the relationships involved. Although puppy walkers did not spontaneously use the term 'fostering', they readily agreed with the analogy when I suggested it to them. Those who took on this role commented that, as active members of the hunt community, providing a home for the puppies was an important (and pleasurable) service they willingly offered the hunt. They were certainly clear that the relationship was one of temporary care and belonging, but they also expressed this in terms of it being warm and enjoyable while it lasted – albeit tempered with wry comments about the damage inflicted on the contents of their houses by quickly growing, robust and boisterous hounds. Many did make another explicit comparison with children when they commented that young hounds soon became like unruly adolescents whom one dearly loved but whom one was equally pleased to see leave home. These animals are never fully incorporated as permanent members of a human family. The puppies always belong to someone else – to the hunt – and ownership is never transferred in this process of puppy walking. This is merely a transfer of guardianship, centred on temporary housing and care; it is not a full initiation into belonging. In terms of naming and the power of names, it is significant that each of these animals is named according to a system developed, or a tradition followed, by the hunt and the huntsman and *not* by those doing the puppy walking. Giving a name to a new puppy, kitten or other pet animal is part of the establishment of ownership of the animal, and a highly individualized relationship with it – and this does not occur with foxhounds. It arrives already named, already spoken of and spoken for. During its time with the family it learns to respond to this name – the one it must respond to later in kennels and on the hunting field.

The puppies will be returned to the huntsman after a few months so that they can be incorporated into their 'natural' family, the social group of hounds, with the huntsman at its head. Although it is acceptable for hounds to have close and sentimental bonds with humans early in their lives, this cannot be allowed to develop to excess. If such bonds did develop they would be unable to express what is regarded as their 'true' nature – their foxhoundness – their 'real' canine identity as a member of a pack of hunting dogs. In an important sense, pet dogs have only one purpose – to be affectionate with their owners and to allow an emotionally satisfying relationship to develop between human and animal. They are generally isolated from other dogs and are certainly not in a position to develop relationships of their own with other dogs. In contrast, for the foxhound to realize its potential as a foxhound, humans must stop responding to it as a unique individual and it must develop a set of complex relationships with the dozens of other animals with which it will live and work. In the end all the hounds must learn to respond to only one individual human, the huntsman. They have a duty and a function to fulfil –

they must become a pack-hunting animal under the direction of the huntsman, who functions as the 'top dog'. The huntsman is the guardian of this particular dog culture, not only in terms of preserving or developing the breed by selective breeding but also in terms of the expressive behaviour of the animals. In his relationships with them he demands and commands what is considered 'proper' hound behaviour, both from each individual and from the pack as a whole.

Some puppy walkers express sadness at losing their charges, but also pride that these animals are soon to take their place in the hunting pack. This return is the end of any long-term relationships with the individual hounds, but they certainly do not lose sight of them. The puppy walkers are usually keen hunt followers or participants and may well seek out 'their' hound at a meet to greet and pat it. They may often ask the huntsman about it and they may pay particular attention to its participation when the pack is hunting. Although the return of the young hounds to the kennels is unmarked, there is a later event that celebrates the association of particular hounds and their walkers – the 'puppy show'. This is a social highlight of the summer for members of the hunt and their guests. The event has the air of a highly formal garden party (with its corresponding formal dress codes), and has been described as a sort of canine Royal Ascot with the Master of Foxhounds standing in for the Royal Family. The event takes place at the hunt kennels, which are on show for the day. The central event is the judging (conducted by invited masters or huntsmen from other hunts) of the new hounds, with the prizes going to the puppy walkers. This celebrates their relationship with the particular hounds and the part they played in its early development, acts as a way for the hunt to thank the walkers for their services, and formally marks the end of their relationships with individual hounds.

Huntsmen comment that despite the hounds being isolated individuals for the first few months of their lives it only takes two or three weeks for most young hounds to adapt to the regime of kennel life and to lose the traces of being a pet. The young hounds will be perhaps a year old when they are returned to the kennels. In larger hunts there may be separate accommodation for these hounds, but most mix them in immediately with the older animals. Although they will not go out hunting during their first season in the kennels, they begin to learn the ways of the pack through their communal living and through the daily exercise walk when the entire pack is taken out. From now on, although the hounds will be recognized as individuals, what is essential is for the huntsman to form them all into a pack. Each foxhound will have its individual character and individual hunting ability, which if positive will be highly valued by the huntsman – but must be put to the service of the pack. As Captain Wallace, a recognized authority on foxhounds, put it:

Foxhounds must behave as a pack, and although some obviously become brilliant and others pretty good as individuals, it is as a unit that they are judged out hunting. A young hound that becomes too sharp in its first season, and then swollen-headed, is dangerous. When I first started hunting I congratulated a young hound in catching an old fox on its own. I was pleased and told it so. It was never any good again. It became too sharp and beyond reformation. (Captain R. E. Wallace, *Countryweek Hunting*, March 1995: 45)

## Forging the Bonds

Having introduced the production of and early socialization of hounds it is now necessary to explore the most important relationship between humans and hounds – the lifelong relationship between the huntsman and the hounds. Although hounds will encounter other people throughout their lives, and have some minimal inter-action with them, their focus of attention will be the huntsman and his assistants, who work with them every day of the year. These animals are never pets of the huntsman, despite the closeness of his daily relationship with them.

There is a marked separation between the huntsman's house (usually located close to the kennels) and the kennels – the home/house of the hounds. The huntsman leaves his house to work with them: they are never allowed into his domestic space; it is he who enters and takes control of their social world. The location of hounds indicates their unusual status as animals in terms of English rural space. Leaving aside the two extremes – pets and wild animals – other rural animals, such as sheep and cattle, live in herds in enclosed fields and are some-times brought into some form of barn for shelter; others, such as poultry and pigs, might live in permanent shelters; and horses will live partly in enclosed fields and partly in individual stables. Hounds are permanently enclosed or housed as a group (although males and females are separated), but they are all taken out for exercise each day into the countryside under the guidance and control of one or two people. Domesticated livestock, living in herds or flocks, are controlled though spatial containment and should be docile and easily managed – there should be no testing of or challenge to the proper relationship of human control and animal sub-servience. Hounds, too, are physically contained in their kennels and yards and should be docile and easily managed when there. However, unlike the relationship of control between humans and livestock there is a continual testing of control and a challenge to the quality of the relationships between human and hound when hunting begins. The ability of the huntsman to maintain control over a pack that is free to run wherever it chooses, and the quality and style of the command he exerts, constitutes an important aesthetic element of foxhunting.

Hounds are neither pets nor livestock, but there are aspects of both of these sta-tuses in their relationships with humans. Pets could be viewed as non-utilitarian animals that are created in order to enter into close emotional relationships of love and companionship with humans. The creation of pets centres on the production of non-human friends. Most livestock are created for utilitarian purposes – for their bodies or the products of their bodies – and their owners, although they might develop close relationships with them, do not keep the animals primarily in order to develop such relationships.[6] The huntsman and his assistants have close, emotional and enduring relationships with the hounds, but not of an individual pet kind, and although hounds are created for a purpose, to hunt foxes, their utility is not directly associated with their bodies as a physical product but with their performance as a group. The creation of a pack of foxhounds centres not simply on the production of animal bodies but on the production of a set of *relationships*, through these trained bodies, that connect humans and hounds and, by implication, wild foxes. The relationship between the huntsman and hounds needs to be explored in two locations: in the kennels and on the hunting field – the first being a preparation for the second.

With its focus on everyday care and management the central activity in the kennels differs little from livestock husbandry. The hounds must be fed and watered, their living quarters must be cleaned and the sick must be attended to. They cannot, in any sense, take care of themselves, and the work to look after them is both intensive and continuous. Not only must their animal bodily needs be attended to but they must also be prepared for their working purpose. Each hound will have to hunt once or twice a week (with some hunts there is hunting four times a week) during the season from early autumn to spring, and this is the busiest period in the kennels. Because hounds cannot simply be turned loose for some form of exercise, they must also be taken out as a group by the huntsman and an assistant. The exact nature of this exercise varies from hunt to hunt but will usually involve a closely controlled journey through country lanes (with the humans on bicycles or horses) and across country, and involve a stop at some suitable location where the hounds are allowed to race about, frolic, play and in other ways 'let off steam'.

The care and attention in kennels not only produces healthy and strong hounds but is also the basis for the production of a set of relationships fundamental for those which the huntsman must have with the hounds when hunting. Crucial to this is the creation of discipline. While the young animal was living with the puppy walkers it was not disciplined much and certainly not trained. Discipline begins when the hound is integrated into the pack, and the kennel is the site of discipline. Although the kennel, with its scores of inhabitants, is often a noisy place, it is never a disorderly place and, except at night, the hounds are always subject to human surveillance. The aim, most huntsmen said, was to create harmony in the kennels – hounds are not allowed to squabble, fight or become unruly and there should be no establishment of hierarchies. The huntsman must assert his authority over the pack as a collectivity and over its individual members – a more complex process than that for the owner of an individual dog – because he must work with so many of them at a time. It is only through his close relationship with each individual animal that the pack is able to hunt as a disciplined group – the collectivity is more important than the individual.

Although all the huntsmen interviewed during this research expressed great affection for hounds and their pack, they did so in ways different from pet-owners. Each hound is known as an individual and partly responded to as an individual member of the pack, but the huntsman cannot, because of the numbers involved, have an intimate, individual and exclusive relationship with each hound. Not only can he not have a 'pet-like' relationship with each animal, neither can he have the same sort of working relationship that shepherds, gamekeepers, game-bird shooters, blind people or the police have with their dogs. It is not a one-to-one relationship either from the perspective of huntsman to hound or hound to huntsman. Although the pack consists of many individual animals, each of which has their relationships with others in the pack, these relationships must never be allowed to unbalance the relationship between pack and huntsman. Although it is relatively easy to maintain order in the kennels, the potential for disorder on the hunting field is enormous. The control of the hounds depends on the huntsman's relationship with them – a relationship that is created by making him the most important person in the lives of each hound. As many huntsmen explained, they were, and had to be, 'top dog'.

Between huntsman and hounds there is a careful balance between an easy, affectionate friendship and discipline, and each party must understand what is necessary or appropriate at different times. Huntsmen must be strict (though certainly not cruel) disciplinarians in order to create the proper working relationship with their hounds. As one Master of Foxhounds complained to me about his huntsman when the hounds were not performing well: 'He's too fond of his hounds, he thinks he can do it with fondness; what he needs is more discipline. He mustn't do everything for them. Hounds must respect you. They mustn't be allowed to do their own thing.' Although huntsmen express deep affection for their hounds, this is balanced by strong notions of how that affection may be expressed. It is captured by the use of 'fond' in the quotation above, suggestive of an over-affectionate, foolishly doting relationship, more appropriate for the individual intimacy of a human–pet dog relationship. In order to maintain what are regarded as the essential and necessary qualities of a foxhound there should be no indulgence in sentimentality. Affection, yes, but not to the extent that any apparent wishes of the animal unbalance the relationship of control and domination by the human over the animal. A quotation from a huntsman, when asked about the fundamental relationship between the huntsman and hounds, expresses a typical view:

[I]t's having hounds that have a great respect for you. It all comes down to how you actually handle them, how you work with them in the kennel. The hounds have got to love you so to speak, so that when you talk to them and ask them to do something, they respond to you and do it. It's no good you being at odds with your hounds at all, because it won't work. They won't work for you. It will up to a point, but they will tend to work independently. You want hounds to do what you want. Obviously to do what they need to do, what's natural for them to do, but you've got to have that control over them – if you've got that, that's half the battle.

Foxhunting is a form of hunting for sport,[7] but it is also configured on the killing of a pest. Such hunting must be effective – foxes must be found, pursued and killed – but crucially it is also a performance, and it is responded to as such by those who participate. Hounds are certainly purposeful when hunting, but that purpose has been established for them. Huntsmen express the view that hounds enjoy hunting and hunt because it is part of their 'nature' but, once again, this must be disciplined enjoyment, and their 'natural instincts' are shaped and controlled by human desires. There must be a careful balance in this activity – they are both hunting for themselves and as the agents of someone else. They must be allowed to express themselves and respond in their own ways when hunting, but they must also remember and respond to the fact that they are also hunting for the huntsman. They should be willingly and fully engaged with the activity, and should do so enthusiastically rather than treating it as a necessary task or a chore. This enthusiasm relates directly to what is seen as their proper relationship with the huntsman. As one commented: 'They want to please you. If you give a command they'll do it because they want to please you. I don't want sulky hounds doing it.'

When they leave the kennels on a hunting day both huntsmen and hounds should be prepared to work and perform, based on a strong sense of mutual understanding, as a team. All the huntsmen with whom I spoke emphasized the intense interrelatedness of man and animal and the idea that something was shared between them in this context. In the words of another huntsman: 'There must be good communication. You must get them so they trust you. You must give them confidence. If I have no enthusiasm why should they?' They are hunting for and with him. The hounds must understand their task, and they understand this not simply by being free to respond to any natural instincts they have but through their disciplined relationship with the huntsman. The notion of confidence was expressed by another huntsman: 'What you want above all with a pack of hounds is high morale, high morale comes from confidence, self-confidence from themselves and confidence in their huntsman.' He went on to explain that such confidence is not achieved through their treatment in kennels: 'This does not just come from feeding and care, but by giving them challenges they can overcome.' The challenges he is referring to are those presented by the difficulties of finding and killing foxes in the complex conditions of the countryside. These are difficulties that the hounds should, ideally, resolve for themselves. They should not wait for him to tell them what to do and how to do it. The huntsman will encourage them in their task, but he should not interfere too much in that process. He should have an understanding of (or perhaps rather a feeling for) both the conditions that are presented to the hounds and their responses to them.

He should not, however, impose himself too much when they are hunting. It is felt that if the huntsman is over-ready to tell the hounds what to do and where to go then they will become lazy and merely wait for his commands. Equally, many huntsmen commented that the huntsman ought to demonstrate trust in his hounds and not always think that he knows better than they do. 'The dimmest hound usually knows more than the best huntsman', as one expressed it to me. Many people in the hunting world refer to 'the invisible thread' that connects the huntsman and his hounds – it is the slackening of this thread, through encouragement, and its tightening, through discipline and command, the ebb and flow of the relationships between them, that constitutes a central aspect of the hunting performance. Although some huntsmen expressed the view that the most perfect form of hunting would be for them to go out alone with their hounds, this does not happen. The huntsman does not develop his bonds with the hounds purely for himself and his own satisfaction. The relationship between them culminates in a performance and everything must be directed towards the perfection of that performance. The relationship is put on show and is responded to and judged by the mounted participants and the other followers. What they have come to see is a demonstration of the relationship between them in action.

## Breaking the Bonds

Finally, it is necessary to return to arguments at the beginning of the chapter in order to explore issues connected with the end of the foxhound. Once hounds have entered the kennels they will spend the rest of their lives there. A good foxhound has a working life of perhaps seven or eight years. Hounds that for various reasons do not fit the desired profile of the pack, or which do not take to the life of a hunting hound, might be sent to another pack or they might be killed by the huntsman early in their lives. When a hound reaches the end of its working life, or when it is too ill or too seriously injured to go out hunting, it will be killed by shooting it and the body incinerated. The end of the life of a hound is highly significant in terms of its life-cycle and its changing relationships with humans. It is never simply removed from the pack and allowed to retire with other unserviceable hounds, as sometimes happens with horses. This made no sense to huntsmen when they were asked about it. Equally inappropriate was the idea that perhaps unwanted hounds could retire and become the creatures they nearly became at the beginning of their lives – pets. The most common explanation given for this is that it would be an act of cruelty to the hound. Huntsmen commented that the pack was their 'natural' and 'proper' home and that if they could no longer live there then it would be cruel to isolate them in a human home where they would be unable to live fully and truly as foxhounds – it would be a diminution of their quality of life. The only acceptable end for an unviable hound is death.

The nature of this death, which huntsmen refer to as 'putting down', again indicates the unusual status of the foxhound. Fit and healthy livestock raised for meat are 'slaughtered' in special establishments, but old, sick or injured livestock are 'put down' where they have lived. The killing of pet animals (once again the horse is an interesting exception here) is rarely referred to as 'putting down' but rather as 'putting to sleep'. The killing of non-individualized livestock is handed over by the owner to a specialist, the vet, who uses a specific form of shooting. The responsibility for the death of a pet is similarly handed over by the owner to a specialist, an animal medical practitioner, who is permitted to kill through the medical technique of lethal injection. The death of a hound is therefore very different from that of a pet and closer to the death of a livestock animal. However, in contrast to livestock, the responsibility is not handed over to a stranger but carried out by the person who has had the closest relationship with the foxhound. The dog lives through him and must die through him.

I conclude with extracts from an interview conducted with a huntsman during a documentary film about foxhunting (*The Hunt*, directed by Niek Koppen, 1997). I conclude with this because, even though it is only one huntsman's view, it captures something of the emotional involvement a huntsman has with the hounds during their lives, showing how this affection, this intense and complex set of relationships, must be shaped by the needs and disciplines of hunting as work for both him and them, and, finally, how despite the closeness of the relationship it must end when they are no longer able to participate and perform together as huntsman and hunting hound. Prior to these questions, the huntsman has been talking about the importance of his family and the support he gets from them:

*Question*: So you said 'My family comes first?'

*Huntsman*: Yeah they do, well I mean, yeah, they come first but the hounds ... they give me my enjoyment, they give me my pleasure ... they become as much part of my life as my wife and two kids you know ... they're lovely friends, they're mates, they're not pets you know, they're not lovely canine creatures, they're friends, they're mates ... this closeness being because I'm here ... seven days a week I'm looking after them you know, and when they're ill I repair them.

*Question*: But if necessary you shoot them as well?

*Huntsman*: Yeah, I don't like doing it, it's ... it's ... that's a hard thing to answer, it's the hardest thing you could ask any hunt servant to do. It's very, very hard. The reason we can't put them down by the needle at the vet is because, you know, they've lived the working life in this kennel with people they know, that they trust, as well as them trusting me, so they deserve the right to be put down in their own environment. So when the time comes that you have to put them down, and it's a time to say, 'Goodbye', it's kind to be put down in the kennels but for me it's hard, but you know life goes on …

*Question*: But is it always necessary?

*Huntsman*: You couldn't have them as a pet, you know, you couldn't. You couldn't put a hound after living in an environment that it's been used to – of hunting and living in a kennel – you couldn't ask them … ask them to … not a foxhound… you couldn't ask them to be pets … there are hounds I've put down that I would have loved to keep as pets but it can't be done …

*Question*: So they never retire after a working career?

*Huntsman*: No, not foxhounds, no, no, no … it's not … it's basically 'Goodbye old friend' … they've given you nine years say, of hard work, 'cos their life is hard work, it's bloody hard work, they've given you nine years of pleasure so, you know, my way of thanking them is putting them down in their own environment, quickly and efficiently, so there's no suffering and no pain and that's the way.

## Acknowledgements

I would like to thank John Knight for inviting me to participate once again in the enormously stimulating panels on human–animal relations that he has carefully constructed at the EASA conferences; to the many huntsmen who have taken the time to talk with me about hound things, and to SSS for her patient listening and critical reading.

## Notes

1. The issue is actually more complex than this and individual Masters of Foxhounds can own foxhounds of the pack for which they are responsible (see regulations 32, 33 in Masters of Foxhounds Association 1999).
2. The only acceptable use of the term 'dog' is when referring specifically to a male foxhound, but even then the correct term would be 'doghound'.
3. See Franklin (1999: 95) for a discussion of the changing fashions of naming pet dogs.
4. A fuller analysis of how the naming of hounds places them in terms of other animals, both wild and domesticated (each of which have their own schemes of naming or non-naming), and the attribution of social status to animals, would need a careful engagement with the analysis Lévi-Strauss (1966: 204–9) made of the names given to birds, cows, dogs and racehorses, for which there is no space here (see also Tester 1991: 33–6).
5. It would probably be better to express this as 'a foxhound which is ideal for the terrain over which a particular hunt operates', but there is no space here to develop the more complex ideas surrounding this point.

6. The horse, not dealt with in this chapter, is an interesting case of an animal placed between the pet and livestock. It is not quite a pet, and certainly not incorporated into human domestic space, but it is created so that its individual body can be used in close relation with that of the human body. Humans also have more enduring and complex relationships with horses than they do with other livestock.
7. In the current political debate about the event in England there is a rhetoric of it being efficient pest control. This debate cannot be entered here, but for an outline of some of the issues see Marvin (2000).

# References

Ahl, F. (1989),'Uilix Mac Leirtis: The Classical Hero in Irish Metamorphosis', in Rosanna Warren (ed.), *The Art of Translation: Voices from the Field*. Boston: Northeastern University Press.

Apsley, Lady (1949), *The Fox-hunters' Bedside Book*. London: Spottiswoode.

Cummins, J. (1988), *The Hound and the Hawk: The Art of Medieval Hunting*. London: Weidenfeld and Nicolson.

Franklin, A. (1999), *Animals and Modern Cultures: A Sociology of Human–Animal Relations in Modernity*. London: Sage.

Lévi-Strauss, C. (1966), *The Savage Mind*. London: Weidenfeld and Nicolson.

Longrigg, R. (1977), *The English Squire and His Sport*. London: Michael Joseph.

Marvin, G. (2000), 'The Problem of Foxes: Legitimate and Illegitimate Killing in the English Countryside', in J. Knight (ed.), *Natural Enemies: People–Wildlife Conflicts in Anthropological Perspective*. London: Routledge.

Masters of Foxhounds Association (1999), *Constitution, Rules and Regulations*. Bagendon (UK).

Phœbus, G. (1984), *The Hunting Book*. London: Regent Books/Hightext Ltd.

De Quoy, A. (1971), *The Irish Wolfhound in Irish Literature and Law*. McLean, Va.: De Quoy Publishing.

Tester, K. (1991), *Animals and Society: The Humanity of Animal Rights*. London: Routledge

*The Hunt* (1997), Directed by Niek Koppen and produced by Kees Ryninks. Amsterdam: Ryninks Films.

# On 'Loving Your Water Buffalo More Than Your Own Mother': Relationships of Animal and Human Care in Nepal

## Ben Campbell

## Introduction

The keeping of domesticated animals has long been a theme within anthropology. Central cultural values have been recognized in attitudes to livestock, giving rise to expressions such as the African 'cattle complex'. Yet the tendency in theoretical analyses is almost always in the end to privilege human sociality, and to render discussion of relationships with animals as predominantly instrumental to the achievement of discretely human goals. One of the Nuer terms at the core of Evans-Pritchard's segmentary lineage theory *gol* is not widely remembered to denote the 'smouldering dung heap' (Evans-Pritchard 1950: 362),[1] in addition to the 'joint family' (Evans-Pritchard 1940: 219). This chapter's focus is on the ethnographic realities and issues of relationship in interspecies social dwelling, that tend to lose out to anthropocentric agendas of meaning and power.

The humanly assisted and modified reproduction of herd kinship among domesticated animals entails reciprocal consequences in the dynamics of labour, wealth and identity categories among human kin. In considering the theme of 'animals in person' and ethnographic perspectives on 'loving animals', my strategy is to discuss how a Tamang-speaking community's living with domesticated animals in the Nepal Himalaya generates a 'kinship' of affectivity, needs and responsibilities between people and livestock.[2] These bonds of connection and mutual dependence carry endemic problems that, as the quoted speech in the title suggests, can result in the perception of more affection being bestowed on ungulate quadrupeds than on human kin. A heated conversation took place within an extended family about how to care for a woman who was too old to stand the discomforts of life involved in looking after the family's mobile herd in the mud, dung, thorns and rocks of the mountainside. Her only son had bought a milking water buffalo, and had become devoted to its needs rather than those of his mother. Retired from the social life of the family's pastoral movements, she had found herself abandoned in the village house, and the old woman's son was accused by his brother-in-law of loving his water buffalo to the detriment of caring for his mother.

How could such a commensurability of 'love' come to be made? How appropriate is it to talk of 'love' for animals in Tamang livestock keeping? Can it adequately describe an ontological unity of care, affection, and reciprocity across species difference? For the Tamang, livestock and human communities are far from consistently dichotomized. Rather, there seems to be an oscillating consciousness between an effective wrapping together of human–livestock interactions in a common field, and strategies of human–livestock category distancing. The instability of dichotomizing practices allows for bonds of intimacy, knowledge of character, and intersubjective communication to occur in keeping livestock, that are not wholly instrumental or metaphorical and that do not amount to an anthropomorphic sentimentalization of animals.

Ingold (2000) offers a provocative contribution to considering a typology of 'modes of engagement' between humans and animals. His central argument, which for all that follows I do not contest, is that pervasive continuities in patterns of sociality straddle human–human and human–animal relationships. His typology is based on a distinction of alternative relationships of trust and domination characterizing hunting and pastoral peoples' respective terms of engagement with animals. '[A]lthough the relations pastoralists establish with animals are quite different from those established by hunters, they rest, at a more fundamental level, on the same premise, namely that animals are, like human beings, endowed with powers of sentience and autonomous action, which have either to be respected, as in hunting, or overcome through superior force, as in pastoralism' (ibid.: 74). He argues against *analogical* comparison between the social and natural because both for hunters and pastoralists environmental engagements preclude the detachment of nature as a separate domain that the dichotomy requires. In order to stress the direct continuities between the treatment of other humans and the treatment of animals he asserts that 'the sense in which hunters claim to know and care for animals is *identical* to the sense in which they know and care for other human beings' (ibid.: 75–6). So as not to set hunters apart from the rest of humanity, he continues with the argument that among Eurasian reindeer herdsmen 'the transition from hunting to pastoralism led to the emergence, in place of egalitarian relations of sharing, of relations of dominance and subordination between herding leaders and their assistants' (ibid.: 76). Whether human–animal relations are marked by caring, sharing trust or by dominance, it is not, according to Ingold, a figurative manner of speech, analogical in effect, but in both cases a fundamental relational disposition.

What this contribution seeks to do is to muddy somewhat the clarity of Ingold's reasoning by exploring the qualities of Tamang–livestock interactions, prompted by the example of the domestic dilemma already described about prioritizing care between human kin and animal charges. The family conflict abruptly disentangled the usually seamless, networked cycles of human–livestock needs and services. It made explicit the awful awareness that keeping water buffaloes at the upland extent of their range entails inordinate amounts of time, effort and attention, which not only makes care of livestock comparable to looking after kin but actually renders caring for kin almost impossible when they most need it and are unable autonomously to look after themselves. The normal straddling of looking after humans and animals as a unitary activity needed to be dispelled in consciousness by a rhetorical strategy of *analogizing* humans and livestock, to acknowledge the old mother's alienation from the family.

The chapter draws attention to the 'domesticity' of Tamang domesticated livestock keeping. It follows the *mostly* inseparable co-ordinations of attending to animals' needs along with, and as part of, those of reproducing everyday domestic social life. This kinship practice of guardian nurture extends across human and domesticated animal categories in ways that could be linked to the etymological root *domus* in 'domination', but it is for the most part more benign features of domestic management that deserve to be highlighted, than the normal English understanding of 'domination' implies, and which Ingold refers to in terms of subordinated involuntary obligation under conditions of pastoralist mastery and control. In examining qualities of pastoral care by the Tamang, the relationship of their livestock practices to national legal and religious norms regarding cow protection in Nepal will be made to contextualize aspects of 'involuntary domination' in human–animal relationships. Although there are relations between people and animals in Nepal which serve to objectify analogically hierarchical differences between categories of people, these are, it is argued, an effect of the symbolic identification of the dominant Hindu culture with the cow, rather than an intrinsic property of social relations among livestock keepers and their animals.

The challenge taken up by this chapter is to think about the processes and linkages that underpin the human–animal moral community as a social life of connection rather than dichotomy (Escobar 1999: 8), while recognizing those instances of moral disjuncture that do produce separations of humans from animals. Descola has written of how, in what he terms 'societies of nature', plants, animals and other entities are part of a socio-cosmic community, subject to the same rules as humans (1994a). Elsewhere (1994b) he has argued, however, that native Amazonian category symbolism has played a part in the absence from that region of developments towards livestock domestication. His point being that having domestic livestock for economic exploitation would require a symbolic objectification to be made at odds with the categorical separation of hunted versus pet animals: those you eat and those you love. For the Tamang, the markedly different moral-categorial co-ordinates of living interdependently with livestock produce continuities of the human and non-human that are, for instance, linguistically reflected in their term for 'carrying' (*naaba*) livestock as you carry a child or other burden on the back, and in the evaluative agency the Tamang exercise in their daily balancing acts of domestic agro-pastoral multi-tasking.

## Past and Present Tamang Herding

The relationship of the Tamang-speaking communities of north-central Nepal to their livestock has undoubtedly undergone massive changes over the last 300 years. Changes in trans-Himalayan trade networks, incorporation into taxation systems, the effects of regulated legal property inheritance, and ratios of population with ecological resources may be presumed to have influenced attitudes to keeping animals. Studies of historical patterns that go back to the early twentieth century indicate that these communities have undergone significant changes in the composition of herds, particularly from beasts of burden for servicing trade to a preference for milch animals (Fricke 1986; Blamont 1986). But whatever the composition, the orientation to looking to livestock for the basis of sustaining livelihoods seems constant in upper Rasuwa District.[3] The productivity of human labour in the pastoral aspect of village economy has a more grounded primacy than it has in relation to the vicissitudes of crop harvests. Herds and flocks are perceived as more evidently social productions and as markers of prestige than are fields. Herds reflect year on year continuities of animal care, management of pastoral labour by family members and/or hired herders (*gothalo*), and strategies of investment and dowry distribution. It is domestic animals more than fields which feature in dowry gifts that circulate among categories of classificatory sisters and daughters (Campbell 2000). It is livestock that replenishes soil fertility and makes possible agronomic intensification, which recent usage of chemical fertilizer by some families does not threaten to change.

While there is no everyday linguistic category in Tamang for 'animal', domestic livestock are collectively *dindu*. The major sub-categories are spoken of in coupled terms *mai–mè* (water buffalo–cattle) and *ra–giu* (goats–sheep). *Yakpo* (yak) and *dzomo* (female yak–cow hybrids) are kept mostly by specialized high-altitude herders. Tengu village, where this research was conducted, has only occasionally had some families herding in the pastoral network of yak–cow hybrids, on account of limited pre-monsoon fresh water supplies in the higher ranges where yak should be kept for their health. Pigs are kept by only a very few people in upper Rasuwa as an oddity, or by the few families of Blacksmith caste. There were none in Tengu. Sheep and long-haired goats are taken from 1,000 metres by the banks of the Trisuli river in winter (*shisang*), to 4,500 metres in summer (*serka*). Before the Chinese occupation of Tibet, goats were kept by some Tengu villagers as pack animals to carry salt and rice through the Himalayan chain to trade. On these visits they encountered Tibetan herders (*drogpa*), seen by Tamang in comparison to themselves as 'real' pastoralists who have no fields, and about whose specialized animal-herding way of life stories circulate suggesting that even their flour is made from powdered meat. Since the mid-twentieth century, geopolitical events, administrative change, and national park regulations have greatly reduced the geographical extent of Tengu village herders' ranges, though the sheep and goat flocks, and occasional yak–cow hybrid herds, do negotiate passage into neighbouring village domains.

Agro-pastoral production has intensified since the mid-1980s, with women's labour in particular increasingly devoted to fodder collection for water buffaloes, brought about through the effects of road development and tourism in creating selling opportunities for fresh milk and potatoes. However, planned economic intensifications for this temperate humid band of the Himalayas through promotions of tree fruit and horticulture over the last twenty years has mostly been resisted by the Tamangs' continuing commitment to their short- and long-range transhumant productive orientation. The specializations of horticulture and tree fruit require sedentarized labour for guarding against wild and domestic animal damage, that would take hands away from attending to the welfare of animals by accessing the vertically distributed seasonal fodder sources on the mountainside through transhumance. The Tamangs' love of their mobile herding way of life thus becomes a cause of developers' regret and failure in their objectively 'rational' project designs for this temperate ecological zone, now linked to Kathmandu by road. Within the development literature commentators lament the locals' 'herds of low productivity' and 'rif-raf cattle', as compared to the profitability of sedentarized, high-input, improved breeds Living so close to their animals makes for a problematic relationship to development modernity, whereas from the inside livestock literally embody values of socio-cosmic reproduction. Animals are sustained by and sustain dense community relationships: by looking after animals people are also looking after themselves and each other. For this reason, whenever a development team arrives in the village of Tengu they are lucky to find even a quarter of the population there. The rest are where it matters for them to be, with the animals.

## Domestic Intimacies

Living in closely dependent domestic proximity with animals generates all kinds of emotion, from joy to despair, and provides viscerally experienced pleasures and pains of dwelling. Many of the professed tenets of Tamang kinship sociality are sustained through practices of livestock domesticity. It is not domination pure and simple, but a convivial, domestic distributional hierarchy based on practices of interpersonal attentiveness, that characterizes this milieu. Notions of love expressed by the Tamang are generated through and by explicit reference to the circulation of substance, care and protection in an emotionally networked human–livestock collectivity. Attendance to this contact contrasts with the attitude of iconic sacralization towards the cow prominent in Hindu symbolism, which will be discussed later (see pp. 93–4). The significance of livestock to embodied practices of mutual trust, closeness and productive sociality can be seen in the language of nurture expressed through the words *naaba, chaaba, whaaba. Naaba* means 'to carry', both in the sense of responsibility and, literally, of transporting a thing. People thus 'carry' their herd in a notion of physical and moral management, as they do their family, the term being also used to refer to raising a child when for instance fostering is perceived as building an enduring responsibility, incurring a reciprocal debt of care. *Chaaba* means 'to look' in the sense of watching animals and children in their activities in a manner of supervisory surveillance, looking out for dangers or straying individuals. It further connotes looking after their well-being and caring for their development. *Whaaba* is a transitive term for 'giving to eat'. It contrasts with more indirect and subtle phrasings for feeding, and conveys the sense of unceremoniously seeing that stomachs and mouths are filled. Thus it covers not only food and drink, and is used to describe how local and bought medicines are administered to children or animals 'for their own good', when there may be an element of force-feeding involved. *Whaaba* also refers to giving food offerings to certain demanding spirits and gods, who are seen

**Figure 4.1** Water Buffalo Calf and Herder in the *Godi* Shelter.

to be in need of attention but who are understood as unlikely to express gratitude other than in terms of leaving humans and animals alone and unmolested for a period.

These everyday responsibilities of *naaba, chaaba, whaaba* (carrying–raising, watchful care, and giving nourishment) are the basic essentials for the reproduction of life in the practice of sustaining bodily health and strength (*pang*) for people and livestock. They are the prerequisites and points of reference for interpreting interpersonal moods, moral evaluations in domestic relations, and the distributive justice of work activity. The social composition of Tamang domestic 'units' is fluid, and many individuals maintain cross-cutting claims to residential rights in various households (Campbell 1993, 1994). Examples of people for whom various households are legitimately claimed to be 'home' include children whose parents no longer live together or who prefer the company of grandparents; women who have married within the village; couples living in part-time semi-detachment from parental hearths; formally independent siblings who nonetheless encamp their *godi* (mobile herding shelters with bamboo mat roofs) as a cluster with their brothers' or sisters'; and people of the village acting as contracted herders (*gothalo*) for other families. In parallel to this human residential fluidity, cows and buffaloes in particular are similarly known as individuals with life-careers in which they have passed between sequences of different herds through inheritance, gift, barter exchange and cash transaction.

**Figure 4.2** Children Minding Adult Water Buffaloes on Stubble Fields.

For many of the categories of people mentioned above whose livelihoods involve shifting relationships of pragmatic alliance to sets of different households, the basis of their domestic attachments are often explicitly contractual, even where direct kinship is involved. One teenage boy who moved between his mother, grandparents, and his father who had remarried, was told he was welcome to choose to stay with his stepmother and half-siblings as long as he worked hard: 'Do work and eat.' He had to earn his keep in other words. Similarly unsentimental and work-related narratives of people's claims to participate in productive domestic inclusion, and to have a stake in the feeding and provisioning nexus of the *godi*, were apparent and became explicit in cases when the terms of contribution and entitlement were seen as being abused. A propertyless widowed mother of a virilocally married woman helped out in her daughter's *godi*, and worked on her daughter's behalf in fulfilling inter-household reciprocal agricultural obligations. She complained bitterly to me one afternoon when I found her returning from the work group to find the *godi* shelter empty, the animals having been taken to pasture, and no cooked food had been left for her. The lack of consideration for all her labours was evidently distressing to her, and brought home to me how sensitive are the micro-politics of everyday life in the *godi*, with readings of care and neglect potentially being made around every meal.

The line for human relations between companionable, considerate conviviality on the one hand and subordinated domination on the other is a territory for delicate negotiation, attendance to detail, and rhetorical commentary on the flow of everyday events. While some individuals manage to manoeuvre effectively between different residential opportunities, others may find themselves less able to vote with their feet. Explicit domination does not sit easily with the strong narratives of personal equality in Tamang social *mores*. They speak of not laughing (at others) while sitting on a rug/skin (an image of comfort and status), and of powerful families losing their status by the time grandchildren are grown up. There are many other proverbialized reminders of humility and the dangers of overweening pride. Put another way, without the possibilities afforded by inclusive social rhetorics of kinship, interpersonal equality, and companionable working conditions, many of the *godi* would simply not be able to find needed extra hands. Domination over people is characteristically unstable in this context.

The significance of livestock to the whole discourse and substance of kinship takes many forms. Many patrilineal clan identities are distinguished by particularized narrative constructions of livestock: the Ploen clan cannot eat buffalo because the orphaned clan founder was raised on the milk of a buffalo; while others (Shyangba and Ghale) require the sacrifice of a sheep to honour the clan god after building a new house. One occasion that revealed a marked consubstantial identification of kin and livestock was when I was invited into the herd shelter of the brother of the family I stayed with to share a handful of the warmed-up colostrum (tasting like a sweet and rich, chewy cream cheese) of a cow that had just given birth the same day. The gathering of *nyang ki mi* ('our inside people') partaking of this supreme life-giving nutritional substance, and adoring the new-born calf, temporarily closed off any sense of endemic, bickering, agnatic squabble in a moment of serenely contemplative, embodied collective nurture. *Dindu-i yang* is the blessing of fertile animals that is requested from the gods at domestic purifications and pilgrimages. Birth is seen as a blessing, a sign of divine cosmic fertility, humans and animals being subject to the same processes of regenerative life force (*tseeh-i chi*). Cosmologically, the shamanic-Buddhist ritual practices endorse an existential commonality among sentient beings subject to similar causes of suffering and well-being, requiring regular ritual housework to keep at bay spirits with malicious intent. Livestock diseases are treated within the same ritual framework as humans: offering, in ways appropriate to the supposed spirit causing trouble, small piles of incense, foods, salt, tobacco, chillis, etc., on flat stones accompanied by chanting, right through to full-blown sacrifice.

## Life in the *Godi*

Whenever I returned to the village settlement after a day's visiting among the encampments of mobile animal shelters (*godi*), people around the houses would routinely ask me: 'Did you eat milk?' The expectation was that I would have been welcomed in to at least a few shelters, and been offered some snack. 'Milk' (*nye*) in this context stands metonymically for any produce of the herding cooking hearth: yoghurt, dried twists of cheese, buttermilk, boiled eggs, or fried-up smoked frogs being characteristic foods of the *godi*. 'Milk' and the herding way of life evoke a proximity to fecund productivity and a provisioning of fresh foodstuffs, as compared to the houses, which are places of set-aside, dried stores.

In the *godi* animals are more intimately dwelt with than when in houses. In the nucleated village, traditional two-storey houses have a stabling area (*wakhang*) at ground level. In the *godi* animals are stalled at night under the same roof, beside the human living area. On approaching one of the shelters, it is important to first call out '*nigi tsungji?*' ('have you got hold of the dog?'). When sitting and talking, or joining in the activities that take place around the *godi* (stripping bamboo poles, weaving a mat, or threshing grain for sowing or eating), you are likely to be nuzzled and licked by a calf, threatened by the sweeping horns of a tethered buffalo, and pestered for bones and scraps of food by dogs and chickens. Walking in the areas of clustered encampments in the middle of the afternoon you will experience the rush hour on the paths, when people take animals to water, as herds of on average five to ten animals negotiate their passing places, and the known aggressive ones are kept to one side by a member of the family, with stick in hand, calling out to others in cheek-sucking, lip-smacking commands. It is important to get to know the capricious personalities of particular animals, especially those with big horns, and to remember to stay uphill of them as you pass, so as not to be toppled downhill.

The *godi* shelters on harvested fields provide children with an environment of human–animal play and learning. My fieldnotes remind me how entranced a twelve-year old girl was by her father bringing back a goat kid from a visit to his ritual friend who kept a substantial flock in a hamlet by the river. It followed the girl from the *godi* all the way down to the wheat fields, where she went to collect fodder, and back again. Children in this way learn techniques of controlling live-stock through intimacy of companionship along with developing an alertness to danger from larger beasts, who are controlled by acquiring skills of hurling stones with considerable accuracy, or by cursing them with imminent deaths 'by an axe!' or 'by a leopard!' By the age of about seven children's play is interrupted by increasing labour duties for the livestock. At this age they can be left in charge of a few goats and even cattle, feeding on cleared fields or the forest edge. They will also join in fodder-collecting trips, especially for the voracious buffaloes, in family groups or age cohorts at an earlier age than that at which, around twelve years, they integrate with the collective agricultural tasks performed in the more regu-lated co-ordination of exchange labour.

From childhood, then, knowledge of the distinctive tasks of looking after spe-cific categories of animals and their best feeding grounds, and awareness of par-ticular animals' desires, tricks and cunning, are learnt through life in the *godi*. Beyond whatever emotional sentiments are built up, an understanding of the desires common to animals, humans and spirits of different types is developed – that is, a common paradigm of attentive provisioning, as evoked by the word *whaaba*. Humans, animals, and gods–spirits (*la-lu*) all require distinctive atten-tions and have their specific dietary requirements and characteristic desires, which if not satisfied lead to the danger of anti-social unrequited need: a world of volatile hungry subjectivities that never know stability but demand constant recognition and feeding for ongoing sociality (Holmberg 1989).

Some examples of appropriate and inappropriate foods were given to me. A man with a pair of excellent ploughing bullocks said that in breaks between their ploughing he gave them *poshoro langdu* (possibly a kind of mulberry), adding that this nutritious plant increased milk yields in females (*nye yuba tsu tse*: 'milk comes from this'), and *sulshing* (leaves of one of the evergreen oaks) which he said fills them up (*phom mremba*). Interestingly this combination very much follows the typical human meal of a filling flour porridge accompanied with a nettle soup or other sauce. He told me for two ploughing bullocks one should give them two bundles of fodder in the morning, around midday give them three bundles, in the evening send them to drink water at the stream, and when stalling or tethering them for the night give four bundles of fodder. Finally, he added, if you don't give them this kind of food to eat it is sinful (*tsaba apinsam paap khaba*). Brewing residues (*palbi*) are a favoured occasional adjunct to the livestock diet, said to give them strength, aside from the entertaining spectacle of seeing calves scampering around half-tipsy.

Even within livestock species particular breeds are often distinguished in terms of their diet and behaviour. Modern introduced Holstein crosses are known not to do well on the local pasturage. One man explained to me that he was not interested in taking the offer of another's bullock (a *male* – a black and white breed) because if they eat wild buckwheat weeds (*tanglemo*) their skin peels, and they walk off, not staying with his herd. The suitability of livestock types for distinctive localities in terms of health is constantly assessed. Thus a herd of goats was moved away from a *godi* beside a stream when their eyes went red from too many leech bites in the monsoon.[4] Later the owner thought the red eyes were not simply from the leeches, and had a malicious spirit exorcism performed (*mang klaaba*), sacrificing a chicken. Tamangs make a distinction between 'disease' (*yam*) such as foot and mouth (*khoren*) and spirit afflictions (*mang shyapji*). Similar distinctions are applied to people, as when the distinctive consumption behaviour of particular types of human herders are remarked on. The transhumant sheep–goat minders, men and women, show a tremendous propensity for binge-drinking of alcohol when visiting back in the village, making up for enforced abstinence, often of several months' duration.

Regimes of livestock control in an open field system, mostly without fencing, obviously create problems with straying animals. There is difficulty in determining who to blame when animals wander and have to be chased off standing crops. The overall village co-ordination of arable rotations partly prevents this, but buffaloes have a tendency to break free at night when a home-made tethering rope breaks. The animal owner's first tack is often to say that the beast is just a naughty character (*baani ajaba*), and try to deflect personal responsibility. But if substantial crop damage has been done, an adjudicated compensation process (*armol*) is set in motion. Alternatively, I witnessed one man pre-empting any such trouble after his bullocks had eaten someone else's paddy seed-beds. The bullock-owner brought his old boyhood friend, and clan-sister's husband, a container of millet beer and they spent the evening reminiscing over their childhood squabbles and games.

## Pooches, Pets and Pampering

Anthropologists are perhaps prone to pick upon the treatment of animals in their fieldwork communities to symbolize cultural difference. We are in this sense compulsive analogical totemizers. When I arrived to do research and found a new hamlet being built beside a road that had been constructed up above the old village, there seemed to be a potent symbolism of the community's relationship to this development in the presence of a three-legged dog (hit by a vehicle) that hobbled around the stone shacks and defunct, rusting steamroller, and that appeared to have a permanent erection. No one of course articulated the interpretation that I read into this animal's condition of crippled excitement (that development left its neglected casualties handicapped with unobtainable desires), but the fact that the creature survived for several years in this state would only have been possible on account of the community's defence of its right to exist and not be tortured by children. I was explicitly told it would be sinful to have the animal put down. The dog had a 'dogged' personality, and a degree of compassion for its fate (a 'dog's life' with a difference of anthropological note) ensured its survival.

This compassion I was to learn did not apply to all canine life. The family I stayed with had a largish bitch, some part mastiff, feared by anybody who was not a regular visitor to the family and known to her. Her capacities as a guard dog prompted several offers of purchase by other herd-keepers. One year she gave birth to six puppies, and I watched as the father of the family stroked, picked up and inspected each of them in turn, with the children huddled round and joining in. My initial reading of this scene as a pet-adoring symbolization of domesticity was rudely dispelled when the father rose with five of the pups in his hands and hurled them down the mountainside. He told me later that this was from compassion for the mother who would only have enough milk to raise one pup healthily. Another incident of abrupt termination occurred one evening after dark, when all of a sudden the cock, tucked away under an upturned basket, crowed out loud as if it were dawn. Within seconds its head had been pulled off. Deviant cocks crowing at the wrong time of day should not be tolerated.

A counter-practice to this unsentimental dispatching of domestic animals was the adoption by children every spring of wild bird chicks found fallen from nests, though I suspect gathered also from nests when cutting fodder up trees. Little stick cages would sometimes be built to house them, where they would be fed scraps of food and wild berries. One year a rather magnificent eagle-owl chick was even brought in, though it did not survive long tied with a length of string round its leg to a house post.

A more elaborately ceremonialized adoration of domestic animals takes place around the autumn Hindu festival of Laxmi puja, when cows and dogs receive garlands of marigold flowers. The full Hindu sequence of ritual attention to animals on subsequent days starts with crows, proceeds through dogs, cows, and ends up with human brothers. The Tamangs seemed to ignore the crows, while they combine the day of the dog and cow. The women spend several days spoiling brothers with gifts of alcohol. The cattle herds were quite spectacularly bedecked with flowers on their day, when they were also fed a mixture of pumpkin, maize flour, salt, and marigold flower-heads and stalks. This event perhaps most closely resembled a 'loving' attitude to animals, but beyond the exceptional ritualization of Laxmi puja, the issue of what love has to do with keeping livestock requires an examination of the Tamangs' fundamental orientation to the herding way of life as a means of kinship practice.

The sheer interpenetration of human–animal discourses needs to be emphasized: a huge proportion of conversations shift between and combine human and animal reference. For the Tamang, human well-being and suffering is intimately connected to the fate of animals. Animals can be made to stand for human relationships, but also contribute in their own right and by their own animating presences to structuring the rhythms and movements of community life. One woman explained to me how great it was to have the sound of a cock crowing in the house again, stressing the feeling of contentment the crowing produced in her. Animals are used as tokens of love between people, and need levels of nurturing and care that underscore the basis of human domestic propensities and responsibility for others.

## Gifts of Connection

As a dwelling locus the *godi* has an open-sky connection to socio-environmental processes. Social visiting is far easier than house-based negotiation of socio-architectural thresholds. The *godi* thus facilitates informality in co-operative relations in groupings and activities of affection, kinship and labour: people sitting around in the sun weaving mats or baskets beside animals chomping on collected fodder, or searching a relative's hair for lice. It accentuates an intimacy with place, with the sight and sound of other *godi*-dwellers' activities, and with daily and seasonal movements in provisioning animals. Conversations characteristically wander with the total sensory landscape, and move back and forth between people, places and animals. When I was interviewing people in these situations, interruptions were constant. On one occasion an old, ragged, wifeless herder looking after his nephew's buffaloes dropped by, interrupting a discussion I was having with the nephew's brother-in-law. The herder had just brought the milking buffaloes up from valley-bottom winter pastures 2,000 feet below, and was having trouble getting the cursed beasts to eat the hard leaves of evergreen oak, after having got used to months of the sub-tropical fodder of wild banana leaves and more lush growth. In the same moaning breath he complained about his one son not staying in the boy's prospective father-in-law's *godi*, where suitors are called upon to demonstrate their suitability as wife-takers with brideservice labours. Kin and livestock populate a discursive continuum of themes and cross-references, encompassing movement, vegetation, diet, sex and recalcitrance.

In Tengu sheep and goats are noticeable as foci of extra-domestic kinship. Although married brothers are normally established in different residential units, their sheep and goats are frequently kept together though nominally distributed under separate ownership. This collective flock management embodies enduring agnatic solidarity in a way that permits further realizations of kinship as loving care mediated by attendance to animals. Twice-yearly sheep shearing collectively activates clan brother–sister (*phamyung–busing*) ties of affection and exchange. Women search out their classificatory brothers among the mêlée of sheep, men and wool, to offer them home-distilled alcohol in return for bundles of wool. Men will also make small gifts of balls of sheep cheese (*ser*) for their *busing*.

Herding is not simply agnatic, and the possibilities afforded by kinship and affinity result in variable emphases placed on sibling affection or wife-taker obligation. People will often need to adjust their management of herding arrangements for all sorts of reasons, such as temporary absence from the village to work as trekking porters, or sickness. Requests for looking after others' animals are best made to those of a trusting intimacy. Paid herders cannot be relied on to give as much concern for the animals' welfare as when moved around between the people whose kin connections are given substance by belonging in the circles within which livestock gifts are also made. The animals or their calves, kids and lambs are thus potential future items of dowry, or, in the case of bullocks, are animals whose work for ploughing their fields might be called on. Ploughing bullocks are not kept by every family, and often are passed around to make up teams or to help perform expressive-instrumental kinship effects. Although each animal will have an individual owner, shared herding arrangements and the creative flexibility towards resources generated by multiple domestic affiliations and inter-household co-operation mean that an ethos of circulating usufruct rights towards the animals often prevails in practice. In instances of temporarily lodging animals at another's *godi*, I perceived that concern and empathy, if not always explicitly spoken about in terms of 'love', are tacitly understood, along with diffuse reciprocal expectation of similar favours in return. An example of this was when a woman explained about some owner's incapacity to see to their animals due to illness with the words: 'Well, they just can't look after them [the animals] for now.'

With dowry animals, however strategically calculating the giving of them may be, they carry in their presence associations of loving responsibility for clan women. From analysing collected histories of livestock dowry gifts, a reasonably well-stocked herd owner might give away seven or more cows or buffaloes in his herding career. The memory of these gifts is well preserved, as are the subsequent lives of the animals. One woman received a dowry cow from her paternal uncle's son that gave birth eleven times. Her father gave her a buffalo, and an additional one after the original animal died, thus being well provided for in a sustained way, to enable the woman to achieve a reputation for conscientious care and socializing nurture.[5] When women receive animal dowry gifts they reciprocate with gallons of home-distilled alcohol and baskets of fried doughnuts, lubricating and nourishing the sustained discursive celebration of livestock and kinship. While men abrogate to themselves the role of generous givers, women alternatively explained to me how they deviously managed to influence their husbands' desire for reputation as good clan providers in a way that specifically benefited the daughters of the wives' own same-clan sisters (*nanchen*) (Campbell 2000). Livestock dowry gifts are among the best occasions for making formalized discursive connections between animals, kin and love, and for talking 'culture' in the sense of 'we do things this way'.

## Domination, Protection and Sacrifice

Contrasting with kin-embedded livestock keeping, sales of all animals, except chickens, are circumscribed by an idea of sinful action expressed in the routine practice of giving a few extra rupees to the seller (*baldso rani*).[6] Sales are most concentrated around the post-monsoon festival of *dasain,* when Tamang villagers from higher up the valley come in search of buffaloes to sacrifice. Even villages like Tengu that do keep buffaloes tend not to use their own beasts to sacrifice, but search downhill for animals to buy more cheaply. In making these transactions prior to *dasain* the value-for-money motive does not preclude extended and sometimes quite tenuous invocations of social connection between virtual strangers involving projections of long-standing alliances between villages. The unrestrained feasting on meat thus becomes wrapped up in discourses of regional solidarity and networks of trust. Talking about and around animals at this festive time becomes a key medium for articulating networks and solidarities within the region, based on historical ties between villages or shared clan identities and interclan alliances among people transacting over animals.

Such talk of solidarities does not displace the fact that issues of the treatment of livestock encapsulate some of the fundamental cultural dilemmas the Tamang face. They are forced to participate in the national Hindu sacrifice of buffaloes at *dasain* (as a demonstration of citizenship), for which they have to atone to their Buddhist consciences by leading a funeral (Campbell 1995). Yet they do not share in the Nepali state's sacralized reverence for the cow, in which the cow is accorded a divine mother status, and as consumers of 'carrion' beef they suffer condemnation as 'mother-eaters'. In terms of their encompassing 'great tradition' cultural environments, Buddhist to the north, Hindu to the south, the Tamang lose out in both directions in these great tradition human–animal morality narratives.

The Tamangs' commitment to livestock as socio-economic practice is awkwardly related to the state religion's bovine totemic icon. In Nepal the dominant cultural and legal system establishes respect for the cow as a principal duty for the social order. More than a mere symbolic equal of humans, in law killing a cow brings the same life sentence as killing a person. Cows are often spoken of, and to, as god-mothers. Walking a forest path in east Nepal I was passed by a perturbed cow obviously intent on finding its strayed calf, stopping, peering around, calling out, back-tracking and searching possible side trails. A Hindu village woman came by and on passing the cow addressed it as 'Ama Laxmi' (mother goddess of fortune), asking 'where are you off to?' in the simple manner of a polite, pedestrian social encounter. The cow epitomizes docile conscientious nurture and care for offspring, and at the same time offers to people milk, butter and curds for themselves and to use as pure offerings to the gods.[7]

This dominant cultural sacralization of the cow, representing bovine nurture as a supreme model both for loving human socialization and for recognition of the divine in non-human beings, is not wholly shared by all the people of Nepal. Among Tamang-speaking communities the prohibition of cow-slaughter still applies, but without the same accompanying cultural reverence. Certain clans (specifically the Ghale former kings of the ancient polity) share the Hindu taboo on eating beef, but the majority of Tamang clans eat the meat of cattle that have died of natural causes. By this practice they bear the stigma of offending primal Hindu moral axioms, and the totemic Hindu complex that fetishizes human–cow love. The law against cow slaughter has been shown to involve numerous uncertainties. Michaels (1996: 90–1) states that a paragraph of the national legal code prohibits the sale of meat from a cow killed accidentally. He points out ambiguities in the detail of the law protecting the cow, including the anomalous position of the yak, and suggests it is not clear whether for instance an accidentally deceased cow can be eaten by its owner.[8] In Tengu the practice has been that dead cattle belonging to non-beef-eating Ghale clans may not be sold, but if the owner is from a beef-eating 'Tamang' clan the meat does get sold. Michaels concludes that bovine protection has primarily had a symbolic role in extending the claim of remote ethnic communities to be considered under the rule of the Nepali state, protecting the orthodox status of the king rather than the actual animals. Unlike other ethnic groups that have variously accommodated to Hindu norms, most Tamang persist in their beef-eating diet regardless of condemnation from others for not respecting the way Nepalis *identify* with the cow as mother. In this regard Tamangs could be said to insist strategically on a harder boundary between human and non-human, and on analogy rather than identity in human–animal relations, given the cultural politics of the treatment of cows.

Sacrificial distributive dismemberment of yaks has been shown to be a key ritual template of the Tamangs' own social order (Macdonald 1987), and mythical variants of the template refer to the trickery of Hindu high-castes in stigmatizing Tamangs as cow-eaters (Holmberg 1989: 34–7). A general point is that in Nepal, as elsewhere, diverse social groups do often evaluate each other analogically by reference to their treatment of animals. The villagers of Tengu, for example, distanced themselves from their more affluent neighbours over the ridge to the east, where the Sherpas of Helambu are said to kill male calves of yak–cow hybrids by feeding them with salt so that they gorge themselves to bursting with milk.[9] Tamang profess a condemnation of this practice that is perhaps phrased more in terms of illegality than immorality

In contrast to the species category prohibition on cow slaughter, there is a cultural practice of the Tamang which reveals an additional dimension to their human–livestock relations – that of attributing special characteristics to a single animal. I only received a slight intimation about *tsehtar* ('liberating animals', or giving them 'life-freedom') during fieldwork, but have since had confirmation of its practice in upper Rasuwa (personal communication, Gyalsang Tamang). *Tsehtar* consists of marking out an individual sheep or goat to be preserved from slaughter or sale. A hole is made in its ear and pieces of coloured cloth are tied through to identify it thereafter as an animal saved from the fate of disposal. The practice, I am told, is often intended for the merit of a dead or still-living person's soul. My research did not pick up on *tsehtar* practice among livestock in Tengu, as I didn't consult the shepherds on this, but the term had been explained to me when used as a person's first name, specifically for the birth of a late and unexpected child.

This attitude to 'liberated animals' could be connected with dialogues of human–animal cosmic moral economy in the Mongolian–Siberian ritual practice of protecting specific animals. The evidence of ritual prohibition on slaughtering special individual animals in the Mongolian–Siberian region is discussed by Tani (1996). He suggests that certain animals are noted for auspicious qualities, and their individualized protection ensures the reproductive potential of the whole herd or flock. Key individual animals are recognized as 'chiefs' among hunted species in Siberia, which should be allowed to live for the sake of the reproductive fertility of the rest (ibid.: 407). Tani claims that this practice indicates a major difference in relationship to livestock domestication, and more generally in attitudes to nature, between the Mongolian–Siberian region and the Mediterranean–Middle Eastern world. It is Tani's theory of contemporaneous developments in ancient Middle Eastern structures of domination over humans using serf-eunuchs, and over flocks using castrated 'guide wethers', which inspired Ingold's reflections on the shift from 'trust' to 'domination'. Tani emphasizes, though, the specificity of the Mediterranean–Middle Eastern attitude of animal domination linked to a view of nature being under godly control but delegated to supervision by humans. He argues that Mongolian pastoralists partake in a different ideology of nature in which 'the reproduction of the animal world is independent of human control and protection, even if this independence might be vulnerable to the human desire to violate it' (ibid.: 410). Ingold's reading of pastoralism as necessarily involving domination therefore needs qualification with reference to such significant ideological distinctions. Echoes of Tani's theory for Siberian–Mongolian special animals can perhaps be recognized in the Tamang ethnography.[10] Not only are specific livestock protected but the idea of animal chiefs was frequently talked about in Tengu by the shepherds. They spoke especially of the packs of wild dogs (*paara*), that prey on sheep and goats, as having a chief noticeably smaller in size than the rest and who directs their attacks. The prohibition of eating certain body parts, which is identified in the Siberian–Mongolian complex (ibid.: 408), might also have an echo in the Tamang custom of never eating brains as food until after a person's own father's death. A firmer exploration of these connections would require more research, but there are sufficient reasons to question Ingold's assertion of a generic dominatory logic in pastoralism as compared to hunter-gatherers.

## Conclusion

A problem with Ingold's typology of trust-based and domination-based human–animal relations is that his argument suggesting an identical sociality across the human–animal divide overlooks the fact that the human arena is significantly differentiated. He draws on Tom Gibson's (1985) ethnography of Buid hunter-gatherers to characterize features of trusting companionship in relations of friendship, in terms of being voluntary, freely terminable and respectful of autonomy, that are extended beyond people to their interactions with animals. By contrast, Ingold points to features of involuntary, non-terminable social obligation in the domination mode of pastoralist engagement. Yet in claiming that qualities of environmental relationship will be manifest also in relations obtaining between people (2000: 61), Ingold has bracketed out the fact that involuntary, non-terminable obligation is how Gibson himself characterizes Buid kinship, as opposed to relations of Buid autonomous companionship. There is thus a problem in not recognizing different modalities of interpersonal relations when an identical and not analogous human–animal relationality is discussed. Ingold's statement that in hunter-gatherer representations 'they see no essential difference between the ways one relates to humans and to non-human constituents of the environment' (ibid.: 75), needs to be qualified by Gibson's original analysis which highlights two very different ways that Buids relate to each other as humans: either as dependent kin or as autonomous companions.

In her reflections on ideas of property, objectification and gendered personhood, Strathern comments on Melanesians' relationships to pigs in terms of socially enchained performative operations: 'The pig is multiply produced … to the open-ended transactions with (multiple) kin of all kinds in which any particular set of transactions … is enveloped' (1988: 160). The Tamangs' relationship to animal keeping appears similarly dividualized through networks and transactional processes of kinship sociality. It is impossible to speak of their kinship without reference to their livestock, and it is not enough to say that their animals serve as embodiments of material and symbolic values. Livestock are the best form of gift for people to show love for each other, blessing another with a gift of life and divine fertility itself. Blessings at weddings routinely contain wishes for transformational abundance among the newly-weds' animals. Should that principle of reproductive bounty obscure people's distinct self-knowledge as living within human kinship – such as when someone appears to love a buffalo more than his own mother – a confusion of identifications deserves to be rudely pointed out. Analogy and identity, rather than being analytical alternatives as Ingold suggests, are complementary interpretive modalities in Tamang perceptions of being and connection. When in analogical mode it is not nature and society that are contrasted (about which I agree with Ingold), nor even human and animal (there is no such clear category of 'animal' in Tamang), but specific groups such as 'our people' (*nyang ki mi*), Hindus (*Jyarti*), or Sherpas, that are put in relationship with particular kinds of animal.

In talking of their livestock the Tamang manage to convey an astute perceptiveness of character and agency that attends to the complex intimacy of animal and human lives (with problems of diet, sex, disease and recalcitrance common to both). The social continuum across species in collective domesticity is an ontological reality for reflexive appropriation. This makes it possible to think of the effects people have on their domestic animals as an interactive whole. Speaking of one family's bullocks as 'thieves', a rather mischievous lama's wife observed that 'it takes people to make a thief'. She thus turned around the idea that the creatures' personalities are intrinsically formed, species-specific, or beyond human training, which would absolve the owners from responsibility for their animals' actions, and asserted instead the influence of their (defective) socialization. This kind of comment could be seen to support Ingold's insistence that 'the domain in which human persons are involved as social beings with one another cannot be rigidly set apart from the domain of their involvement with non-human components of the environment' (2000: 61). Yet the qualitative range of social being in the ethnographic context described here does not straightforwardly conform to a paradigm of domination. The suggestion in this chapter has been that Tamang domestic social dwelling with animals involves modalities of both identification and separation. It is not possible to impose a stable grid of supra-species category distinctions over the multiple contexts of animate meaning generated through human–livestock conviviality. Further to this, attending to the Tamangs' coexistence with livestock in their domestic practices makes for a knowledge of their humanity as a species-thick engagement that is little understood by others. Indeed, it is dominating outsiders who place on the Tamang an identification with animality that the Tamang themselves are at pains to counter. Rather than pastoral activities necessarily being accompanied by domination in social practices, the political economy of marginal mountain agro-pastoralism offers an unstable basis for enduring relations of inequality among the communities of producers themselves. They are caught in a trap of extending their pastoral base at the expense of looking after their own mothers.

## Acknowledgements

The research for this chapter was enabled by funding from ESRC as a postgraduate student at UEA (1989–92), and later as a research fellow at Manchester (1997–8).

## Notes

1. Evans-Pritchard states that 'the primary meaning of [this] word is the heap of smouldering cattle-dung and the hearth around it that is a feature of every byre' (1950: 326).
2. Tamang is the Tibeto-Burman language spoken in upland Rasuwa, apart from a few pockets of Tibetan speakers. To avoid repetition I hereafter refer to Tamang-speakers as Tamang, though technically this would offend people of clans who claim royal descent status as Ghale (Campbell 1996).
3. Some evidence to the contrary in the Helambu valley to the east is given in Bishop (1998), where the population has for decades been more integrated into the wider South Asian economy of migratory trading.
4. Short-haired goats are kept with village herds, while long-haired ones go on long transhumance with the sheep, always keeping at higher altitudes than the ascent of the leeches with the onset of the monsoon.
5. There are perceptions of animal care as gendered, in the sense of particular intimacies being recognized between women and their herd, characterized by distinctly personalized bonds of intersubjectivity and protectiveness, that are spoken of as especially reciprocated in the case of women who look after yak–cow hybrids. I was often told to be wary of approaching these women too suddenly as the animals would defend their keepers aggressively.
6. *Baldso rani* – if selling a cow or buffalo, an amount of 10–20 rupees extra would be paid by the buyer after the transaction to avoid sin coming to the seller, with 2–4 rupees extra being paid for sheep or goats.
7. The capacity attributed to other animals of expressing deep maternal feelings was dramatically revealed to me when climbing some temple steps in northern Kathmandu. I saw a female rhesus monkey with a little puppy in her arms, and feared for the puppy's fate. I explained my concern to a local temple visitor, who told me the monkey must have lost its own child and had adopted the puppy to care for instead.
8. After the initiation of multiparty democracy in 1990, new district officials in Rasuwa began insisting that even female buffaloes should not be killed.

9. Bishop (1998), in a study of Helambu herders, does not mention the use of salt, but refers to other means of indirect culling.
10. Though distinctly Buddhist in the Himalayan region, Chinese accounts report similar but deliberately 'de-Buddhicized' versions (Handlin-Smith 1999).

# References

Bishop, N. (1998), *Himalayan Herders*. Fort Worth: Harcourt Brace.

Blamont, D. (1986), 'Facteurs de différenciation des systèmes agro-pastoraux des hauts pays du Centre Népal', in J. Dobremez (ed.), *Les Collines du Népal Central: écosystèmes, structures sociales et systèmes agraires*. Paris: INRA.

Campbell, B. (1993), 'The Dynamics of Cooperation: Households and Economy in a Tamang Community of Nepal'. Ph.D. thesis, University of East Anglia.

Campbell, B. (1994), 'Forms of Cooperation in a Tamang Community', in M. Allen (ed.), *The Anthropology of Nepal: Peoples, Problems and Processes*. Kathmandu: Mandala.

Campbell, B. (1995), 'Dismembering the Body Politic: Contestations of Legitimacy in Tamang Celebrations of Dasain'. *Kailash* XVII(3–4): 133–46.

Campbell, B. (1996), 'The Heavy Loads of Tamang Identity', in D. Gellner, J. Pfaff-Czarnecka and J. Whelpton (eds), *Nationalism and Ethnicity in a Hindu State*. Chur, Nepal: Harwood Academic Publishers.

Campbell, B. (2000), 'Properties of Identity: Gender, Inheritance and Livelihood in Nepal', in V. Goddard (ed.), *Gender, Agency and Change*. London: Routledge.

Descola, P. (1994a), *In the Society of Nature: A Native Ecology in Amazonia*. Cambridge: Cambridge University Press.

Descola, P. (1994b), 'Pourquoi les Indiens d'Amazonie n'ont-ils pas domestiqué le pécari? Généalogie des objets et anthropologie de l'objectivation', in B. Latour and P. Lemonnier (eds), *De la Préhistoire aux Missiles Balistiques. L'Intelligence sociale des techniques*. Paris: La Découverte.

Escobar, A. (1999), 'After Nature: Steps to an Anti-Essentialist Political Ecology'. *Current Anthropology* 40(1): 1–30.

Evans-Pritchard, E. E. (1940), *The Nuer: A Description of the Modes of Livelihood and Political Institutions of a Nilotic People*. Oxford: Clarendon Press.

Evans-Pritchard, E. E. (1950), 'Kinship and the Local Community among the Nuer', in A. Radcliffe-Brown and D.Forde (eds), *African Systems of Kinship and Marriage*. Oxford: Oxford University Press.

Fricke. T. (1986), *Himalayan Households: Tamang Demography and Domestic Processes*. New York: Columbia University Press.

Gibson, T. (1985), 'The Sharing of Substance versus the Sharing of Activity among the Buid'. *Man* 20: 391–411.

Handlin-Smith, J. (1999), 'Liberating Animals in Ming-Qing China'. *Journal of Asian Studies* 58(1): 51–84.

Holmberg, A. (1989), *Order in Paradox: Myth, Ritual and Exchange among Nepal's Tamang.* Ithaca: Cornell University Press.

Ingold, T. (2000), *The Perception of the Environment: Essays in Livelihood, Dwelling and Skill.* London: Routledge.

Macdonald, A. (1987), 'Creative Dismemberment Among the Tamang and Sherpas of Nepal'. In *Essays on the Ethnology of Nepal and South Asia.* Kathmandu: Ratna Pustak Bhandar.

Michaels, A. (1996), 'The King and the Cow: On a Crucial Symbol of Hinduization', in D. Gellner, J. Pfaff-Czarnecka and J. Whelpton (eds), *Nationalism and Ethnicity in a Hindu State.* Chur, Nepal: Harwood Academic Publishers.

Strathern, M. (1988), *The Gender of the Gift.* Berkeley: University of California Press.

Tani, Y. (1996), 'Domestic Animal as Serf: Ideologies of Nature in the Mediterranean and the Middle East', in R. Ellen and K. Fukui (eds), *Redefining Nature: Ecology, Culture and Domestication.* Oxford: Berg.

# –5–

# Loved to Death? Veterinary Visions of Pet-keeping in Modern Dutch Society

## Joanna Swabe

## Introduction

The presence of pet animals in modern Dutch society is generally taken very much for granted. Indeed, one could argue that the practice of sharing homes and gardens with select members of other species is deeply embedded in what social theorist Pierre Bourdieu (1984) has described as the nation's *habitus*. It is something that the vast majority of the population leaves unquestioned in their everyday lives. While not all members of Dutch society are inclined to keep an animal as a pet, they will undoubtedly recognize that it is a normative and socially acceptable practice to do so. Indeed, in recent decades, the Dutch media has increasingly tapped into the public fascination and affection for small furry or unusual animals, producing a wealth of television programmes, newspaper articles and even specialist publications to satisfy the human curiosity and interest in pet animal species. Likewise, a thriving pet industry has developed within the Netherlands to provide for and service pet animal needs From the breeders, who produce tailor-made animals, to the pet food manufacturers who feed them, entrepreneurs have realized that there are considerable profits to be made by exploiting attachments to small animals and encouraging people to keep them as pets (Swabe 1999: 180–1) As the levels of both affluence and inquisitiveness about animals have increased, the range of creatures kept as pets in the Netherlands has also expanded to include a whole host of exotic rodents, reptiles, amphibians and birds. Today, even horses are often considered 'companion animals', where once they were only kept for recreation, sport and labour purposes.

Yet whilst the practice of pet-keeping is very much a taken-for-granted one in the Netherlands, there are great variations in the kind of attention and affection that pet animals will receive from their lowland owners. Some of these creatures are lavished with affection and accorded the status of quasi-human beings, others are neglected, maltreated or even abandoned (Swabe 1996, 2000). However, companionship is not always the reason why the most familiar pet animal species, such as dogs and cats, are kept within this modern industrial society. The age-old functions of these mammals as the protectors of property, hunting companions and the agents of pest control may still remain as the prime motivation for keeping them. Even at the start of the twenty-first century dogs are still bred and used for fighting purposes, in spite of social and legal prohibitions on the practice. In present-day Dutch society, dogs and, to a lesser degree, cats are also employed for therapeutic purposes. Interaction with these species has been found to improve the mental and physical well-being of socially marginalized and institutionalized members of society (Robinson 1995). Dogs are also routinely employed as helpers: they guide the blind or help the deaf and disabled to perform everyday tasks (Sanders 1999). Besides these functions, pet animal species are kept for ornamental purposes, or function as status symbols or are kept simply as playthings (CSS Report 1988: 3–7). We should also not turn a blind eye to the use of species, which are commonly kept as pets, within scientific experimentation and even food production. Rabbits, for example, which have become increasingly popular as pets within the past couple of decades, are routinely bred for both laboratory experiments and the dinner plate.

In sum, the relationship between humans and pet animals within Dutch society is not always as straightforward as one may like to believe. As sociologists Arnold Arluke and Clinton R. Sanders have observed, when we more generally consider modern Western attitudes towards animals, 'one of the most glaring consistencies is inconsistency' (Arluke and Sanders 1996: 4). Yet we do not necessarily have to look to animal abuse, laboratory science or rabbit stew to illustrate the paradoxical nature of this human–pet relationship. The contradictions and ambiguities with which this relationship is often replete may also be observed in everyday settings where decisions about the health and prospects of animals are in play. This chapter will thus specifically consider human–animal interactions that take place within a veterinary context. It will explore the attitudes of Dutch small-animal practitioners towards pet-keeping and pet-keepers, examining the extent to which the boundaries between humans and animals are contested within this cultural context.

The qualitative data upon which this chapter is based derives from three different research projects into the nature of human–animal relationships. Some of the data were collected between 1993 and 1994 during an ethnographic study of veterinary interaction, which formed part of my doctoral research. The veterinary practices studied were located in the provinces of North Holland and South Holland, mainly in urban settings. The second data set derives from ethnographic material collected from 1999 to the present-day whilst working part-time as a volunteer on the Amsterdam Animal Ambulance service. This charitable organization is a member of a nationwide network of volunteer animal ambulances – unique to the Netherlands – and exists to serve the needs of pet, stray and wild animals in crisis situations and, for a small fee, to provide transportation for animals and owners, particularly to veterinary surgeries. Finally, the third and most recent data set derives from in-depth interviews conducted in 2001 with small animal practitioners throughout the length and breadth of the country (in both urban and rural areas), as part of a research study into the social and ethical acceptability of killing domestic animals.[1]

All the veterinarians who participated in this research received their veterinary medical training at the Faculty of Veterinary Medicine, Utrecht University. This is the only place within the Netherlands where veterinary medicine can actually be studied (though occasionally Dutch students intent on pursuing a veterinary career will train across the border at the Belgian University of Ghent when no places in Utrecht are available). In the latter data set, from which the bulk of the data in this piece derives, a total of sixteen veterinarians were interviewed. Roughly half of the sample was female, the majority having graduated within the past fifteen years. This clearly reflects the process of feminization that the Dutch veterinary profession has undergone throughout the past two decades. There was also significant variation in the length of time in which my veterinary informants had been working in veterinary practice: those interviewed received their diplomas between 1965 and 1995. Demographically speaking, the interviewees were selected according to province and the size of the community they served, which ranged from under 10,000 to more than 600,000 inhabitants. The practices in which they worked varied in terms of character. Some, particularly the urban practices dealing exclusively with pet animals, were one- or two-man shows. Others, in rural areas, employed between four and eighteen veterinarians. In such rural practices, most of the vets did not work exclusively in small animal practice but also specialized in, for example, pigs or cattle. Additionally, one veterinary oncologist from the veterinary school was interviewed. Further to this, several of the veterinarians over 50 years of age had previously worked with livestock before choosing to work with pets, which – they argued – offered them a much quieter life.

Despite the common educational background, the sample was far from homogeneous, differing considerably in religious and cultural backgrounds and attitudes towards certain veterinary procedures. However, as will be illustrated, there was striking consistency in their moral attitudes towards pet-keeping, particularly with regard to the moral responsibility of owners towards their pets and the necessity of their recognizing that they are indeed animals which have species-bound needs and requirements. As we shall see, these veterinarians were acutely aware and deeply critical of behaviour that breaches the human–animal divide. In general, the veterinarians tended to regard themselves as the advocates of the animals, their role being in part to regulate the conduct of pet owners towards their animal charges and to protect animal welfare. Indeed, it is evident that these veterinarians act very much as the mediators in what is essentially an intimate and deeply personal relationship between pet and person.

## Crossing the Human–Animal Divide

At the very outset of my sociological inquiries into human–animal relations, one of my central objectives was to establish whether any truth lay behind the widely held notion that people treat pets as if they were children. Historically speaking, there is considerable evidence dating from ancient times that people – especially women – have been prone to dote on small animals with no utilitarian function, particularly lapdogs. Such devotion to pets was often met with considerable disdain. Accusations that people had a tendency to care more for their pet dogs than their own children abound in the historical literature (Caius 1576; Thomas 1983). Indeed, the practice of pet-keeping has often been seen as an extremely potent symbol of 'man's inhumanity to man'. As James Serpell has argued, since antiquity members of the ruling elite have tended to lavish their pet animals with care and attention, whilst at the same time displaying indifference to the lot of the impoverished masses (Serpell [1986]1996: 55). By the twentieth century, however, the practice of pet-keeping had trickled down to all strata of Western society; the Netherlands is certainly no exception in this regard. As a consequence of this, keeping animals of no utilitarian value is seldom frowned upon as a luxury in modern-day Dutch society. However, that is not to say that there is no room for critique within this culture about the esteem in which pet animals may be held by their owners. Whilst it may be necessary as a responsible animal owner to safeguard one's naturally inquisitive pet from potential dangers, like a parent protects a human child, this does not necessarily mean that the animal should be treated as a child.

The chief point of critique revolves around the belief that some, though by no means all, pet owners fail to accept the quiddity of the animal. In other words, by affording an animal a quasi-human status, the distinction between human and animal can become so blurred that the owner's decisions pertaining to the animal are not necessarily made in the interests of the animal. On a more trivial level, one can witness the imposition of human whims on animals when owners force their animals to wear items such as fancy coats, hats and bejewelled collars. Likewise, it seems that some pet owners also feel the need to impose on their animals human celebrations such as birthdays, Christmas, and, in the United States, even bar mitzvahs and weddings (Dresser 2000). The existence of such human rituals for animals perfectly illustrates just how the boundaries between humans and animals are increasingly being crossed within modern Dutch society. Aside from the special attention that the animal may possibly enjoy, such rituals seem to take place more for the benefit of the owner than the animal. Whilst we may view such phenomena as harmless, they are perhaps symptomatic of more insidious transgressions of the divide between humans and other animals, transgressions that may in fact be harmful to the animal's health.

The question here is whether we are capable of *loving our pet animals to death*. By ignoring the basic needs and natures of animals, pet owners may well compromise their health and well-being. It could well be said that we are capable of killing our pet animals with kindness. Throughout the past decade or so, Dutch veterinarians have increasingly been confronted with medical conditions, such as obesity and diabetes. Such problems are often the direct consequence of incorrect diet, over-eating or lack of exercise. Similarly, animals can become neurotic from confinement and the excessive attentions of their owners (Serpell [1986]1996). Within the highly urbanized Dutch society, the popularity of cats has now exceeded that of dogs, since this species is viewed as suitable for keeping permanently indoors in an urban environment. Indeed, for urban dog lovers miniature breeds such as chihuahuas have recently been promoted as the ideal pet, since they too can be kept more or less like cats. According to one proud chihuahua breeder interviewed in 2001 for *Alle Dieren Tellen Mee (Every Animal Counts)*, a popular Dutch prime-time television show, once the dog is trained to use a litter tray, one does not, at least in theory, even need to let it out to relieve itself. The question remains as to whether it is contrary to the animal's nature or damaging to its well-being to prevent it from enjoying fresh air and open spaces.

In the following, I consider in greater detail some of the paradoxes and problems that emerge as a consequence of such human–animal intimacy with respect to dilemmas encountered within veterinary settings in the Netherlands. The central issue discussed concerns the lengths to which some Dutch pet owners are prepared to go in order to retain the company of their cherished pets. In such situations one can clearly identify the problematic nature of pet-keeping as the individuals' actions, taken out of 'love', may very well have a negative impact on the health and well-being of the animal. In this regard, issues such as the use of chemotherapy, pet 'wheelchairs' and kidney transplantation will be considered. Though extremely relevant to a discussion of the changing nature of pet-keeping in modern Dutch society, such veterinary therapies are not necessarily desirable for all pet owners or welcomed with open arms by every vet. Thus, before I embark upon my discussion of such issues, I shall briefly outline the wide range of attitudes towards pets in the Netherlands, particularly with respect to veterinary care. In so doing, it will become evident that there is not always any truth behind the received notion that people treat their animals as if they were children.

## The Broad Spectrum of Human–Animal Relations

As the discussion has already suggested, relationships between humans and other animals are far from homogeneous. Attitudes towards pet animals can vary considerably throughout a society, though, as will be illustrated, it is difficult to make any generalized statements about the lengths to which Dutch pet-keepers are prepared to go for their animals. From examining veterinary settings in the Netherlands, it is evident that there is also great variance with regard to the amount of time, effort and money that is expended on pet animals within Dutch society. However, basing one's analysis of pet–people relations purely upon what goes on in veterinary settings has its limitations. Whilst veterinary settings provide a great context to observe and gain an understanding of the nature of human–animal interactions, it should not be assumed that all pet owners will actually seek regular veterinary guidance or treatment for their animals.

In fact, in the Netherlands – as I suspect in other modern industrial societies also – a category of pet owners exists that apparently never take their animals to vets. Just what percentage of the Dutch pet-keeping population this category represents, and what kind of animals they own, is difficult to determine with any certainty. It also cannot be concluded that simply because a person does not take an animal to a veterinarian that they are not at all concerned with the animal's health. Owners may, for example, not feel the need to visit the vet since they can purchase special diet foods, vitamins, anti-flea treatments, worm tablets, etc. from pet shops, although veterinarians are inclined to argue that these products are inferior to those available from a veterinary surgery.

One may also speculate that the owners of rabbits and rodents, which are obtained at low cost and have short life expectancies, will be disinclined to spend much money on veterinary treatment. Indeed, such creatures have only recently begun to find their way into Dutch veterinary surgeries, whereas in the past this would have been unthinkable. Yet we should remind ourselves of the fact that small animal practice in itself is only a phenomenon of the past hundred or so years. Even at the turn of the twentieth century, the medical treatment of dogs and cats was regarded with considerable contempt by the Dutch veterinary establishment. At that time, in spite of an increasing sentimentality towards small animals and a huge increase in pet-keeping, most veterinary practitioners only saw profit, in both monetary and societal terms, in treating creatures of clear economic value. Throughout the nineteenth century the profession had striven hard to be taken seriously, and veterinarians did not wish to lower themselves by tending to 'useless' animals (Porter 1993; Offringa 1983; Swabe 1999).

Just as it is difficult to establish what kinds of animals are going untreated, it is also difficult to draw any conclusions about or socially categorize the pet owners who fail to visit veterinary surgeries. Pet owners in the Netherlands are not legally obliged to seek veterinary assistance, unless failure to do so results in a situation that may unambiguously be classified as animal cruelty. The Dutch veterinarians interviewed commonly report that owners often only ask for veterinary assistance for the first time when an elderly animal is truly on its last legs. A pet animal can therefore live for more than ten years without ever gracing a veterinary surgery, and when it does so euthanasia may well be the only viable solution to its problem.

Likewise, many of the animal owners I encountered on the animal ambulance in Amsterdam do not have a regular vet and will only seek veterinary help during crisis situations. Ironically, this can, for example, occur when an animal – commonly a kitten or puppy purchased from a pet shop or disreputable breeder – suddenly becomes very sick, displaying the symptoms of a serious infectious disease such as feline panleucopenia (infectious enteritis), feline viral rhinotractheitis (cat flu) or parvovirus. Such potentially fatal diseases can easily be prevented through routine vaccinations (and may be avoided by only obtaining young animals from reputable sources where the mother has been vaccinated), which makes it difficult for ambulance personnel to fully sympathize with the owner's predicament. This leads to the passing of moral judgements on the owner's competence to own an animal (naturally behind the owner's back) and overt attempts at re-education.

In passing such moral judgements they assume the existence of a social norm for preventive veterinary care, also presupposing that the owners do not adequately care for their animals. Whilst this may be true with respect to the veterinary care available, and deemed necessary by veterinary experts for good animal care, the failure to get one's animal properly vaccinated is not necessarily to be equated with neglect or lack of affection, but more with an ignorance of optimal animal care. In recent years, partly due to the increasing societal and media fascination for (pet) animals and the work of vets, animal owners in the Netherlands are becoming more aware of animal health issues and cognizant of veterinary knowledge. With this increasing proto-professionalization (de Swaan 1988: 144–6) of veterinary medicine, one may speculate that the numbers of pet owners who do not seek routine veterinary care, such as vaccination, will diminish (Swabe 1999: 183).

The issue of who is actually fit to own a pet will, however, likely persist. The veterinary practitioners who participated in the research were apt to pass moral judgements on the competence of animal owners. For example, they consistently lamented that there are no kind of legal restrictions as to who may acquire an animal, pointing out that there is no requirement for a pet owner to undergo any form of education or training. Furthermore, many of the veterinarians were angered by the fact that people do not require any kind of diploma to breed animals. Such remarks were generally made during discussions about canine aggression and fashionable problem breeds of dog, such as pitbulls, rotweilers, dogo argentinos, fila brasileiros, Staffordshire bull terriers and, perhaps more surprisingly, golden retrievers. They tended not so much to dismiss the viability of particular breeds as suitable pets, rather the appropriateness of breeding practices and the 'wrong' kinds of people who tended to acquire such animals for the 'wrong' reasons, with little understanding of how the animal should be kept.

It is noteworthy that the older veterinarians who participated in the research studies, especially those practising in rural areas of the Netherlands, were able to describe significant changes in the attitudes of clients towards the veterinary treatment of their animals. In particular, they noted how throughout the past few decades urban attitudes and sentimentality towards animals have increasingly trickled down to livestock holders, who tend to be rather more pragmatic with respect to their animals. They report that where once a farmer would at best only reluctantly administer a course of antibiotics on veterinary advice to help his ailing dog (or at worst dispose of the animal brutally), today they appear to display a far greater willingness to pursue more complex and costly veterinary treatments to improve the well-being of their animals. The rural vets observed that the farmers still tend to call it a day quicker than their urbanized counterparts, but stated that their sensitivities towards pet animal species tend to be far greater than a decade or two ago.

Another example that several rural veterinarians gave was with regard to the euthanasia of new-born kittens. In the past, they suggested that farmers were inclined to drown them, whilst today their increased delicacy of feeling will sometimes lead them to request that euthanasia is used instead. This service is also sometimes offered for free by rural vets to encourage people to seek a humane solution to the problem of unwanted animals. It should also be noted that requests for the euthanasia of new-born kittens have also significantly diminished as sterilization of cats has become the norm. Farmers, the rural veterinarians add, have also increasingly participated in the sterilization programmes subsidized by the Dierenbescherming (Society for Prevention of Cruelty to Animals). Interestingly, the euthanasia of new-born kittens is a practice that was generally abhorred by the purely urban practitioners, particularly those who had more recently qualified. In areas where there is already a surplus of (feral) cats, euthanasia is reluctantly performed on the condition that an appointment immediately be made for the queen to be sterilized. In other areas, where people are clamouring for kittens, the veterinarians tend to refuse to kill the kittens and will make alternative arrangements to have them hand-reared. All vets interviewed claim that they refuse to kill kittens by euthanasia once their eyes are already open.

Sociologically speaking, the changing attitude of Dutch farmers towards pet animal species is particularly relevant. It points to a subtle, though significant, transformation in the personality structure of livestock farmers. These farmers are forced to deal with the harsh everyday realities of keeping animals for food production, yet now seem increasingly to display the same kind of sensibilities to the lot of non-food animals as their urban counterparts. The contrasts between those who work the land and those who are divorced from it therefore seem to be diminishing. Whether this is a result of the impingement of urban dwellers into rural areas and their ideas about animals, or the influence of the mass media, or even a rise in people's disposable income is unclear. What is clear is that these farmers appear to have developed a heightened delicacy of feeling towards animals and are allowing sentiment to play a role in their decisions. On the other hand, one could argue – in line with the writings of Norbert Elias (1994) – that there is increasing pressure within Dutch society for farmers to regulate their own behaviour in accordance with the demands of others. This social pressure for self-restraint may well play a role in decisions to allow a vet to kill new-born kittens by euthanasia, instead of the owner taking matters into his/her own hands. The decision not to drown the kittens may thus not be purely a question of an aversion to brutality, but may well be tempered by the desire to avoid social censure.

Aside from the diminishing contrasts between rural and urban animal owners, according to the veterinarians there does not always seem to be a direct link between income or social status when it comes to the preparedness of a pet owner to embark upon a course of veterinary treatment which may enhance or extend their pet's life. It should, however, be noted that the expense of specialist treatment may ultimately make it prohibitive to some animal owners, eventually leading to the employment of alternative therapies or euthanasia. As various veterinarians independently remarked, it never fails to surprise them that the people who can least afford to pay for costly veterinary treatments are often the ones who wish to proceed with them, whereas the client who arrives at the practice in an expensive Mercedes will often display little interest in spending money on his pet. The vets, though, generally concur that irrespective of a client's ability to pay for veterinary treatment, there is little point in trying to encourage them to proceed with it if they are indifferent to it. If an owner is not prepared to go along with the course of action proposed by the veterinarian, then the animal may go untreated, or if lack of adequate treatment means that the animal will get worse and suffer then euthanasia will be suggested as the preferable course of action. This is especially so if there is little possibility of the animal being re-homed elsewhere.

A good example of this derives from the qualitative interviews regarding the social and ethical acceptability of terminating animal life. During these interviews, veterinarians were presented with a number of scenarios in order to gauge the circumstances under which they believed that euthanasia was morally justifiable. One of these scenarios dealt with a cat, which had been diagnosed with diabetes mellitus. Just as with humans, this is a chronic condition that is fairly easily treated by way of daily insulin injections. However, the animal owner must be willing and able to administer these injections, which may well involve them significantly altering their own daily routine. In most cases, depending on the severity of the animal's affliction, the veterinarians responded that if the owner proved unable to administer regular shots, then euthanasia would be an appropriate course of action. This was because an animal with such a chronic condition cannot easily be re-homed, and that if it is left untreated then it will progressively deteriorate and suffer as a consequence. The cost of the treatment and a personal aversion for administering injections were viewed as inadequate reasons to opt for euthanasia immediately. Only when the owners had repeatedly attempted and failed to inject the animal (e.g. it was too aggressive), or that the condition proved extremely difficult to regulate, did they deem euthanasia appropriate. However, if an owner bluntly refuses to take any action whatsoever, then there may be little choice other than to kill the animal.

There, in fact, lies the crux of the veterinarian's dilemma. Even if it is in the best interests of the animal to pursue a particular course of therapy, they cannot force an animal owner to comply. The animal remains the legal property of the owner and ultimately it is he or she who is responsible for making the decision about an animal's future. Their only power lies in the art of persuasion, by informing the client of the consequences of failing to act in accordance with veterinary advice. If a pet owner declines to allow his or her animal to be treated, or refuses to relinquish ownership, then the veterinarian may be forced to employ euthanasia to prevent further suffering even though there may be a perfectly good course of treatment available to enhance its well-being. Whether a pet lives or dies can thus be rather arbitrary and is largely dependent on the owner's willingness to proceed with and/or pay for treatment.

The arbitrariness of an animal's future prospects can be illustrated by people's attitudes towards elderly animals. Here too one can detect very little consistency. At the one extreme, there are owners who are prepared to put up with any inconvenience that an animal may bring. For example, they will constantly clean up the trail of urine or excreta that an elderly, incontinent animal may leave in its wake. They will try out specially formulated diet foods and turn to the use of painkillers or muscle-strengthening drugs to help their pet get around better. At the other extreme are the owners who attempt to dispose of their animal when it becomes elderly and thus no longer meets with their requirements. Veterinarians routinely receive requests to dispose of elderly animals by euthanasia. In some instances, it is clear that these requests are both medically and ethically justifiable. My veterinary respondents contended that owners will often bring their elderly animals for euthanasia far too late. The common example given was cats suffering from chronic renal disease, who are little more than skin and bones when they arrive, having maybe only days or even hours left to live. In such instances the owner's desire to not have to part with the animal seems to take precedence over having it put out of its misery. On the other hand, there are also owners who will request euthanasia for animals, which despite being elderly are still full of the joys of spring.

Generally speaking, the veterinarians interviewed seemed exasperated by such requests. Several stated that they would not allow their surgeries to be treated as dumping grounds for unwanted pets. The general attitude espoused was that people all too often treat animals as if they were throwaway items, which may be disposed of when they are no longer of sufficient interest. According to my respondents, pet owners have a moral responsibility towards their animals throughout their entire lives. Old age is part of the package. The vets reported that they often have to persuade, or rather re-educate, clients to accept this as a fact. There are also various veterinary drugs available, which in many cases can reduce the problems associated with old age. Some veterinarians observed that clients, presenting an elderly animal for euthanasia, were often relieved to discover that there were therapies that could alleviate their animal's problems. When they arrive at the surgery, such clients believe that euthanasia is the only option available to them.

Veterinarians, however, also pointed to less wholesome reasons for requesting euthanasia for elderly pets. They consistently report that such requests, particularly for dogs, are frequently made shortly before the summer holidays. Euthanasia, it seems, costs less than placing an animal in a kennel or cattery for several weeks. Some vets remarked that after the summer holidays people will suddenly reappear with a completely new pet. The original animal having been dumped at an animal shelter, or put to sleep by another veterinarian. On the animal ambulance, a clear increase in 'stray' animals can be detected during the summer months, particularly for house cats who have been put on the streets to fend for themselves while their owners go on holiday.

While virtually all veterinarians interviewed clearly objected to owners attempting to get rid of their elderly pets, several conceded that they were some-times prepared to put down such animals if people were set on getting rid of them. There were two main considerations in this regard. The first is related to the via-bility of re-homing the animal, particularly dogs. Elderly animals can be very dif-ficult to find new homes for, and it was viewed as morally irresponsible to incarcerate some animals in the kennel of an animal sanctuary for the rest of their short lives. According to them, this would effectively mean that the quality of the animal's life would be so reduced that the animal would – in their eyes – ultimately be better off dead. The second consideration for killing elderly animals was also related to the quality of an animal's life. If the owners no longer took pleasure in the animal, particularly if it suffered incontinence or a dermatological condition, and thus was cast out as an undesirable, it was seen as reasonable to terminate the animal's life. The veterinarians reasoned that it was wrong for an animal, which had spent its entire life in the close company of people, to be exiled to the garage or bathroom because it was incontinent or smelled bad. Again, in such an instance, it was seen as doing not only the owner but also the animal a favour by ending its life. Such owners, however, would have been expected to do all they could to min-imize the animal's complaints through, for example, drug therapies, before euthanasia would become a viable option. Telephone requests to put down any animal were, all veterinarians claimed, rejected out of hand, unless the history of the animal was known to them. No small animal practitioner participating in the research, or encountered during animal ambulance activities, admitted to killing animals to order. Those also connected with animal shelters, however, acknowledged that they put down animals at the shelter, which, if they had seen them at their own practice, they would likely have kept alive.

## Only an Animal?

The future of an animal can thus be rather arbitrary. Depending on the owner, a pet animal may either be discarded when it no longer amuses or is too expensive or inconvenient to treat, or every trick in the book will be used and no expense spared to keep it on its four paws for as long as possible. Within modern Dutch society, there appear to be enough of the latter breed of pet owners to allow the small animal practice to flourish. Indeed, small animal practitioners now constitute the largest group within the Dutch veterinary profession. During the past few decades, small animal medicine has expanded rapidly and can today be characterized by a high degree of specialization and feminization. This is certainly a far cry from a mere century ago when dogs, cats and birds, let alone rabbits, rodents and reptiles, were pretty much shunned by the veterinary profession as unworthy of treatment. Today, there is such a demand and market for small animal veterinary services, at least for a segment of the pet-loving population, that the veterinary profession has been able to specialize in a manner analogous to human medicine. There is a whole range of therapeutic options now available to pet animals and their owners. One can, for example, get a tiger's bad breath sorted out by a specialist in veterinary dentistry, or take Fido to a veterinary homeopath or acupuncturist. Complicated fractures can be skilfully fixed with metal pins by the orthopaedic veterinary surgeon and skin conditions cured by the veterinary dermatologist. The market for such services is definitely in existence, and some pet owners in the Netherlands – though by no means all, as has been shown above – are prepared to shell out for them (Swabe 1999: 182).

Whilst some of the specialist veterinary treatments available are generally designed to allow otherwise healthy animals to get back on their feet again or to lead a healthier life, there are therapies which may be viewed as more questionable. In the remainder of this chapter I shall examine three such therapeutic options, which are disputed within the veterinary world. These are chemotherapy, the use of animal 'wheelchairs', and the pioneering of kidney transplants for cats with renal disease, a practice that is currently restricted to the United States. The extension of the use of such medical treatments to small animal medicine from human medicine has raised serious ethical and societal questions about the extent to which one should go to preserve animal life. Just because it is scientifically possible to extend a pet's life by employing such therapies, it does not necessarily mean that it is morally responsible to do so.

Here we return to the issue of appreciating the quiddity of the animal, raised earlier in this chapter. If a pet animal is treated as a quasi-human, thus rendering the divide between human and animal indistinct, then it is possible for decisions about the animal to be taken that are not necessarily appropriate. Irrespective of the projection of human characteristics on it, or the existence of a tangible bond between pet and owner, a cat is biologically a cat and not a person. As several of the Dutch veterinarians participating in my research remarked, an animal must be able to lead a life that is dignified. In this regard, many of the veterinarians displayed a clear aversion to the innovative therapies, such as chemotherapy, which may be employed to extend an animal's existence. Even a veterinary oncologist interviewed in connection with the research into killing animals, who himself administers chemotherapy treatments, stated categorically that one must always consider whether the prolonging of life is truly in the interests of the animal.

The use of chemotherapy to treat cancer in pet animals is perhaps one of the most contentious developments in veterinary medicine in recent years. Even the veterinary oncologist conceded that there is a risk that the animal can become the victim of attempts to extend the bounds of medical treatment by the use of inno- vative therapies. Few tumours occurring in animals can actually be cured by chemotherapy. While it seems that animals will generally tolerate chemotherapy fairly well, the majority of patients will only experience a partial or temporary remission from their symptoms. In the short term, this may prolong survival and improve the quality of an animal's life. Nevertheless, it is often not a curative therapy. Moreover, when one considers that chemotherapy necessarily involves the use of potentially harmful cytotoxic drugs, it is not unreasonable to question the ethics of such treatment (Dobson and Gorman 1993). There was considerable vari- ation in the attitudes of the small animal practitioners towards the use of chemotherapy. Not all vets interviewed were convinced that it was fair to subject an animal to it.

For instance, one young female vet, J.v.L., who graduated in 1995 and is based in the city of Amsterdam, had borne witness to the terrible impact of chemotherapy on her late father and thus found it morally irresponsible to expose animals to such an aggressive treatment. Mainly, she argued, because – unlike people – you cannot explain the side-effects to animals. The proponents of pet chemotherapy tend to argue that such a perception is inaccurate. Animal chemotherapy, they contend, is much milder than human chemotherapy, and has different objectives. Another veterinarian, W.K., who qualified 1983 and is cur- rently based in a mixed rural practice in the eastern province of Overijssel, asserted that it was highly irresponsible to expose pet animals to cytotoxic drugs.

He found it outrageous and ethically unacceptable that where the excreta of a person being treated with such drugs is treated as chemical waste, a pet cat treated with them can wander round a home with children and use its litter tray or garden as usual. Other vets were unconvinced of the value of chemotherapy, since they did not believe that it would extend an animal's life more than a couple of months and was simply postponing the inevitable. At the same time, it would involve subjecting an animal to a treatment which they considered particularly unpleasant and stressful for the animal. Chemotherapy was also viewed as a costly – in two cases reprehensible – exercise for which the client and animal ultimately got little in return. In spite of this, many of the veterinarians – even those with qualms about the therapy – were inclined to present it as an option to animal owners and to provide them with a view of the prognosis for the animal if treated. They argued that it was ultimately the owner's choice whether to pursue a particular course of treatment and that they must be presented with all the options. If the client opted for chemotherapy, then the vets would refer them to the veterinary school in Utrecht. (This is the only location where this treatment is currently available in the Netherlands; while it is a small country, pet owners in certain regions may still have to subject their animals to two to three hours of travel before even reaching Utrecht.) Even for the oncologist, his main consideration when assessing whether it is worthwhile to treat cancer in pets with chemotherapy is whether the animal stands a chance of survival for at least a year. However, ultimately, as J.M., who qualified as a vet in 1992 and works as a small animal practitioner in North Holland, astutely observed, the most important consideration when deciding on an appropriate therapy is extending the quality of the animal's life, not the quantity thereof.

Another controversial issue is the use of pet 'wheelchairs' to allow dogs, though sometimes also cats, with mobility problems to get around. These special carts first emerged in North America during the 1970s, designed by specialist veterinary orthopaedic surgeons to help mobility-impaired pets walk. Such devices are intended for permanently impaired animals for whom surgery is not a viable option, and for owners who are unwilling to give up on their pets just because they can no longer walk properly. The temporary use of such devices purely as a rehabilitative aid after injury or surgery is less controversial, since it is anticipated that the animal will walk normally within the foreseeable future. For the Dutch veterinarians interviewed, the ability for an animal to walk unaided and without unbearable pain was viewed as one of the key indicators of quality of life.

The concept of quality of life was, they unanimously admitted, a highly subjective and relative one. However, the ability to carry out normal physical functions, such as walking (speed, distance and frequency were less important), eating and drinking voluntarily, the ability to urinate and defecate without permanent discomfort, the display of pleasure in life (e.g. canine tail-wagging, feline purring), were consistently listed as factors according to which the quality of life could be assessed. In this regard, aside from breeds of very large dog, animals that required the amputation of a limb were believed to be able to function on three legs with a high quality of life after rehabilitation.

Animals with a transverse spinal lesion, which will never be able to walk again unassisted nor have control over bladder function due to irreparable nerve damage, are potential candidates for a pet wheelchair. However, when asked about the use of such devices the vets were far from enthusiastic. For example, J.T., a vet who qualified in 1976 and currently works in the northern city of Groningen, argued that animals should be allowed to live according to their nature, which means that they should be able to walk unaided. Whilst wheelchairs are appropriate for human use, she said, they are wholly inappropriate for animals. J.W., a colleague who graduated in 1973 and is based in a small town in the rural province of Drenthe, could not see any value in such devices because he believed that the animal would not get any more pleasure out of life because of them. Again, what came to the forefront in discussions with vets was that the use of such devices was not worthy of the animal and its nature. Nevertheless, the sting in the tail for veterinarians is that they cannot prevent owners from acquiring such a device, if they so wish. All that can be done is to discourage the owner from doing so by highlighting the negative side to them. As F.v.A., a Surinamese vet who graduated in 1973 and works as a small animal practitioner in the province of Flevoland, pointed out, when an animal has irreparable spinal damage, you know what the end result will be (i.e. euthanasia). He argued that you have to protect the owners from themselves. Even though such pet wheelchairs can be used successfully for a while, the animal may deteriorate or the owner will tire of having to deal with a permanently incontinent animal. After all the effort the end result will be the same, while in the meantime the animal will have suffered.

Finally, we may turn to perhaps one of the most contentious recent developments in small animal medicine: feline kidney transplants. Renal transplantation has also been carried out on dogs, but it appears to be less effective due to problems with immuno-suppression. Chronic renal disease is one of the main causes of death in cats, for which there are few effective treatments. While renal transplantation is not yet available in the Netherlands, it does not mean to say that it is a development that has gone unnoticed by Dutch veterinarians. In the United States, cat owners who are confronted with the realities of losing their cherished pet to renal failure now have the controversial option of having their pet undergo a kidney transplant. This technique was originally developed by veterinary scientists at the University of California at Davis and has since been employed by several practices throughout the United States.[2] The only snag is that new kidneys do not grow on trees or in laboratories, but in other cats. Thus, feline kidney transplants require that a healthy, living donor cat must relinquish one of its kidneys. The donor cat may, for example, come from a shelter. If so, the recipient cat's owner is expected to adopt the donor cat and look after it for the rest of its life. It is argued that the health risk to the donor cat is very low, but the recipient cat – even though subjected to drug therapy – may reject the organ. Needless to say, this is a very costly exercise.

The cost, however, is not just in terms of how much capital such a procedure entails. One must also consider the moral costs of subjecting a healthy animal to surgery and depriving it of one of its vital organs in order to extend the life of another. Just because the procedure is scientifically possible it does not necessarily make it ethically acceptable. As my Dutch respondents observed, there seems to be something seriously askew with the idea that one animal can be valued so much that another member of the same species has to be put at risk in order to keep it alive for a couple more years or months – even more so when it is considered that the life expectancy of pet animals is relatively short (in comparison to humans, that is). Indeed, there lies the rub. If one is not prepared to accept that an animal is only an animal and not a human person, then the boundaries between the species become ever more indistinct. From such a perspective, it may been seen as reasonable to do everything to preserve the animal as an individual personality, rather than simply as a member of a particular species. Within the pragmatic society of the Netherlands, the veterinary establishment has – at least for the time being – drawn the ethical line at transplants for animals.

## Conclusion

The boundaries between pet animals and humans seem to have become increasingly blurred within modern Dutch society. The fundamental problem with people–pet relationships, particularly those that are characterized by deep devotion to the animal, is that the biological needs and nature of animals may be inadequately recognized or appreciated. As the above discussion reveals, the problems may range from over-feeding an animal to the failure to accept that a pet animal's life is finite. Moreover, by trying to keep their cherished companions at their sides for as long as possible, pet owners can run the risk of inflicting unnecessary suffering on them. People are capable of loving their pets to death. The excesses and extremes of pet ownership are easily highlighted, but are not, as I have suggested, necessarily representative of the entire body of Dutch pet owners. In truth, it is very difficult to draw any firm conclusions about the nature of pet-keeping in the Dutch cultural context, since there is considerable variation with regard to the esteem in which pet animals are held within Dutch society.

What can perhaps be surmised is that there is increasing pressure within society for pet owners to regulate their conduct towards animals in accordance with current norms for veterinary care and animal welfare. Failure to care adequately for an animal may result in social or even legal censure, particularly in a social climate where there is increasing sensitivity to animal suffering and shared knowledge of the possibilities of veterinary care. Paradoxically, for those who claim to love their pets to death, to seek more radical treatments or to attempt to 'unreasonably' prolong animal life may also result in societal critique. Keeping an animal going because one cannot bear to part with it may also be perceived by some as an act of cruelty. As H.U., a small-animal practitioner who qualified in 1972 and is today based in a large town in the province of South Holland, observed in relation to canine amputees, owners out walking such dogs (who can – it is commonly argued – enjoy a high quality of life on three legs) are frequently subjected to the extreme reactions of complete strangers, including accusations of animal cruelty. Finally, as observations on the changing behaviour of farmers in the Netherlands suggests, there appear to be diminishing contrasts and increasing similarities in attitudes towards and treatment of animals within society as a whole. Sentimentality towards animals, and willingness to seek complex veterinary care for pet animals, is no longer the sole preserve of the urban or affluent segments of Dutch society. Anyone, it seems, is capable of loving their pet to death.

## Notes

1. This research project on the killing of animals, funded by the Netherlands Organization for Scientific Research (NWO) programme for Ethics and Public Policy, was jointly conducted with veterinary ethicist Dr L. J. E. Rutgers DVM and Professor E. N. Noordhuizen-Stassen DVM, Faculty of Veterinary Medicine, Utrecht University.
2. For details on feline kidney transplants: http://www.vmth.ucdavis.edu/vmth/info/felrenaltransplant.htm

## References

Arluke, A. and C. R. Sanders (1996), *Regarding Animals*. Philadelphia: Temple University Press.

Bourdieu, P. (1984), *Distinction: A Social Critique of the Judgement of Taste*. London: Routledge and Kegan Paul.

Caius, J. (1576), *Of Englishe Dogges, the Diversities, the Names, the Natures and the Properties* (Newly drawn into English by Abraham Fleming, student). London: Richard Johnes.

Council for Science and Society Report (CSS) (1988), *Companion Animals in Society*. Oxford: Oxford University Press.

Dobson, J. M. and N. T. Gorman (1993), *Cancer Chemotherapy in Small Animal Practice*. Oxford: Blackwell Scientific Publications.

Dresser, N. (2000), 'The Horse *Bar Mitzvah*: A Celebratory Exploration of the Human–Animal Bond', in A. L. Podberscek, E. S. Paul and J. A. Serpell (eds), *Companion Animals and Us: Exploring the Relationships Between People and Pets*. Cambridge: Cambridge University Press.

Elias, N. (1994), *The Civilising Process* (translated by E. Jephcott; German original published 1939). Oxford: Basil Blackwell.

Offringa, C. (1983), 'Ars Veterinaria: Ambacht, Professie, Beroep. Sociologische Theorie en Historische Praktijk'. *Tijdschrift voor Geschiedenis* 96: 407–32.

Porter, R. (1993), 'Man, Animals and Medicine at the Time of the Founding of the Royal Veterinary College', in A. R. Michell (ed.), *History of the Healing Professions: Parallels between Veterinary and Medical History* (Volume 3). London: CAB International.

Robinson, I. (ed.) (1995), *The Waltham Book of Human–Animal Interaction: Benefits and Responsibilities of Pet-Ownership*. Oxford: Pergamon.

Sanders, C. R. (1999), *Understanding Dogs: Living and Working with Canine Companions*. Philadelphia: Temple University Press.

Serpell, J. A. ([1986]1996), *In the Company of Animals: A Study of Human–Animal Relationships*. Cambridge: Cambridge University Press.

De Swaan, A. (1988), *In Care of the State: Health Care, Education and Welfare in Europe and the USA in the Modern Era*. New York: Oxford University Press.

Swabe, J. M. (1996), 'Dieren als een Natuurlijke Hulpbron: Ambivalentie in de Relatie tussen Mens en Dier, binnen en buiten de Veterinaire Praktijk', in B. van. Heerikhuizen *et al.* (eds), *Milieu als Mensenwerk*. Groningen: Wolters-Noordhoff.

Swabe, J. M. (1999), *Animals, Disease and Human Society: Human–Animal Relations and the Rise of Veterinary Medicine*. London: Routledge.

Swabe, J. M. (2000) 'Veterinary Dilemmas: Ambiguity and Ambivalence in Human–Animal Interaction', in A. L. Podberscek, E. S. Paul and J. A. Serpell (eds), *Companion Animals and Us: Exploring the Relationships between People and Pets*. Cambridge: Cambridge University Press.

Thomas, K. (1983), *Man and the Natural World: Changing Attitudes in England 1500–1800*. London: Penguin.

# 6

# From Trap to Lap: The Changing Sociogenic Identity of the Rat

*Birgitta Edelman*

## Introduction

The brown rat (*Rattus norvegicus*) is the most widely distributed rodent on earth.[1] In most parts of the world, albeit not everywhere,[2] the rat is considered to be an ugly, filthy, dangerous and disease-carrying specimen of vermin.[3] The aim of this chapter is to describe developments that today allow rats to be depicted also as 'clean, intelligent, affectionate' and 'extremely rewarding pets [that] will repay any attention and affection you give them a thousand fold' (Swierzy and Horn 1998). It seems that during the last century and a half it is not the case that one view of the rat has progressively replaced another, but rather that 'the beastly rat' and 'the fancy rat' have developed along separate lines. Today the contrasting images coexist, even if they seem to be rather uncomfortable bedfellows, trying their best to ignore and turn their backs on each other. I shall argue that although the rat has been transformed through breeding to fit the requirements for human use, as a laboratory animal and a pet, the new fascination for the rat still feeds upon the same images that made it feared and hated. When introduced into new fields it is no accident that the rat has carried its vermin traits with it; the rat has been entered as an already symbolically loaded pawn into a novel social discourse. It still draws on its association with the sewer, and, despite the fact that physically and symbolically it has been purged and cleaned, and its sociogenic identity radically transformed, it will always remain an imaginary connecting link to the dark world down under.[4]

There is no lack of theories that touch upon the banishment of certain animals, such as the rat, the bat, the spider, the snake and the pig to the underworld, or to a dark, cold and dirty place, uninhabitable for human animals.[5] As we know, the pioneering ideas that Durkheim and Mauss put forward in *Primitive Classification* (1963) inspired not only Lévi-Strauss but an entire generation of structuralist anthropologists, who in turn influenced most, if not all, later writers dealing with cognition, symbols and classifications, acceptability and rejection, honour and shame, distinction and abjection, regardless of whether they agreed or disagreed with the structuralist axioms. (These later writers include most of the most influential names in anthropology, such as Bourdieu, Douglas, Elias, Foucault, Goffman, Leach, Needham, Ortner, Tambiah, and Turner.[6]) If there are many explanations of why certain phenomena have come to be ideally excluded from our sight, touch, or smell, there are relatively few writers who have dealt with the reintroduction of such earlier discarded phenomena into 'decent society'. Since I claim that the rat has made an inverted trip from rejection to acceptance, from sewer to parlour, or from trap to lap, I shall look at some thoughts regarding such a process of diminishing contempt put forward by Peter Stallybrass and Allon White in *The Politics and Poetics of Transgression* (1986) and by William Ian Miller in *The Anatomy of Disgust* (1998). But first I think it wise to have a quick glance at some of the historical mileposts on the rat's journey from the sewer to the parlour.

## A Short History of Rats in Britain

The transformation of the sociogenic identity of the rat seems to have begun in Britain in the middle of the nineteenth century. At this time London held some forty ratpits, where enthusiasts could enjoy the 'ratting sport', ratbaiting. The typical ratpit was connected to a pub and consisted simply of a small enclosure where a specific number of rats were introduced in order to be killed by dogs.[7] The ratting game itself implied betting how many rats a particular dog would be able to kill in a specific amount of time. For example, one celebrity, a dog named Billy, was claimed to have killed 100 rats in five and a half minutes.[8] Heads of particularly talented dogs were sometimes stuffed and could be admired on the walls of the inns were the ratting sport was exercised (Mayhew 1861, III: 6).

Jimmy Shaw, the owner of one of the largest 'sporting public-houses' (i.e. ratpits) estimated that he used between 300 and 700 rats a week (that is, broadly speaking, something between 15,000 and 36,000 rats a year) for the ratting sport. Despite the fact that rats are quite prolific – a doe (female) theoretically being able to produce an offspring of more than two hundred kittens (baby rats) during her lifetime of approximately two and a half years – it seems that Jimmy Shaw bought the rats he needed from people who caught the rats in the wild, rather than bred them for the purpose of ratbaiting. At the time rats fetched a price of 3–6d. each in London, the lowest price still being a penny more than farmers paid for rats caught on their premises. The prime areas for ratcatchers, according to Jimmy Shaw, were Clavering, Essex, and Enfield, from where, he said, 'I have hundreds of thousands of rats sent to me in wire cages fitted into baskets' (Mayhew 1861, III: 9). The deliverers of rats to Jimmy Shaw and other ratpit proprietors in London were said to be poor country people. Shaw called them 'barn-door labouring poor' and described them as the most ignorant people he ever came across, saying that their language was almost unintelligible to him. Today it seems difficult to comprehend that farm hands managed to collect hundreds of thousands of rats in the 'hedges and ditches' in the English countryside, and send them alive to London by horse and cart. One ratcatcher claimed that he had made cages of iron-wire that would take up to 1,000 rats, stacked 'solid like', adding the rather apt comment: 'No one would ever believe it … it's astonishing, so it is!'[9] Jimmy Shaw said that he had kept as many as 2,000 rats in his house at one time, and that he fed them one sack of barley per week. The price of a sack of barley being 34s. 5d. in 1845,[10] it is reasonable to assume that it would have been good business to breed rats for the pits, rather than to go out and catch them, but this was not how it was done. Rats for the pits were caught, not bred (ibid.: 9–10, 21).

It is interesting to note that the same persons who provided the ratpits with rats by the thousand also occupied themselves with breeding rats. These rats were, however, handled differently, since selective breeding necessarily demands that the individual animal is observed, controlled and attentively cared for. These rats were also sold singly and fetched naturally much higher prices than the sewer or barn-rats mentioned earlier. Mayhew reports about Jimmy Shaw:

[He] showed me some very curious specimens of tame rats – some piebald, and others quite white, with pink eyes, which he kept in cages in his sitting-room. He took them out of their cages and handled them without the least fear … In one of these boxes a black and a white rat were confined together, and the proprietor, pointing to them, remarked, 'I hope they'll breed, for though white rats is very scarce, only occurring in fact by a freak of nature, I fancy I shall be able, with time and trouble, to breed 'em myself. The old English rat is a small jet-black rat; but the first white rat as I heard of come out of a burial-ground.' (ibid.: 10–11)

Jack Black, Her Majesty's ratcatcher,[11] also said he bred rats for quite other purposes than to be massacred in the pits. (He was otherwise one of the urban suppliers of rats to Jimmy Shaw.) He had bred white rats as well as pied specimens, 1,100 of them, and Mayhew quotes him as saying:

I have ris some of the largest tailed rats ever seen. I've sent them to all parts of the globe, and near every town in England. When I sold 'em off, three hundred went to France. I ketched the first white rat I had at Hampstead; and the black ones at Messrs. Hodges and Lowman's, in Regent-street, and them I bred in. I have 'em fawn and white, black and white, brown and white, red and white, blue-black and white, black-white and red … They got very tame and you could do anythink with them. I've sold many to ladies for keeping in squirrel cages. Years ago I sold 'em for five and ten shillings a-piece, but towards the end of my breeding them, I let them go for two-and-six. (ibid.: 20)

There seems to have been pet rats on a not insignificant scale already in the mid-1800s, although we cannot know the destinies of the rats that Jack Black sent to all corners of England, and even to France. It is also difficult to tell the difference between keeping rats as pets and keeping them for the purpose of breeding. Today these two purposes go hand in hand, and there seems to be some indication that the rats of Jack Black had the status of pets – being very tame and having their living quarters in the sitting-room in Mr Black's house – but at the same time Black had a rather unsentimental view on killing rats, poisoning them with his special 'composition' and selling them off to ratpits.

In the present-day, the keeping of fancy rats is supposedly a serious hobby, built on a strong foundation of love and respect for the little rodents, but the possibility remains that breeders with unsentimental attitudes will sell the less-attractive kittens out of the litters for snake food. Since a doe, given good living conditions and good health, can produce about a hundred kittens a year, the temptation to breed new colours and new varieties on a reckless trial-and-error[12] basis seems to be present. I shall nevertheless assume that most breeders of fancy rats are what the fanciers today define as 'serious', i.e. that they are concerned about the well-being and fate of the animals they breed. The rats they keep are 'pets', and although they might not actually all be considered members of the family the demand is that they should be tame and enjoy being handled by people. During the earliest rat shows at the beginning of the twentieth century it was not unusual for judges to be bitten by the rats they were examining. Such behaviour would immediately disqualify a fancy rat today.[13] The purpose of breeding is therefore not only to improve looks and bring out new fur colours or varieties but also to select rats with a pleasant temperament.[14] Fancy rats are *supposed* to be pets, in addition to being objects for exhibition and competition. It is with reference to this selective breeding that the fancy or pet rats of today are seen as different from their wild ancestors.

Although it is difficult to discern the beginnings of keeping rats as pets there is some documentation about the rat fancy from 1900 onwards. At this time Beatrix Potter started to publish her books about Peter Rabbit and other little animals, including the two wild rats Samuel Whiskers and his wife Martha. Interestingly enough she dedicated *Samuel Whiskers* to her pet rat Sammy, describing him as: 'The intelligent pink-eyed representative of a persecuted (but irrepressible) race, an affectionate little friend and most accomplished thief.' Being pink-eyed, could Sammy have been a descendant of Jimmy Shaw's pied rats? asks Nick Mays, author of *The Proper Care of Fancy Rats* (Mays 1997: 50). One must say that the possibility exists, but we have seen that rats by this time must have been bred in quite large numbers, judging by the fact that Jack Black claimed to have bred as many as 1,100 rats already several decades earlier. Even if he were a descendant of Jimmy Shaw's rats, little Sammy would have been at least as many generations removed from them as we are from our ancestors around the birth of Christ.

The pet rat got a boost in the early 1900s, when the legendary Mary Douglas[15] managed to introduce rats to the National Mouse Club (NMC, founded in 1895).[16] Nick Mays writes (1997: 54–5): 'The first-ever classes for fancy rats were staged at the Aylesbury Town Show on 24 October 1901. Miss Douglas's "black and white even marked" (the forerunner to today's Hooded variety), won Best In Show against several others entered.' Mary Douglas is responsible for the NMC changing its name to the National Mouse and Rat Club (NMRC) in 1912. During her time as honorary secretary, as well as president of the NMRC, Douglas worked actively to promote interest in fancy rats. She donated 'good stock' to youngsters who wanted to start their own breeding, as well as donating awards for shows. Over a period of twenty years she wrote numerous articles about rats for the fanciers' magazine *Fur and Feather*. Her 'Rat Résumé' column in the same magazine was famous, and she also edited a column, called 'Junior Fanciers', which was designed to attract youngsters to the rat fancy. Despite all her efforts, interest in fancy rats very much stood and fell with Mary Douglas. After her death in 1921 the fancy started to fall into decline, although a few NMRC members continued with rat breeding for some time.

Simultaneous with the decline of the rat fancy in the 1920s there were internal problems in the NMRC and, in connection with a reorganization in 1929, the name National Mouse Club was readopted, once again throwing the rats out into the cold. The 1930s and 1940s saw further decline of the rat fancy. By the end of the 1940s most of the varieties of fancy rats had died out, and in 1957 the NMC erased all references to rats from their constitution. It was only in 1974, when two rat fanciers, Joan Pearce and Geoff Izzard, started to exhibit rats that things began to stir in the fancy rat world. Two years later, in 1976, the National Fancy Rat Society was founded. Only a week after the inauguration the society staged its first exhibition, showing the new rex (curly-coated) variety. The first ever show with rats only was set up in 1978, and since then the interest in breeding and exhibiting rats has been growing steadily. The interest in rats as pets seems to go hand in hand with an interest in breeding, and the statutes of the NFRS also stress the importance of the rat as a pet – not just as an object for exhibition.

Most fancy rats are sold by private breeders directly to the customers, but many pet rats change hands in pet shops. The pet shops no longer consider rats 'vermin', which was a reaction Joan Pearce was said to encounter regularly when she tried to obtain rats in English pet shops in the early 1970s. If pet shop rats are considered 'vermin' today it is by rat breeders, who think that pet shops are careless in their choice of rats, offering animals that are not up to decent standards, physically or temperamentally. The fact that pet shops also sell rats for snake-food makes them suspicious in the eyes of rat-lovers (Himsel 1991: 14–15) I believe it is safe to say that serious owners of pet rats and pedigree rats avoid pet shops and mostly communicate through rat societies, rat magazines and 'ratpages' on the Internet.

At the moment the interest for rats as pets, as well as for breeding, seems to be greatest in Britain, Germany, the Netherlands, Belgium, Sweden, Finland, Switzerland, Australia and the United States, if one is to judge from the fact that there are one or several fancy rat clubs in all these countries, and that websites belonging to citizens from these countries dominate the ratpages on the Internet.[17] The varieties that had vanished during the years when the fancy dwindled have been brought back, and there are some new additions to the standards. In all there are now more than thirty colours, a handful of varieties, and about a dozen different markings, which are accepted for exhibitions.[18]

## Separation and Contagion

There is obviously a long history of breeding rats in England. The fact that both Jimmy Shaw and Jack Black took an interest in breeding different colours might indicate that there was a tradition for such a 'hobby' already when they got started in the early 1800s. The existence of an established fancy is also supported by the fact that there was a market for tame rats, which were acquired by ladies – not necessarily 'young' ladies, as Nick Mays incorrectly quotes Mayhew (Mays 1997: 50) – who kept them in 'squirrel cages'. There was also an export market for rats, and, counting overheads for transport, feeding and sales, we must assume that the exported rats fetched rather high prices in the country of their final destination. Being 'pedigree' rats, coming in assorted colours, such rats could hardly have been used en masse for baiting. Despite this, rats remained a despised and hated species during the nineteenth century.

However, Stallybrass and White (1986: 143) believe that 'the symbolic meaning of the rat was refashioned in relation to the sanitary and medical developments of the nineteenth century'. From being a despised animal on account of its intrusion into houses and barns, eating and soiling produce intended for livestock or human consumption, the rat was now transformed into a creature which held a position in the animal world that was a homologue to the position of dirt and refuse in the new hygienic order of society. The rat was no longer just a nuisance and an enemy to the farmer, it was a dirty species of vermin, disgusting and abhorrent. The symbolic role of the rat seems to have grown in importance at a rate matching the importance of the novel draining system, the sewers, which gloriously separated and veiled the waste products from the sight and smell of the inhabitants above. The construction of the sewer system implied that dirt and refuse was rejected and deviated into a physical underworld, inhabited by rats and pigs.[19] At times the sewers would overflow and deposit their filth in the streets, and this experience was paralleled in the imaginary world of horrors to include a fear of a transgression of the separation of the upperworld and the underworld. The fear that the rats would leave the dirt and the darkness of the sewers and attack the light and clean world

above made the disgusting little rodent suitable to play a role in all kinds of narratives of horror, such as the legend about Dracula and the stories by Edgar Allan
Poe. Not surprisingly it also pops up as a main actor in a couple of the accounts
from the consulting-room of Sigmund Freud, such as 'Rat Man' and 'Frau Emmy
von N' (ibid.: 143–6).

According to Stallybrass and White there is a relation between the censoring of
the 'low' parts of the body and the emphasis and fascination for the 'low' parts of
the city in bourgeois life and imagination. While the lower parts of the body are
cleaned, covered up, unmentioned and unmentionable, we find an increasingly
obsessive preoccupation and fascination for the lower parts of the city, such as 'the
slum, the rag-picker, the prostitute and the sewer'. 'The hierarchy of the body [is]
transcoded through the hierarchy of the city' (ibid.: 145) The fear of the rat is then
a fear of the rejected part below; a fear that uses the sewer as a mediator of an
unmentionable part of the body. In this scheme of things the low is equalled with
dirt, and the demonization of the rat thus follows as a corollary of its attachment
to the sewers. Mere disliking has turned into disgust as the bourgeoisie has
ascended to a position excluding all refuse from bodily waste to the social 'great
unwashed'. Miller has explored in detail the fascination, curiosity, and even desire
towards the disgusting (Miller 1998: 109–42),[20] a fascination which may well
explain the inclusion of rats in horror stories and in the dreams or fantasies of
Freud's patients. But how are we to interpret the fact that the rat turns from being
despised to being disgusting during the very period it is brought into the homes of
bourgeois ladies? Not all objects of disgust could possibly pass over the household
threshold and be put on display.

Rats may well be dirty and despicable things when swarming in the sewers and
the underworld, but seen in the singular a rat is a small rodent – not unlike a
squirrel or a field mouse. Miller writes: 'the variation in elicitors of disgust across
cultures will hardly look like a random sampling of all things or all actions in the
world' (1998: 16). The rat has the obvious potential of being classified as something other than an object of disgust, as opposed to, for example, rubbish and
faeces. The rat is connected to rubbish by means of contagion, by its connection
to the sewers, but it is still possible to consider the rat as separate from the sewer.
As such it may even be considered funny or cute. Since we are familiar with the
homologous position of rats and the lower classes we could perhaps point at the
fact that there is also a homology in how members of these groups are considered
when seen as individuals versus when taken as collectives or groups. The working
class is not entirely the sum of its parts. Individual members of it may be sweet
children, beautiful young women, friendly old men – in reality, and also in the
world of stereotypes. The maid is a representative of, but not identical with, the
dirty and the low, just as the rat in its cage is a representative of, but not identical
with, the dirty and the low. This ambivalence implies that they can be introduced

into high society, albeit not unconditionally. The maid, as well as the rat, has undergone a process of cleansing. A clean, standardized uniform, or a hair coat of a new breed, and a limited space, such as the maid's quarters or a cage, guarantee that the order is not upset. The contagion is reduced to a minimum and the upper still holds full control of the lower, the master/mistress over the servant, the human over the animal. In the Victorian world the rat was actually perhaps more like Eliza was to Professor Higgins in *Pygmalion* than the Victorian maid was to her master, since the rat was not kept in order to work or provide any service for its master. It was invited because of a conviction that it could be tamed and well behaved, and that once the dirt was scrubbed off and the diet and the table manners corrected, a delightful little creature would appear: Eliza – the rat!

The majority of the rats were not scrubbed and purged, but remained disgusting and poisonous. These were the animals that were baited in the pits, introduced as 'these 'ere are none of the cleanest' and 'Get out, you varmint!' (Mayhew 1861, III: 7). They were mass creatures as opposed to the individuals. However, the rats in Jack Black and Jimmy Shaw's parlours were no class-climbers and did not have to clean up their act in order to be accepted. They were not retrieved from recently having been expelled into an imaginary world of disgust. They were certainly 'spiteful' and 'poisonous' creatures, which could give you a bad bite, but they came from the real world around the people who caught them: from rich people's abodes, from 'shores' (equalled with sewers) and 'ditches and fields' – they did not come to you in horrifying dreams. These rats were not pets in and for themselves, and when they were turned into pets (animals that you could do 'anythink' with) they were so in order to bring an income to their breeders. The parlours of Jack Black and Jimmy Shaw constituted a completely different site of discourse from the discourse of the bourgeois parlours, and while the rats in the latter were controlled in conformity with the demands of hygiene and domestic order, the rats in the former were controlled in the way one controls a resource and turns it into a good-quality sales item. They were raw material being manufactured into pets.

## Jack Black: Her Majesty's Ratcatcher

As mentioned, Jack Black killed, caught, bred and sold rats both to ratpits and to ladies. He was Her Majesty's ratcatcher and wore a uniform – which he had made himself. His qualification for earning this impressive title was the fact that he could master and control rats. He wandered around London, demonstrating his skills. He describes his 'act' as a very silent one, since he relied mainly on visual effects. He poisoned rats with his 'composition', showing that the rats died immediately after tasting it, but he also showed the audience that he could handle rats – and wild rats at that – without being bitten. He was a master of the species and he could keep rats under control. We could compare Jack Black to a physician or to a

medicine man, who with the aid of a 'medicine' (the composition) could extermi-
nate the disease (the rats) and do it without being contaminated or affected
himself. He could handle the danger without fear. Jack Black describes one
instance when he demonstrates his powers in front of a stunned audience. He says:

> I drove the cart, after selling the composition, to the King's Arms, Hanwell, and there
> was a feller there – a tailor by trade – what had turned rat-ketcher. He had got with him
> some fifty or sixty rats – the miserablest mangey brutes you ever seed in a tub – taking
> 'em up to London to sell. I, hearing of it, was determined to have a lark, so I goes up
> and takes out ten of them rats, and puts them inside my shirt, next to my buzzum, and
> then I walks into the parlour and sits down, and begins drinking my ale as if nothink
> had happened. I scarce had seated myself, when the landlord – who was in the lay –
> says, "I know a man who'll ketch rats quicker than anybody in the world". This put the
> tailor chap up, so he offers to bet a half-a-gallon of ale he would, and I takes him. He
> goes to the tub and brings out a very large rat, and walks with it into the room to show
> to the company. "Well", says I to the man, "why I, who ain't a rat-ketcher, I've got a
> bigger one here", and I pulls one out from my buzzum. "And here's another, and
> another, and another", says I, till I had placed the whole ten on the table. "That's the
> way I ketch 'em", says I – "they comes of their own accord to me". He tried to handle
> the warmints, but the poor fellow was bit, and his hands were bleeding fur'ously, and I
> without a mark. A gentleman as knowed me said, "This must be the Queen's rat-
> ketcher, and that spilt the fun. The poor fellow seemed regular done up, and said, I shall
> give up rat-ketching, you've beat me! Here I've been travelling with rats all my life, and
> I never see such a thing afore." (in Mayhew 1861, III: 16–17)

This story elegantly describes the aspirations of Jack Black. He proves his point:
he deserves his title as Her Majesty's ratcatcher. He, and nobody else, possesses
absolute power over the rat kingdom. He can without hesitation handle rats that he
secretly has 'borrowed' from a pretender, who shamefully ends up being bitten by
his own rats. Jack Black's triumph is complete and the fact that his 'lark' was
exposed does not in any way diminish his feat. We see that the uniform and the
proud title 'Her Majesty's ratcatcher' was no joke. Jack Black was the capital's
symbolic Master of the Underworld, and in that capacity he was a man even the
Queen could not afford to ignore.

## Mary Douglas: Mother of the Rat Fancy

We might be able discern a tendency for a gender division in handling rats.
Catching, baiting and breeding rats seem to have been male occupations, while
keeping them as pets seem to have been done particularly, although far from exclusively, by women. One interesting case is the 'Mother of the Rat Fancy', Miss
Mary Douglas. She obviously had rats as pets, as well as for breeding, but being,

in her own words, 'a spinster of independent means' (her father was Dean of Worcester Cathedral) she did not primarily breed rats for profit. On the contrary, she donated rats and trophies in order to promote the rat fancy. (She also organized charitable work for the benefit of other animals. During the First World War, for example, she organized shows for the Blue Cross, in aid of injured war horses on the Western Front.) Her dual interest in the more male occupation of breeding and organizing shows, as well as the female fancy for keeping rats as pets, seems to have been reflected in her rather masculine appearance and lifestyle. Mays writes: '[S]he would often drive a pony and trap into town [Lostwithiel, Cornwall], clad in breeches, leggings and a wide straw hat, often puffing away on a clay pipe!' (1997: 56). It seems like a peculiar coincidence that the two differently gendered strands of rat interest come together in this very influential and eccentrically androgynous personality.

The pictures we have of Mary Douglas (a photograph) and Jack Black (an etching said to be 'from a photograph') show the discrepancy between the two personalities rather distinctly.[21] Jack Black appears in his uniform; across his shoulder is a belt, with cast pewter rats, the letters V and R and a crown on it. He is depicted without any signs that would indicate the setting, but one would assume that he is somewhere in the streets of London. He is accompanied by a small black dog (probably his excellent Billy, which, however, was hardly identical to the record-holding dog with the same name), and he holds a basket containing an unspecified number of rather minute rats in his hand. The photograph of Mary Douglas shows a very proud-looking woman (but easily mistaken for a man) leaning with one arm on a table that is crowned by a sizeable trophy. A dark rat sits comfortably on Miss Douglas's arm. It is about as big as the half dozen rats that Jack Black carries in his cage. The rat of Mary Douglas is depicted as an individual and a free-ranging pet. Jack Black's rats are a bunch of vermin, caught and confined to a cage. The relations between the owners and their rats were in both these cases known to be close and regular. From that knowledge, is it possible to say that these relationships were similar in any other respect? Did Jack Black's rats develop into pets? Does closeness 'breed' affection and empathy?

## Interacting with Rats

In an article entitled 'Understanding dogs', Clinton R. Sanders presents the interactionist view that routine relationships between dogs and their caretakers – like the routine relationships between alingual persons and their caretakers – constitute, through the 'natural rituals' that they offer, a growing ground for the construction of sociogenic identities. The caretaker attributes thinking to the dog/alingual person, sees it/him/her as an individual with a distinct personality, considers the relationship to be reciprocal in that the caretaker receives something back for the care and attention provided, and finally incorporates the dog/alingual person into a social body, involving it/him/her in 'ongoing domestic rituals and routines' (Sanders 1993: 210–11). Claiming that there exists such a mutual recognition between a dog and its caretaker, or, for that matter between a linguistically disabled person and his/her caretaker, does not strike me as implausible and I would actually argue that we today consider such communication natural, belonging to the stock of assumptions that we take for granted.[22] However, Sanders adds a comment, which relates directly to the word 'today' in the previous sentence. He writes:

> Those who routinely interact with alingual companions draw from their ongoing experience information about the other, *effectively disconfirming folk beliefs, occupational ideologies, or academic doctrines* that present the inability to talk as rendering one mindless and incompetent. (Sanders 1993: 222–3, emphasis added)

This quote seems to entail that the natural rituals in a situation of caretaking in some ways manage to penetrate through and transcend a whole set of pre-existing views about the person or animal that is being taken care of. Folk beliefs, ideologies and academic doctrines are explicitly mentioned as examples of beliefs that the mutual interaction manages to disconfirm.

This view might be correct from a very limited interactionist perspective, but it has a rather unfortunate ahistorical bias, which makes it nonsensical when we consider, for example, Jack Black and Jimmy Shaw and compare the sociogenic identities of their tame rats with how 'the other' (i.e. in this case the rat) is constructed in the letter from someone calling herself 'the crazy rat lady', when she writes to the Rat Fan Club:

> They [the rats] are very playful, playing the attack rat, jumping, popping up in the air, playing Boo with me, pretending to run away, only to quickly turn back thinking they fooled me. I love their wet cold noses. They are alive and can think, comfort you when sad, make you laugh, have little hands with fingers to reach out to you. They make me feel loved and when all is calm and quiet and they're in my lap and I can feel their warm breath on my skin, I cannot express the feelings I get. (Shannon Danyluik, Pomona, California, quoted in Ducommon 1999–2004)

I do not think we can claim that the caretaking situation, generally and uniformly throughout history, works as some magic potion enabling the caretaker to cut through or free himself entirely from pre-existing beliefs. There are, I claim, expectations and ideological patterns that direct, and to a certain extent determine, the construction of the new sociogenic identities as well. The determination we are talking about here is, however, more of a limiting than a prescribing nature. We are in the field of last-instance determination. This implies, in our cases, that long before a person becomes a dog-owner, or a caretaker of a dog, and long before one becomes the caretaker of an Alzheimer patient or a child with limited or absent linguistic ability, one has, as a part of one's habitus, certain expectations, beliefs and ideologically tainted views about what the relationship to a dog or a person of the aforementioned kind *could* possibly entail. Furthermore, the ability to read the situation in such a way that the experience is seen as contradictory to one's preconceived ideas and expectations is not a given entity either, but a part of habitus and as such socially constructed.

How does this relate to my argument above? It seems to me that we could read Sanders as talking about the transformation of habitus through the experience of a 'gap' between expectations and experience, and I do not reject the thought of either the gap or the transformation of habitus as described by him. I feel, however, that in order to understand why the experience of taking care of rats meant something different to Jack Black we have to acknowledge the fact that his habitus did *not* allow a similar gap between his expectations and his experience. Whatever gap he experienced he most evidently attributed a different meaning to it. One can claim that I do not have any evidence of how he felt about his relation to his rats, but I think that, were I to attribute 'the crazy rat lady's' quote to Jack Black, at least some historians would raise their eyebrows in surprise (their habitus immediately creating a gap between their expectations and experience …). Jack Black was not likely, gender expectations aside, to consider his rats to be thinking creatures that 'comfort you when sad, make you laugh, have little hands with fingers to reach out to you'. In case he did, we will find it difficult to explain that he made an income of selling rats that were to be torn apart by pit bull terriers, or that he found rats good to eat (saying he used to taste them, 'unbeknown to his wife' – Mayhew 1861, III: 12). The 'crazy rat lady' could hardly conceive of getting involved in either enterprise.

One might argue that the 'ladies' who bought rats in order to keep them in 'squirrel cages' had a different view of rats to that of Jack Black. As I have argued, I believe that we here meet a different habitus, one which is more of a class habitus than a gender habitus. This is the habitus that redeems the rat from its position as disgusting vermin. It is an attraction which, as we have seen, originally may spring from disgust, but which overcomes that very feeling by giving way to the competing feelings of fascination and perhaps even compassion. We have an eye that suddenly sees a small creature behind the stigma and the rat is brought out into the light, ready to play a part among all the other little animals that depict an allegorical scenery of human society in children's books. Beatrix Potter writes about Peter Rabbit, Squirrel Nutkin and Samuel Whiskers – and these characters will be followed by a rich tradition of anthropomorphized animals. From this one might draw the primary conclusion that it is not the caretaking in itself that creates the relationship of understanding and empathy between the caretaker and the rat, nor is the sociogenic identity of the rat simply a result of the situation of caretaking itself. Rather, it is the nature and quality of the caretaking of the rat that is a function of the rat's sociogenic identity, which in the last instance is determined by wider societal factors, but which, nevertheless, may be modified by direct experience resulting from intimate handling and caretaking. Whether direct experience is allowed to influence and adjust the sociogenic identity of the rat depends on whether there is a conceived gap between expectations and experience, and furthermore how this gap is handled.

## The Pet Rat

Today the rat has entered the vast field of pets, which in the case of the rat I take to include fancy ratting, the family pet status, as well as the role of image enhancer for punks and goths. Here we clearly see the cleansing process, where the ugly sewer rat has been transformed into fancy pedigree rats displaying furs of colours and qualities that would complement a queen. Also the temperament of the animal has been improved through selective breeding.[23] The role as an image enhancer is perhaps the only area the rat has entered without going through a thorough purgation. Here it is very much the 'sewer' and beast character of the rat that provides the effect. Punks and goths do consequently prefer brown rats, which look like their wild cousins, and would probably not use the fancy term 'agouti' to designate their colour. Naturally, the rats that are used for this purpose are not wild rats, but fancy rats (clandestinely, one may suppose) bought in a pet shop. This does not alter the fact that it is the wild image that is strived for. (The rat on the shoulder of a punk or goth is *not* to be equalled with a hamster, guinea pig or rabbit. It would probably be quite humiliating for a punk if a middle-aged lady like myself were to approach the little 'beast' in order to pet and fondle it.)

Fancy rats are kept out of reach of wild rats of course – partly because of the diseases that the wild rats might carry, but mainly because the pet rat is a more docile animal. The breeding process that brought it to where it stands today would thus be reversed. The idea of 'getting fresh blood' into the strain of fancy rats pops up every now and then on the Internet pages, but all the societies and experts warn against such attempts. Pet rats are domesticated, and this term implies a process of purgation. The domestic rat is thus kept in a meticulously clean cage, offered food from a dish, water from a clean bottle, and its environment is carefully arranged so that it is safe, interesting and stimulating. The kittens are offered educational toys (ropes and ladders that may improve climbing skills, for example) and the elderly have hammocks where they may rest when they become infirm and immobile (ages 2 years and over). Pet rats are often anthropomorphized (this seems to be the case with pets of the 'family member' type more than with fancy rats), and they are described as having human emotions and reactions such as 'a sense of humour' or 'love for the United States'. One can also find numerous photographs on the Internet of rats dressed up in different outfits, for example impersonating

'Captain Hook', Jack from *Pirates of the Caribbean*, or Super Jane Rat – or even parading in a pot with vegetables and twigs of rosemary as 'Rat Stew' (Ducommon 2004).

The pet rat is divided by a sharp break from the wild rat and has entered a world where anthropomorphized animals are treated like children, ascribed consumer needs like any other member of society (Christmas presents, birthday cakes, toys, 'quality time', etc.), and commemorated with obituaries and gravestones. A closer look reveals that the pet rat, too, has retained some of its vermin status inside the world of pets. The struggle the rat-fanciers had to be accepted as members of the National Mouse Club (NMC), only to be excluded some time later, shows that there was a strong reluctance on the part of the majority of mouse-fanciers to be associated with rats. Only when the rats got their own society did they have a chance to establish themselves as close to equals. Almost every rat-page on the Internet has a chapter on the history of the rat, and although it is often claimed that the purpose of this is to dispel misconceptions and prejudices (that the rat carried the plague, that the brown rat killed and extinguished the black rat from Northern Europe, etc.), one can read the sense of pride that is taken in presenting the 'roots' of the rat (see, for example, Jordan 1999; Olsher 2004–2005; NFRS 1997–2005; Swierzy and Horn 1998). The domesticated rat may be separated from the wild rat, but its ancestors are still revered. As long as the connection with the wild rat is recognized, the fancy rat will have a status as a slightly odd pet, not on a par with the dog, cat or budgie. Again we see that the separation between the pet and vermin is radical, but that there nevertheless is a colouring or a contamination which gives the rat a lowly, but somehow perhaps also special and fascinating, position within the new field it has entered.

## Gaps between Expectations and Experience

Throughout the period we have been discussing (from about the 1830s to the present) the rat has been a despised and abhorred animal. There have nevertheless always been people who have been in close contact with rats, and this contact has sometimes been of a peaceful, and even friendly or affectionate, character. I can accept the idea, presented by Miller, and by Stallybrass and White, that stigmatization of certain phenomena may create the opposite (i.e. a fascination for and an attraction to these very same things). This would explain the Victorian disgust for the rat in general, but also the thrill of watching the disgusting rats being torn to bits by dogs, as well as the *Pygmalion* scenario where rats are kept in the home as a delightful curiosity.

Changing class relations, or according to Miller the general 'democratization' process in society, would then lead to modifications of the image of the rat so that today it can be conceived of both as a pet and a rodent with its own rightful place in nature. According to Miller the democratization of society is an ongoing process of increasingly blurred class distinctions, accompanied by an increased acceptance of earlier expelled categories, such as ethnic groups and sexual minorities (Miller 1998: 235–7). The matter from 'down under' is allowed to surface. For the rat this entails (pun permitted) that it becomes more of an (adorable) animal than a disgusting species of vermin. The creation of the rat as a demonized and disgustingly desirable 'other' is thus seen as determined by class relations and the hierarchy of the city and the body. However, the corollary of the exclusion–attraction mechanism seems to be that almost every possible instance of affiliation with rats in the hierarchical class society could be read as an expression or consequence of either of the poles in the dualism so produced. This is a determination that is very rigid at the same time as it is unpredictable.

I believe that the rat as a sign of filth and disgust is a very significant social construction, to the point of almost being a 'key symbol', but there are undeniably other cultural expectations that modify, clash or blend with the rat as the personification of the sewer. The rat is an animal, and a rodent, and among the different expectations arising from that fact we could point at several ideas that are more likely to induce feelings of sympathy than of disgust. The rat is small and furry, and it has a human-like diet and exists in a society, taking good care of its offspring. It is intelligent and playful and bonds easily to humans. We need not make the list longer, it suffices to point out that cultural expectations are multiple and far from uniform. We encounter a field of contradictions and ambiguities, indicating that we had better look at the cultural expectations as a box of several possible readings rather than as one prescribed set of interpretations. The possible readings form part of situated discourses, but again we must stress the open-ended character of these discourses instead of seeing them as socially determined. If we think of cultural expectations as multiple, situated and negotiated it becomes easier to appreciate why rat–human relations have been articulated in various ways. The different forms of rat–human relations do, however, differ in terms of one important variable: to the degree that the relation comprehends direct experience and personal involvement. Of the examples discussed in this chapter we have seen that some relations imply close physical contact, while others are based mainly on observation or narratives.

Jack Black bred rats and killed them. But he also transported and exhibited them in the street, bought and sold them, and he even ate them and used them as moulds for his pewter casts. Mayhew's description of the man and his abode gives us the feeling that we here have a man who had an impressive knowledge of animals. He has extensive experience of all kinds of animals and intimate knowledge of their respective habits; knowledge that comes from catching, handling and breeding them. Nevertheless, Jack Black does not see animals as persons.[24] For all the closeness and intensive interaction, observation and knowledge, there does not seem to be any identification with the animals. Jack Black's cultural expectations do not allow for such emotional development. Animals are his livelihood and trade, and his zoological knowledge is not part of some disconnected 'academic' science but connected with his craftsmanship and skills. He uses it to catch better, breed better and eat better. His prank in the pub is not just an innocent joke, it is a way of stating an example and getting rid of competitors in the trade.

The ratbaiters were already several steps above the sewers compared to Jack Black, who knew the 'shores' as well as his own pockets. Ratbaiting could perhaps be compared to the carnival, as described and analysed by Stallybrass and White (1986: 171–202), in the way this brutal and carnal dog 'sport' displayed and stressed the low and the disgusting, the crude and the burlesque. It presented fearless conquerors and mighty heroes – among small rodents and dirty sewers. Ratbaiting is perhaps the best example of the attraction of the disgusting.

The other example of the attraction of the expelled was the *Pygmalion* parlour rat, kept by 'ladies', and we may also add Beatrix Potter and Mary Douglas and her fancy rats to this category. These ladies were part of a different social discourse, and their distance and removal from the sewers was so far and absolute as to allow them to sympathize and take an interest in creatures that were despised and expelled. We can also assume that the ladies who kept rats in squirrel cages had physical contact with the rats, and that they learned about the habits and behaviour of their little pets. Beatrix Potter describes her rat, which has a name, as a good friend and an accomplished thief. She clearly sees her pet as a person. Whatever the expectations prescribe concerning the disgusting character of the rat, there are other, conflicting, expectations concerning pets. It is the latter expectations that seem to be enhanced by close encounter with the animals, by intimacy and experience. The disgusting character of the rat is now seen as a 'misunderstanding', and Mary Douglas spends a large part of her life as an advocate for the rat.[25]

The rat of the new millennium is no less at the crossroads of cultural expectations. The democratization process entitles it a ticket to the ark along with all other creatures; but even if the categories of dirt and 'matter out of place' of today are less concerned with sewers and the underclass and more with viruses and illegal immigration, the vermin label and the fear of the plague still seem to be dominant in the imagination of the common man and woman. But the gap between expectation and experience can be bridged. The following little story from the Internet tells us how conflicting expectations can be mediated by experience and direct perception:

If you need to find a home for baby rats, here is a strategy that worked well for Rosalie Elliott, a RFC member in Florida who used to breed rats. She ran an ad in the newspaper that said POCKET PETS. PLAYFUL TRAINABLE AFFECTIONATE MUNCHKINS. Available to selected homes for $5 up … DON'T YOU JUST HAVE TO BE ONE OF THOSE SELECTED HOMES? When Rosalie first told people they were rats, they would hang up on her. So now she doesn't tell them they're rats until they come see how wonderful and cute they are. She called them raffins which is a name I made up that means domestic rats. You could also use 'Ratzel', which is a German nickname for rats. Or, you could just use 'pocket pets.' When people asked 'What's a raffin,' she said, 'Why don't you come see?' Once they come saw [*sic*] how cute and wonderful rats are, they fell in love with them and didn't care that they're rats. She had a waiting list of people who wanted her babies! (Ducommon 2001)

Here we find a way to introduce a new set of expectations to disperse a former set that on its own effectively blocks new experiences. The hope is that the new expectations will be able to make the 'victims' approach the rats long enough to create a gap between their present experience and their former expectations. As Bourdieu has said (2000: 148–9), it is in the gap between expectations and experience that we find the principle of transformation. The words 'pocket pet', 'munchkin', and 'raffin' are brought in to work like magic formulas, closing the gap and turning the rats from being disgusting vermin into enchanting little pets.

## Notes

1. The brown rat came originally from Asia, from where it spread to Europe, arriving in England in 1728. In 1775 it had made it across the Atlantic to America. It is now to be found all over the world, except for the most extreme Arctic and Antarctic areas (Zinsser 1963: 201–2).
2. One often-cited example of rats having positive connotations is the rat cult in a Jain temple in Deshnoke, Rajastan, where rats are objects of worship. However, this cult is limited only to the ancestors of Karni Mata, who believe they are reincarnated as rats and that rats again reincarnate as children of Karni Mata. The rats are therefore ancestors, or dead relatives, of the worshippers. One cannot deduce from this example that rats are worshipped, or even liked and appreciated, throughout India.
3. See John Knight concerning pestilence discourses (Knight 2000: 8–11).
4. Most of the material for this chapter comes from the UK, the United States and Sweden, but I hope in time to expand my research to include other Western countries as well.
5. Since the denominations 'human animal' and 'non-human animal' are somewhat clumsy I shall instead speak of 'humans' and 'animals'.
6. We need only mention Bourdieu (*Distinction*), Douglas (*Purity and Danger*), Elias (*The Civilizing Process*), Foucault (*Discipline and Punish*) Goffman (*Stigma*), Leach (*Anthropological aspects of language*), Needham (*Right and left*), Ortner (*Key Symbols*), Tambiah (*Animals are good to think and good to prohibit*) and Turner (*The Ritual Process*), and we see that we have listed some of the most influential figures in social theory during the last century.

7. These dogs were often, but not exclusively, terriers or terrier-mixes; the term 'pit bull terrier' refers to a mix that was commonly used, but not identical with the pit bull terriers of today.

8. According to Mayhew, Billy killed 500 rats in five and a half minutes. This sounds slightly exaggerated, and I have therefore chosen to quote a lower number, stated by Hodgson, who also dates the match: 22 April 1823. That was, according to her, Billy's ninth match (Mayhew 1861, III: 6; Hodgson 1997: 78).

9. Jack Black, quoted by Mayhew (1861, III: 19).

10. I want to thank Marthe Arends and Ralph Harrington who kindly helped me in the search for barley prices in London in the mid-nineteenth century. The figure quoted was published in the 'Markets' column of the *Globe* in 1845.

11. While most ratcatchers were of very low status, Jack Black had managed to be appointed 'V.R. Rat and mole destroyer to Her Majesty', wearing a home-made uniform with leather breeches, green coat and waistcoat, a gold band around the hat and a belt with cast metal rats over the shoulder. ('So I took a mould from a dead rat in plaster, and then I got some of my wife's sarsepans, and, by G-, I cast 'em with some of my own pewter-pots' (Mayhew 1861, III: 16).

12. When talking about trial and error in this respect I do not primarily mean a complete random breeding. I am rather referring to recessive genes 'popping up', producing surprising (wanted or unwanted) physical traits in the off-spring. One might add that the offspring will hardly keep a decent show standard in case the doe is forced into too many pregnancies. The realistic number of kittens per year is therefore in all probability much lower than the pure biological limit.

13. 'Intractability' is listed as one of five disqualifying faults in the Standards of Excellence of the National Fancy Rat Society of Great Britain. See also Mays (1997: 55).

14. It is widely accepted that there is a marked difference in temperament between *Rattus rattus* and *Rattus norvegicus*. The former is more' flighty', 'frenetic' and 'quarrelsome', and 'seems to have only two speeds: complete comatose, or ricocheting off the walls', while the latter has a 'jolly, sociable and laid-back nature ... [making them] ideal candidates for domestication' (Jordan 1999).

15. This is a different Mary Douglas to the aforementioned anthropologist.

16. In my account of the history of the NM(R)C I have relied on Mays (1997: 51–70).

17. I am talking about pages in English and German, Dutch and Swedish, which often are found to be interlinked. If there are pages in other languages they have not made it into this particular Western circuit.

18. There is some confusion concerning the vocabulary. In the United States alone there are several standards. For example the Rat and Mouse Club of America (RMCA) recognizes only four 'varieties' (standard, rex, hairless and tailless), which are divided into six 'sections' (self, ticked, shaded, silvered, marked and odd-eye). Adding the different colours and markings we see that we have a large amount of different-looking rats. The British standards are the standards of the NFRS, distinguishing between 'self' (i.e. one colour) and 'marked'. Among the former we have dark eyed and pink eyed, with several colours, and among the 'marked' we find Berkshire, Irish, hooded, capped, variegated, silver, and other (including, agouti, cinnamon, Himalayan, Siamese, etc.) as well as 'coat' varieties (e.g. the curly rex) (Mays 1997: 142–64). See also NFRS at (1997–2005), the RMCA (1995–2005), and the American colourings pictured in Olsher (2004–2005). I think it is safe to conclude that the variation is rather puzzling for a layman.

19. Mayhew reports that there was said to exist a hoard of feral pigs in the sewers of Hampstead. They were said to live and breed there 'and have become almost as ferocious as they are numerous' (Mayhew 1861, II: 154). Rats and pigs, the two most common 'dirty' animals, were then both inhabitants of this new underworld.

20. The same view is found in Stallybrass and White: '[D]isgust always bears the imprint of desire. These low [i.e. the 'dirty, repulsive, noisy, contaminating'] domains, apparently expelled as "Other", return as the object of nostalgia, longing and fascination' (1986: 191).

21. The photograph of Mary Douglas is reprinted in Mays (1997: 54), while the picture of Jack Black can be found in Mayhew (1861, III: 8).

22. Kay Milton has discussed the role of experience in the emergence of identification with animals and environment in the Western world (Milton 2002: 40ff.).

23. There seem to be certain 'negative' side effects, though, since it is reported that 'healthy wild Norway rats will bring food to sick members of their pack – rather than swiping food from them, as pet rats tend to do' (Jordan 1999).

24. An exception to this may be the only animal that seems to have a name (i.e. his dog, Billy), but we do not know if Billy was seen as a person. Victorian London displayed a great variety of attitudes towards dogs (see, for example, Howell 2000: 35–52).

25. One could compare this to the tripartite process of demonization, inversion and hybridization that Stallybrass and White mention (1986: 57). The first part describes a process of exclusion, the second one a celebration of the inversion of the terms in a system and the third a reorganization of the terms. We would find the rat as (a) an expelled pest, (b) as an adored pet on a pedestal in the parlour, and finally (c) redefined as a respectable breeding object of a fancy, on par with dogs, cats and rabbits.

# References

Bourdieu, P. (2000), *Pascalian Meditations* (trans. R. Nice). Cambridge: Polity Press.

Ducommon, D. (1999–2004), *Mail Chatter*, The Rat Report, The Rat Fan Club. Available at: http://www.ratfanclub.org

Ducommon, D. (2001), *Adopt a Rat*, 6 March 2001. Available at: http://www.ratfanclub.org/adopt.html

Ducommon, D. (2004), *Costume Contest Pictures*, 7 November 2004. The Rat Fan Club. Available at: http://www.ratfanclub.org/costumes.html

Durkheim, É. and M. Mauss (1963), *Primitive Classification* (trans. R. Needham). Chicago: University of Chicago Press.

Himsel, C. A. (1991), *Rats: A Complete Pet Owner's Manual*. New York: Barron's.

Hodgson, B. (1997), *The Rat: A Perverse Miscellany*. Vancouver: Greystone Books.

Howell, P. (2000), 'Flush and the *Banditti*: Dog-stealing in Victorian London', in C. Philo and C. Wilbert (eds), *Animal Spaces, Beastly Places: New Geographies of Human–Animal Relations*. London and New York: Routledge.

Jordan, C. M. (1999), *Introduction to the Rat Race*. Available at: http//members.madasafish.com/~cj_whitehound/Rats Nest/Ship Rats/Menu.htm

Knight, J. (2000), 'Introduction', in J. Knight (ed.), *Natural Enemies: People–Wildlife Conflicts in Anthropological Perspective*. London and New York: Routledge.

Mayhew, H. (1861), *London Labour and the London Poor*, Vols II and III. New York: Dover Publications, Inc. (Originally: *London Labour and the London Poor; A Cyclopædia of the Conditions and Earnings of Those that Will Work, Those that Cannot Work, and Those that Will Not Work*. London: Griffin, Bohn, and Company.)

Mays, N. (1997), *The Proper Care of Fancy Rats*. Neptune City, NJ: T.H.F. Publications, Inc.

Miller, W. I. (1998), *The Anatomy of Disgust*. Cambridge, MA: Harvard University Press.

Milton, K. (2002), *Loving Nature*. London and New York: Routledge.

NFRS (1997–2005), *Varieties*, National Fancy Rat Society. Available at: http//nfrs.org/varieties.html

Olsher, S. (2004–2005), *Markings & Colors*. Fat Rat Central. Available at: http//www.fatratcentral.com/info_pages/about/markings_colors.html

Poe, E. A. ([1843]1927), 'The Pit and the Pendulum'. *The Work of Edgar Allan Poe*. Oxford: Oxford University Press.

RMCA (1995–2005), *RMCA Rat Standards*, Rat & Mouse Club of America. Available at: http//www.rmca.org/Standard/Rat/

Sanders, C. R. (1993), 'Understanding Dogs: Caretakers' Attributions of Mindedness in Canine–Human Relationships'. *Journal of Contemporary Ethnography* 22(2): 205–26.

Stallybrass, P. and A. White (1986), *The Politics and Poetics of Transgression*. London: Methuen.

Swierzy, A. and A. Horn (1998), *Pet Rat Information Sheet*. Available at: http//www.quite.co.uk/rats

Zinsser, H. (1963), *Rats, Lice and History: Being a Study in Biography, which, after Twelve Preliminary Chapters Indispensable for the Preparation of the Lay Reader, Deals With the Life History of Typhus Fever, also Known ...* Boston, Mass.: Little, Brown and Co.

# 7

# The Unbearable Likeness of Being: Children, Teddy Bears and *The Sooty Show*

## *Candi Forrest, Laurence Goldman and Michael Emmison*

And thus I learned. However much like us the Teddy Bears might appear to be, they were in fact the totally enigmatic Other. That they might live in nuclear families with mummies and daddies … and so on, meant nothing. These superficialities only served to mask the unpenetrable Otherness of Beardom.

Fox, 'Anthropology and the "Teddy Bear" Picnic'

## Introduction

Like Lascaux palaeolithic cave art, the playroom landscapes of many Euro-American pre-school children betray the ubiquity of animal representations in Western culture. So prevalent are these symbols in the real and fantasy ecologies of children that we might indeed forgive them for entertaining the thought that in the struggle for sovereignty between humans and animals the war must have long since been lost. The fauna of the bedroom discloses both visual and tactile evidence of the colonizing hegemony of the animal kingdom. Such nuanced readings of the human–animal relationship are perhaps further reinforced by media advertisements which commonly present animal figures in ready-made fantasy scripts (Kline and Pentecost 1990; Kline 1993) that explicitly solicit the child to 'come buy me and let's pretend'. Animals, it seems, appear in marketers' narratives as proactive agents for, and of, make-believe play. Only later does the child become aware of the programmed way in which care-givers are institutionally manipulated. Positive role models compel adults, then, to nurture child development by means of a variety of inanimate animal-like objects. Whilst these fulfil perhaps some early function as transitional objects (Winnicott 1971) the child is enculturated into understanding that recognizable and acceptable 'play' behaviour involves fantasy interaction with anthropomorphized cuddly toys. Adults, too, are enjoined to scaffold children's behaviour by drawing affinities between the child and the animal 'other'. Like them or hate them, teddy bears[1] are an inescapable part of the

Western childhood experience. Within this ecology of stuffed animal companions – including those which attempt verisimilitude, those which are purely fictional, and those which become endowed with their own pre-existing society – the 'bear' has longed reigned pre-eminent.

Providing some understanding of why it is that adults engender and utilize animal-based models for children – and most especially why bears occupy a privileged place in this pantheon – is now very much a multi-disciplinary endeavour. Philosophers have here been concerned with children *playing as* a bear – rather than *playing with* their bears – in unravelling the conundrums of *mimesis, imagination* and *play* (Goldman 1998). Throughout the history of theorizing about the perennial issues of truth and representation, the paradigm of child make-believe – for example, taking the role of the animal other – has served as both a prototypical and ontogenetic picture of humankind's mimetic behaviour. Role-play of the bear kind was thus for Ryle (1949) a way of talking obliquely about the ingenuous performance of bears themselves, and as such a critique of the Cartesian notion of imagination as 'other-worldly'. Psychologists have been wont to interpret such animal play as 'a biologically pre-programmed activity' (Flavell *et al.* 1987: 817), the pathology of which is an attempt to transform a primary reality into a fabricated 'second reality'. Adopting an animal identity is causally implicated in psycho-social development – cognitive, affective, linguistic and symbolic competencies. In playing as a bear, 'the real I is supplanted by the apparent I' (Groos 1901: 388) so that this *taking the role of an other* (Mead 1934) provides one conduit by which the child learns to develop an awareness of self and ultimately to understand pretence in others. The focus is on what cognitive models and competencies are invoked in behaviour to the effect of 'I am a bear therefore I am.'

These cognitivist paradigms with their intellectual debts to Piaget (1962) and Vygotsky (1966) have been at the heart of anthropological perspectives on how humans take animal shape (Mullin 1999; Shanklin 1985). The complex analyses of myth and ritual index a human propensity to exploit nature and animality for the purposes of social categorization and differentiation. Animals are the primordial metaphors, the play resources, and '*points de repère* in the pronouns' (the essential inchoate subjects') quest for identity' (Fernandez 1974: 121). A succinct expression of these theoretical findings might suggest that *playing as* a bear is a form of primordial predication which the child performs as cognitive agent in the quest to disambiguate dichotomies such as the real:irreal, nature:culture, male:female, wild:domestic and human:animal. These dualities are commonly presented as somehow fundamental to understanding the culturally encumbered identity of self.

Those analysts who have by contrast, read and deconstructed the texts of *playing with* bears – most especially in popular culture – argue by extension from the above that we encounter here the instantiation of pan-cultural anthropomorphizing proclivities (see Brabant and Mooney 1989). Human sociality is represented through animal embodiment. Far from attempting to penetrate the unpenetrable otherness of beardom, animals function as disguised humans, symbols that obliquely reference ourselves rather than didactic natural behaviour models (Blount 1975). Bear are not just a reflection of our own omnivorous versatility, they are also a reflected model[2] of human development through transformation. We dance on the boundaries of otherness to map the extent of similarity and difference as well as to reflect on shape-shifting itself in human life cycles. We are cerebrally hard-wired to engender mythic and symbolic skeins about the relationship of animal to human – the Lévi-Straussian notion of animals as good food for thought – and to reproduce these meanings linguistically in taxonomies, proverbs, adages, folk-tales, nursery rhymes, spells, etc. (see Bryant 1979). These cultural artefacts, then, have provided a rich resource for scholars to fixate on how play with animal representations informs us about the socio-cultural construction of human–animal relationships.

Research in decoding animal symbolism in popular culture has tended primarily, though not exclusively, to concentrate on the visual and literary representations found in television advertising (Lerner and Kalof 1999), children's literature (McCrindle and Odendaal 1994), nursery stories (Bilmes 1982), tabloid pictures (Herzog and Galvin 1992), children's television (Paul 1996), and greeting cards (Brabant and Mooney 1989). These studies provide a thick description of the dimensions of anthropomorphism – attitudinal differences to, and frequency and distribution of, specific animal species, gender-inflected narratives and animal stereotyping, and associated functions of indirect and didactic communication of value frameworks. Frequently, fine discriminations are made within the media between animal representations that are humanized/personified – where the natural animal form is given characteristics such as speech or thought – and anthropomorphic portrayals where animal form is adapted through modalities of dress, bipedalism, or behavioural patterns (McCrindle and Odendaal 1994: 139). This now-burgeoning literature is beginning to provide a number of important insights into the nexus of human–animal relationships.

First, the view that the fictional and non-fictional worlds of human–animal relationships are not discrete but rather evidence mutually implicated influences. Tate, for example, speculates that the 'teddy-bear syndrome' (1983: 216) preconditions human perceptions of real-world bears. Second, the recognition that animals are anthropomorphically represented in fictions designed for both child and adult audiences as part of a 'soft' allegorical approach to portraying didactic and commercial messages. Anthropomorphized animals, in other words, can convey messages about human activities and behaviours which could appear threatening or politically incorrect if human actors were used instead (Brabant and Mooney 1989; McCrindle and Odendaal 1994). Third, a point of specific relevance to the present chapter, the suggestion that recurrent TV characters engender affective attachments from their viewers either in the form of *wishful identification* – vicarious participation, experiential sharing and desire to be like – or *parasocial interaction* – imaginative and intimate co-participation with a media character (Hoffner 1996) which promotes socialization and cognitive development. This is a strain of research that clearly also encompasses a range of invented and standardized *imaginary others/friends* (Thompson and Johnson 1977). Finally, this renewed interest in the role of TV has been accompanied by a corresponding interest in cognitive discriminations about reality and fantasy, false beliefs, and associated 'theory of mind' problems (Howard 1994,1996; Szarkowicz 1998; Goldman 1998).

The contours of academic research concerning adult-generated representations of animals clearly touch on both the manner in which humans are role-taking beings, as well as how they culturally re-manufacture the 'dissimilar similarity' (Rapp 1984) between humans and animals. The fictional modality of TV, like games of make-believe, abrogates to itself the power to recontextualize experience that is part fidelity and part fantasy, a slippage 'between "what was", "what is" and "what if"' (Goldman 1998: 10). These anthropomorphic performances typify animals as culturally iconic of the sentient and social life of humans, thus servicing both metonymic as well as metaphorical operations. Whether it is themes of rebirth and regeneration symbolized by the snake in myths found in the highlands cultures of Papua New Guinea, or the migratory and hibernation behaviours of bears which underscored their prominence in palaeolithic and North American mythologies (Shepard 1998), the alchemy of animal assimilation reflects the importance of human play with transformative images of themselves.

## Hello Boys and Girls

In a series of related articles (Emmison and Goldman 1996, 1997; Smith *et al.* 2001), the authors have argued that the popular long-running TV programme *The Sooty Show*[3] provides a unique vehicle for analysing the interaction between children, the medium of TV, and the all-important phenomenological and cognitive axis of the real and imagined. This British children's TV programme featured the antics of three glove puppets who differed crucially in their verbal abilities. *Sooty*, a yellow bear, does not speak but is perceived to whisper in the ear of his handler, the presenter of the show Matthew Corbett (hereafter MC). MC in turn acts as both a mouthpiece and decoding gatekeeper for Sooty. Sooty is joined in the show by his friend and partner in mischief *Sweep*, ostensibly a spaniel-cross dog who has a conversational style that consists entirely of squeaks. Sweep presents as minimally communicative, for the squeaks which he produces appear to mimic the syllabic patterns of words including prosodic features such as intonation, stress, volume and extension. However, the majority of Sweep's squeaks are subject to a similar 'translation' on the part of MC and Soo. In contrast to the male-gendered Sweep and Sooty,[4] *Soo* is a female panda (bear) and is totally verbal and able to converse on equal terms both with the other puppets and MC, as well as act as surrogate mouthpiece in those sections of the show when the puppets appear by themselves without MC.

In one sense our research was very much about answering the philosophically encumbered question posed by Fink – 'is the exotic land of irreality the consecrated place for conjuring up and rendering present the essences of all things that exist?' (Fink 1968: 28). In *The Sooty Show* we encounter issues of realism and verisimilitude, referentiality and illusion, and abstractly the priority of the word in the accomplishment and commerce of fictional representation. The findings made are directly germane to the concerns of the present chapter and can be summarized as follows.

First, despite the inability of two of the puppets to 'speak' in ways recognizable to a human audience, this deficiency in verbal competencies presents no problems for the smooth flow of conversation and action. By the artful use of conversational devices all participants in the show succeed in generating a sense of spontaneous naturally occurring interaction for the viewers. This credibility turns on the manner in which MC (a) converses with his puppet interlocutors 'as if' it is obvious they are verbally competent and (b) disguises his translations of what they appear to say through the generic device of repetition. MC renders his interaction with the dumb Sooty as utterly mundane – there is nothing extraordinary about what Sooty has 'whispered' or Sweep has 'squeaked'. The show thus relies on the children's internalized models of ordinary conversational practices to communicate the dramatic reality of talking animals in moments that suspend their disbelief. In the text example below we see how MC paraphrases, repeats or recycles a turn of Sooty or Sweep as if it were a reaction on his part, but which clearly also functions to inform the overhearing audience as to what either of the interlocutors actually said.

*Example 1: The Cuddly Toy Machine*

> *Soo*: Well it all sounds rather <u>complicated</u> Matthew
> *MC*: Oh not really Soo on the contrary – I mean once I've built the machine you see
> Soo all you have to do is feed the material in at ONE end[5] (.) and then out the
> <u>oth</u>er end (.) comes a cuddly toy
> *Sweep*: ➜➜➜➜::
> *MC*: *What shall we make?*
> *Sweep*: ➜
> *MC*: Well we could make anything (.) w'cud make cuddly fro::gs or cuddly <u>du::</u>cks or
> [what-
> *Sooty*: [( )
> *MC*: *Cu- cuddly teddy bears*
> *Sweep*: ➜

*MC*: Good idea yes good idea
*Soo*: Yee:s that is a good idea

Implicit in fabricated discourse which has the intention of simulating non-fictional talk is a model of what ordinary talk is like, a model relied upon to convince the audience of a verisimilitude.

Second, if children rely on their intersubjective models of turn-taking to experience Sooty as 'real', they are equally compelled to draw on their internalized ethnographies of child behaviour. The humorous violations of adult behaviour codes by what are essentially animal-children reflect back cultural mores. The moral world inhabited by the fictional puppets is an entirely conventional one but now indirectly accessed through the make-believe play of puppets who serially transform from animal, to child to adult. *The Sooty Show* thereby makes an implicit appeal to children's internalized models of pretence that incorporate an ability to characterize and manipulate others' cognitive relations to information. Once again fictional resources constitute invaluable tools for the investigation of social interaction.

The dramatic reality of *The Sooty Show* for young children[6] is also dependent on certain inherent technical advantages of the TV medium which allows for the portrayal of a variety of characters' differentiated mental states (imagining, deceiving, dreaming and pretending). Importantly, TV technology enables the portrayal of multiple layers of pseudoreality so that (a) the action of the show is framed as continuous with a reality that pre-exists and is outside of that frame – the animal characters are constructed as lives ongoing when the camera is absent; and (b) the TV medium through visual and aural devices (for example, gaze, theme music, camera angles) re-presents a variety of irrealities (dreams, 'as if' scenarios, etc.) as encapsulated within the pretence of the show itself (Smith *et al.* 2001).

While we have stressed the importance of understanding that this constant shifting between the real–irreal boundary scaffolds the development and acquisition of pretence capabilities, our key contribution in this line of enquiry related more to 'how' this is achieved. *The Sooty Show* emerged as a text that plays with play itself. However, it is only when pretence becomes an object of itself – when there is pretence within pretence – that the compelling need for disambiguation work is established. The child must process and discriminate between complex and multiple layers of irreality by reference to the 'state of mind' consciousness of the animal participants. The pre-condition for successful 'pretending to pretend' to be so recognized by viewers is that the boundary of the pretend and non-pretend cannot be blurred (Smith *et al.* 2001).

This chapter builds on the above legacy by more specifically examining the previously less-explored dimension of the central characters' identities as 'animals'. The paradox which encumbers *The Sooty Show* is precisely that, again, in the face of what appears self-evidently a fabricated reality (the domestic life of anthropomorphic puppets co-habiting and talking with humans), strategies are devised to make the child audience feel it is watching quite normal interaction. Insofar as one might want to argue that nature: culture or human: animal oppositions are being worked out by the viewers, then, this is achieved primarily by having such boundaries re-presented and re-fabricated. In effect, the TV show becomes the default reality setting which can then generate fantasy situations such as the very human-like 'animal-children' differentiating themselves from non-speaking non-anthropomorphized animal 'others'.

## Some Bear Facts

Technological advancements have now reshaped the material culture of child play so that it is very much an 'endless consumption … [of] transmedia intertextuality' (Kinder 1991: 39). The 'bear' in nursery rhyme or folklore is now reshaped, simultaneously duplicated and readily accessed through literature, TV, films, cartoons, audio tapes or CD, clothing, food, household goods and an assortment of toys. The child thus consumes beardom in both the literal and figurative senses. No ethnographer of Western child fantasy fauna can fail to be impressed by the veritable panoply of bear representations. Without labouring the point drawn attention to by other writers (see Warner 1995, 1998; Crist 1999; Shepard 1998), one might list here the famous bears in literature such as *Rupert Bear, Winnie-the-Pooh, Paddington Bear, Berenstein Bears, Goldilocks and the Three Bears, Wilberforce*; TV bears such as *Yogi Bear, Bear in the Big Blue House, Lu, Amy and Morgan, Bananas in Pyjamas, Humphrey B Bear, Care Bears*; edible food bears such as Arnotts' *Tiny Teddy* biscuits, Dick Smith's *Teddies*, Mannatech *Phyto Bears*, etc.; and, lastly, the advertising bears used in the packing imagery of Coca-Cola, Sanitarium foods, Bundy Rum, Mars bars, porridge, etc.

The 'teddy bear' motif pervades and is culturally iconic of Western childhood, and yet this most mundane of facts seems to have drawn little scholastic comment. For many adults, the teddy-bear dolls function as transitional objects between the child and caretakers/outside adult world. They are comforters that supposedly ease anxiety. The giving of teddy bears in adult therapy is thought similarly to invoke a form of regression for 're-birth', just as Rowan Atkinson's famous Mr Bean 'Teddy' communicates an image of an adult unable to progress beyond the pre-adolescent stage. Why have teddy bears assumed such importance in the cognitive ethology of Western childhood in view of the fact that bears are one of the largest land-dwelling predators of humans? Cross-culturally animal dolls are not prevalent in the same caregiving contexts, and even in Anglo-American societies bears are not common family pets. Their identity seems very much the combined result of both historical circumstance and heritage as well as certain naturally endowed biophysical features.

The historical transformation in the image of 'bears' is charted by Warner (1995) as one from a 'predator' – the fifteenth- to seventeenth-century images of bestiality, cannibalism and eroticism – to the more 'playful' nineteenth-century connotations associated with carnival (circus, fair, zoo) appearances. The bear's earlier metaphysical stature (see Carroll 1986) was variously predicated on this animal's subsistence and life-cycle patterns – it was a forager whose movements were the 'gnosis of a wise eater' (Shepard 1998: 22). Equally, the bear was morphologically human-like – tailless, omnivorous, upright, and a traveller. The metaphor of hibernation became a marker of human transformation and ontogeny. Against this background of cultural history, the commercial popularization of the modern 'teddy bear' is more usually referenced to the famous episode involving Theodore 'Teddy' Roosevelt who in 1902 refused to shoot dead a captive bear. Folklore records that this incident was seized upon by Morris Michtom who advertised 'Teddy's bear' in his window that year with much commercial success. Mitchom later founded the Ideal Toy Company (Teddy Bear UK 2000a; see Bauman 1995).

Equally significant, however, has been the gradual development of the 'teddy bear' over the last century from partially realistic animal-doll – massive shoulder joints, back humps, etc. – to the modern incarnations with stubby legs and arms, non-gendered and seated, and a 'skin' of mohair or some synthetic acrylic (Teddy Bear UK 2000b). What seems reflected in such transitions of form has been the tendency of doll manufacturers to imbue the teddy bear with a more pronounced humanoid structure and with characteristics of neotony: large rounded head relative to body size, eyes, nose and mouth forward, short trunk and appendages. The point is less that researchers have found these traits to be coded as 'cute' by children or adults (Herzog and Galvin 1992: 81), than that in the selection of some animal species for human aesthetic 'play' such natural anthropomorphic physical features may enhance the candidature of bears and bear-like creatures.[7] Succinctly stated, the ursine constitution of Sooty is less a product of accidental whim and more the conspiring influence of historical circumstance and body morphology.

## Izzy Wizzy Let's Get Busy

For a mute, fluffy yellow ursine hand-puppet Sooty tells us a lot about the kind of humanity being portrayed in the show. This is the world of domestic play in which the three puppets are effectively constituted as children living with, and under the supervision of, the adult MC. They are visually animal but behaviourally human, having made this categorial crossing without the transition being highlighted. Like normal children they are usually represented as boisterous or mischevious; so that the absence of these traits is a cause for comment:

*MC*: (voice over)

> Well look at this (.) Sooty and Sweep both enjoying a quiet read in their lovely
> new bedroom (0.5) it's not often that you see such a peaceful sight I think you
> (audience) should consider yourselves very lucky

The fact of this dual identity becomes unremarkable for the audience. 'Indeed, the
peculiar paradox of the programme's success is that it depends on concealment of
what is self-evidently the case – that animals don't talk like humans!' (Emmison
and Goldman 1997: 329). What the viewing audience is presented with are puppet-
actors engaged in pretend-play scenarios essentially 'playing society' – making
narrative and ethical sense of the world around them. The moral caregiving provided by MC is that conventionally associated with adult child relations:

*Example 2: The New Bedroom*

*Soo*: OH Matthew Matthew
*MC*: Yes
*Soo*: We've bought you a present – give it to him Sooty
*MC*: Really?
*Sweep*: [➜::
*Soo*: [Bit touristy
*MC*: A present? OH hey look at thi: : s (0.5) a pencil (.) a souven↑::ir? (.) of Scotland
(1.0) hang on a minute you didn't go to Scotland you went to London
*Sweep*: ➜➜➜➜➜➚➘
*MC*: *That's why you got it cheaply?*
*Soo*: Heh heh but it's the thought that counts isn't it Matthew that's what you're always
telling us isn't it?
*MC*: Ye::s a reduced rate pencil (.) yes it is the thought that counts you've all been
extre::mely thoughtful

This fiction of domestic animal-children is maintained through disguise of an
initial bear-to-child transformation which becomes established as the default
reality setting for the audience. Thus in one episode involving the puppets 'playing
restaurants' the 'children' sustain a piece of collaborative make-believe through
further symbolic role-play. There is then a further transmutation of the play-frame
*animal = child*:

*Example 3: The Restaurant*

*MC*: Look who it is (.) Sweep
*Sweep*: ➜➜➚➘?
*MC*: Why- *can you join me*=
*Sweep*: =➜:

*MC*: Well er (1.0) alright then you can join me (.) sit down (.) why are you dressed like that anyway?

*Sweep*: →→↗↘→

*MC*: *You're a city gent*

*Sweep*: →::

*MC*: Sweep's a city gent

*Aud.*: xxxxxxx

*MC*: Go on make yourself at home Sweep

*Sweep*: →→ =

*MC*: =Bit slow the service in here (.) I'll see if I can find the waiter (.) WAITER (1) WAITER (1) I –

*Aud.*: [ xxxxxxxxx

*MC*: [Oh (.) not <u>you</u> (.) are you the waiter?

*Sooty*: ( )

*MC*: Sooty's the waiter (.) well let's have a look at the menu then go and get the menu

As illustrated in Figure 7.1, the first transformation is opaque and unmarked in the sense that there is no overt signalling of the puppet's acquired anthropomorphism. The more they appear to indulge in childlike behaviour the less ursine and canine they seem. The second transformation is by contrast linguistically marked in the precise sense that the adopted role identity as 'waiter' or 'city gent' is negotiated as a move between the fantasy participants. The initial animal-to-child transition represents the 'unsaid' of the text as the animal's identity becomes fully parasitic on what the child viewer has internalized about children in his/her peer group.

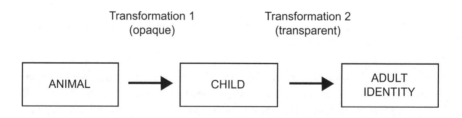

**Figure 7.1** Schema of Transformations.

Like Paddington, Sooty and his friends each succeed in becoming a 'person', but persons frozen in developmental time. In so far as their humorous pranks become blameworthy, they cannot escape reprimand or judgement by relying on their animal constitution. They are subject like any 'child' to parental discipline:

*Example 4: The Miracle Cleaner*

> *MC*: and get something for stinging bottoms would you?
> *Sweep*: ↗↘↗↘?
> *MC*: That's right (.) *stinging bottoms* =
> *Sweep*: [➔::::
> *MC*: [=because that's what <u>you</u> two are going to have when I catch you!

*The Sooty Show* parades its reality credentials by quarantining the puppets' primary animality from their assumed humanity. We deliberately avoid describing this in terms of an *effacement* of identity because the transition is never complete. The potential to suddenly reverse the primary transformation, to remove the veneer of humanity, remains. In the data we examined reference to the puppets' animality is invariably done directly to produce humour through the incongruity of mixed animal/human behaviour associations (McCrindle and Odendaal 1994: 144). In the following extract Sweep's food order betrays his liminal status as dog-child because of a predilection for 'bones' most *especially* with foodstuffs usually craved by human children.

*Example 5: The Restaurant*

> *MC*: Yes err he wants bones first
> *Sweep*: [↗::
> *MC*: [Bones squash
> *Sweep*: ↗➔➔↗➔➔↗
> *MC*: Followed by bones and chips
> *Sweep*: ↗::
> *MC*: Write that down Sooty (.) bone and chips
> *Sweep*: ➔↗➔↗↘
> *MC*: Bone flan and [ custard to finish up with
> *Sweep*: [↗:
> *MC*: Al[right
> *Sweep*: [➔➔
> *MC*: Bone flan and custard (1.0) have you got all that?
> *Sooty*: (   )
> *MC*: *He has the same everyday*? (.) well why did you have to bother writing it do:wn
> *MC*: Where are you going? (1.0) just a minute where are you going as well (2.0) Waiter come here
> *Sweep*: ((humming))
> *MC*: Where's that creature gone?
> *Sooty*: (   )
> *MC*: *He's gone to eat his bones under the table*
> Sooty: ((*nods*))

MC: <u>City gents</u> don't eat their bones underneath the table (.) anyway I want something to eat go and get my fish course

Sooty reminds MC that Sweep is canine and thus consumes food 'on the ground'. More intriguing is MC's use of 'creature', which recalls Sweep's animality as well as, perhaps more obliquely, the tendency for adults frequently to reference young children as 'animals' (for example, *beasts, creature, monkey, etc.*) which, as Warner (1998: 150–2) notes, is a motif in Western children's literature wherein children as 'little beasts' are commonly likened to animals. Though infrequent, other episodes similarly reference the puppets' animality in two types of very different scenarios. First, where MC wishes to play with the initial transformation from animal to child – as in the example below where 'crossing one's palm/hand with money' is changed to 'crossing the paw':

*Example 6: Lucky Things*

MC: ((*to viewers*)) HEY this is really exciting we rang this lady fortune teller (.) she's actua(hh)lly agreed to come round here and tell my fortune
MC: Well no I take your point (.) but actually I would like to see her. When is she going to come round?
Sooty: (   )
MC: *I've got to cross your paw with silver* (.) what does that mean?
Sweep: ➔➔⬀⬂
MC: *Cost me 10p?*

Or in the extract below where the verbal utterance of Sooty is immediately corrected by MC changing 'paws' back to 'fingers' thereby reorienting the children back to the hypothetical human identities of the participants.

*Example 7: Cuddly Toy Machine*

(*All add materials to the toy machine*)
MC: Switch it on OK (.) there we go
Sooty: (   )
MC: *Should be alright this time*
Sooty: ((*nods*))
MC: Yea – keep your paws crossed you three (.) please keep your paws crossed it could be a success (.) <u>this time</u> (.) got to wait 'n see
Sooty: (   )
MC: *And just keep our paws crossed* (.) alright keep your fingers crossed there we are the machine's jus – HANG on there's summin happening – there's something happening

Third, the animal name becomes the object of punning routines such as that presented below:

*Example 8: Lucky Things*

> (*Soo appears 'dressed up' as Madame Futura, a fortune teller, who fortells Matthew's future*)
> *Soo*: let me look into my <u>crystal ball</u>
> *MC*: good idea I'll have a look as well
> *Soo*: Oh yes
> *MC*: Oh yes
> *Soo*: And I see a person entering the crystal ball
> *MC*: Yes
> *Soo*: Yes
> *MC*: who is it?
> *Soo*: very special
> MC: to do with me?
> *Soo*: to do with you (.) someone with whom you will have a unique relationship
> *MC*: hey hey is she er tall and dark and good looking mm?
> *Soo*: SHE? It's not a she lovey it's a <u>he</u> and he's small blond and totally bare
> *MC*: small and blond and totally=
> *Soo*: =hey ((*Sooty pops up*))
> *MC*: oh Sooty
> *Soo*: YA SEE (.) I was right he's a bear <u>totally</u>

While the above allusions to the animal identity of the puppets appear to transgress if not subvert the very frames the show endeavours to maintain – the illusion of reality through concealment of animal-to-child transitions – they are almost always used for humorous routines and puns, and their infrequent occurrence renders them innocuous and no more than temporary suspensions of disbelief for the child audience.

## Creature, What Creature?

More significant for the processing of categorial distinctions and cultural knowledge about the animal environment are the references to animals which the pseudo-animal puppets themselves generate. Clearly the puppets treat animals as 'others' which are bereft of the communication skills and sentient capacities exemplified by Soo, Sweep and Sooty. By this means the puppets are again marked off as human-like. In the following extract there is no evident incongruity for the child viewer in a panda bear puppet exhibiting violent intentions towards another animal. The message being relayed is that of conventional adult culture – among animals some are pets, some are part of the food chain, some provide sport for human endeavours.

*Example 9: The Animal Catcher*

> *MC*: A computerised animal catch: er?
> *Soo*: Yes
> *MC*: How does it work Soo?
> *Soo*: Well (1.0) to get the animals close (.) you must invent food (.) drink (.) and a mating call=
> *MC*: =I see
> *Soo*: and then you've got to give them the right scent=
> *MC*: =yes
> *Soo*: and perhaps a decoy that you see
> *MC*: yes but the thing I don' understa –
> *Soo*: and then (.) when you've got them close (.) you can operate my patent stu::nner

What the animal-children purvey for the audience through multiple *Sooty* episodes are the conventional cultural attitudes to particular species. For example, associations between some birds and black cats with 'good fortune' figure prominently, as does the humorous potentiality of skunks, flies, chickens, etc.

*Example 10: Lucky Things*

> (*Scene: The new bedroom*)
> *MC*: (*voice over*)
> Well look at this (.) Sooty and Sweep both enjoying a quite read in their lovely new bedroom (0.5) it's not often that you see such a peaceful sight I think you should consider yourselves very lucky
> (*Soo arrives*)
> *Soo*: Hello you two
> *Sweep*: ↗↘
> *Soo*: Hey guess what I've just seen I've just seen two magpies I feel so lucky
> (1.0)
> *Sweep*: ↗↘
> *Soo*: Yes Sweep *lucky* it's lucky to see two magpies
> *Sweep*: →↗→→↗↘
> *Soo*: *You think it's rubbish?*
>
> (*Scene: Lounge*)
> *MC*: (*to viewers*) Oh hello there (.) I expect you're wondering what I'm doing are you (.) well the truth is I'm looking at the lawn (.) well actually at the birds on the lawn there's quite a lot and right in the middle is this great big magpie y'know

> the black and white birds (.) and I know this is going to sound silly but well (.)
> seeing one magpie (.) is meant to be unlucky (.) only <u>two</u> magpies that's very
> lucky but one magpie –
>
> *Soo*: Hello Matthew were you talking to somebody?
> *MC*: Well I was just actually saying that I've seen a magpie on the lawn Soo
> *Soo*: Was it just one?
> *MC*: Yes
> *Soo*: That's supposed to be unlucky isn't it?
> *MC*: We: : ll they do say so but I don't believe in any of that Soo
> *Soo*: Well I do because I saw two magpies and I found a five pound note (.) which I
> thought was lost
> *MC*: Oh that's rubbish (.) where's Sooty anyway?

The unwritten rule for script-writing about other animals is that no mention is ever
made of violence towards the puppet's co-species members. When reference is
made to co-species members the puppet is singled out as special by virtue of its
obvious abilities to communicate with MC, but most particularly because it is a
'named' individual. MC does this work of dealing with the ultimate reality of
Sooty's ursine constitution when breaking into one of the signature *Sooty* songs:

> There is only one real genuine Sooty in the world.
> I'd know you anywhere
> You stand out in a crowd of Bears
> You're a Bear who's quite unique
> No-one's ever heard you speak

This is exploited in marketing strategies which duplicate TV show characters as
stuffed toys – it is never 'own a frog or own a bear' but 'own Sooty or Kermit'.

## Achieving Some Bearings

In the development of children's television over the last half-century animal puppet
shows have continued their popularity – for example, *The Muppet Show* – and far
outnumber other programmes such as *Johnson and Friends* which feature inanimate talking participants. From an anthropological viewpoint, this dramatic
activity can appear functionally continuous with the play lessons of non-Western
oral traditions (myths, fables, etc.) which similarly adopt a symbolic attitude to
animals. Telling stories about 'ourselves', masked as animals, to children, making
narrative sense of the world through humanized 'others', certainly has cross-cul-
tural instantiation. The conventional explanation for why animals are used to
service these roles includes the rationales that they are less threatening to children
(even dinosaurs, lions and crocodiles are rendered 'friendly' in TV shows), they

sustain and attract their attention,[8] and they provide a parsimonious model of human sociality (Brabant and Mooney 1989; McCrindle and Odendaal 1994). Notwithstanding the variety of species which are subject to TV anthropomorphism – turtles, horses, worms – this selection appears anything but random and unprincipled. Those animals which tend to be part of the human food chain – fish, chickens, etc.[9] – are less frequently portrayed, as are invertebrates. This endorses the finding that TV reflects our culture's 'phylogenetic hierarchy' (Paul 1996; Lerner and Koalf 1999) in terms of the moral dispositions we take towards certain animals. The human-like animals of fictional TV tend to be closer to humans on the phylogenetic scale and tend to be mammals and/or pets.

So entrenched is the teddy bear in our caregiving psyche, and so widely diffused are the iconic images of bears in the fantasy fauna, that it makes little analytic sense for us to now attempt to discern chicken from egg in the complex of contributing and causal factors. While the domestication of this wild animal appears part of the aetiology for symbolic adoption, the reasons for its persistence owe more to the efficacy of intertextuality as the child moves effortlessly between TV programme, film, book and toy. This consumption further extends to apparel, foodstuffs and décor. Sooty, Paddington, Rupert and Winnie are merely reinforcing exemplars of adults' creative activity to provide mimetic myths for children. In this process folklore fact supersedes any natural scientific model of ursine nature and behaviour as popular culture media create for the child a fantasy-zoological system that is often for the Western child the first horizon of experience of the animal 'other'. What is ingenuous is mostly perceived through the window of the mock performance. How much this relates to the increased mechanization of the West and the consequential marginalization of real animals in the lives of urban children (Berger 1980; de Courcy 1995: 105; Fernandez 1974: 121–2; Shepard 1998: 143–4) is debatable.

## Conclusion

Our focus in the continuing analysis of *Sooty* has been on how such anthropomorphism, as part of the wider art of pretence-making, refracts as well as conveys boundaries between reality and fantasy, the human and the animal. Precisely because the intention of the show is that the viewers sustain the illusion that the performers before them are 'like themselves' – that in effect the pretend is the real – the messages of identity and taxonomy have to be re-manufactured or re-institutionalized through the mouths of the players themselves. A pretence must be created within a pretence, just as the animal actors have to make comment on animal 'others' as part of the process of differentiation. We know that the human: animal distinction is significant precisely because the pseudo-animal puppets reproduce this bifurcation from the perspective of assumed human identities. This kind of dramatic illusion operationalizes conceptual distinctions because the viewer can only make sense of what is happening through cognitive processes which disambiguate and differentiate. In a quite profound sense, *Sooty* is a symbol of the permanence of illusion in the world, of the transforming power of human imagination, and of the need for the child to grasp modalities of reality through fiction. Animals here service the requirement for a model of transformation as they are dramatically reshaped and moulded by adults to project the dynamics of becoming and identity formation. The ultimate lesson for the child is, as Fox reminds us, very much like that for the anthropologist attempting to rationalize the Other: 'with Bears you never can tell. They may look like us, but they are really very, very different, so leave them alone' (Fox 1992: 47).

## Appendix: Transcription Details

In producing the transcripts we have followed the system originally devised by Gail Jefferson, full details of which can be found in *Structures of Social Action* (Atkinson and Heritage 1984). In the interests of clarity we have simplified the system used by excluding features which are not directly relevant to our analysis.

The principal symbols used in relation to the talk of MC and Soo are as follows:

| | |
|---|---|
| [ | Onset of overlapped talk |
| (1.0) | Timed pause within a speaker's talk or between speaker turns |
| (.) | A micro-pause |
| - | A dash indicates the cut-off of the prior sound or word |
| wo:::rd | Extension or stretching of the sound or syllable |
| <u>word</u> | Emphasis in delivery |
| *word* | Italics used to indicate the component of MC or Soo's turn which contain the repetition forms |
| ↑ | The upward arrow in MC's turn indicates a marked rising shift in intonation immediately following the arrow. |

For describing Sooty we have used the following symbols:

| | |
|---|---|
| ( ) | An empty bracket indicates any whispered (i.e. presumed spoken) turn |
| (*nods*) | Head nod, used as confirmation (i.e. presumed to be a 'yes') |

In the case of Sweep we have endeavoured to capture something of the prosodic nature of his vocalizations by representing his syllabic squeaks with the following symbols:

| → | A non-intonated squeak |
| ↗ | An upwardly intonated squeak |
| ↘ | A downwardly intonated squeak |
| →::: | Long or elongated squeaks |

Audience laughter has been represented as follows:

Aud.:      xxxxxxxxx

## Notes

1. The term is used in its generic sense for any cuddly toy which may include animals other than just bears or bear-like creatures.
2. Or 'mirror and window' (Mullin 1999).
3. The TV show ran between the 1950s and the 1980s, with first Harry Corbett as presenter and then his son Matthew Corbett. In many instances it was filmed in front of a live audience and would present internationally as a stand-alone puppet show. All rights to Sooty were sold in the 1990s to a Japanese media organization after which a number of cartoon videos were produced. It was the longest-running children's programme in history to that point and very much a British institution, with associated Sooty museums and Sooty fan clubs variously established around the UK.
4. Later episodes of the show introduced a fourth playmate known as 'Butch' who was a male dog.
5. See the appendix on p. 157–8 for a transcription of the symbols used to indicate the modes of communication between MC, Sooty, Sweep and Soo.
6. Buckingham has noted that 7–12-year-olds found Sooty to be popular but 'childish or babyish' (1993: 76–7). We surmise that unlike 3–5-year-olds, children in this age bracket have less problem disambiguating the pretend–real distinction.
7. Across the highlands cultures of Papua New Guinea marsupials invariably provide a model for self-decoration, ritual symbolism and paraphernalia, and categorial systems. For example, the Huli term for the tree kangaroo is *andaya*, which means 'human-like'.
8. David Attenborough (private communication) indicates as much for adults as well when he notes that TV shows about animals always rate higher audiences than TV shows about other cultures or other peoples.
9. Ms Piggy and Babe were very much exceptions to the rule.

# References

Atkinson, M. and J. C. Heritage (eds) (1984), *Structures of Social Action: Studies in Conversation Analysis*. Cambridge: Cambridge University Press.

Bauman, T. (1995), 'The History of the Teddy Bear'. *Teddy Bears on the Net* [online], Available at http: //www.tbonnet.com/second_index.html (accessed 30 April 2001).

Berger, J. (1980), 'Why Look at Animals?' In J. Berger (ed.), *About Looking*. New York: Pantheon.

Bilmes, J. (1982), 'The Joke's On You, Goldilocks: A Reinterpretation of *The Three Bears*'. *Semiotics* 39: 269–83.

Blount, M. (1975), *Animal Land: The Creatures of Children's Fiction*. New York: William Morrow and Company, Inc.

Brabant, S. and L. Mooney (1989), 'When "Critters" Act like People: Anthropomorphism in Greeting Cards'. *Sociological Spectrum*. 9: 477–94.

Bryant, C. D. (1979), 'The Zoological Connection: Animal Related Human Behaviour'. *Social Forces* 58: 399–421.

Buckingham, D. (1993), *Children Talking Television: The Making of Television Literacy*. Washington, DC: Falmer Press.

Carroll, M. P. (1986), 'The Bear Cult That Wasn't: A Study in the Psychohistory of Anthropology'. *The Journal of Psychoanalytic Anthropology* 9: 19–34.

Crist, E. (1999), *Images of Animals: Anthropomorphism and Animal Mind*. Philadelphia: Temple University Press.

De Courcy, C. (1995), *Zoo Story: The Animals, the History, the People*. Ringwood, Victoria: Penguin Books Australia Ltd.

Emmison, M. and L. Goldman (1996), 'What's That You Said Sooty? Puppets, Parlance and Pretence'. *Language and Communication* 16: 17–35.

Emmison, M. and L. Goldman (1997), '*The Sooty Show* Laid Bear: Children, Puppets and Make-believe'. *Childhood* 4: 325–32.

Fernandez, J. (1974), 'The Mission of Metaphor in Expressive Culture'. *Current Anthropology* 15: 119–33.

Fink, E. (1968), 'The Oasis of Happiness: Toward an Ontology of Play'. *Yale French Studies* 41: 19–30.

Flavell, J., E. Flavell and F. Green (1987), 'Young Children's Knowledge About the Apparent-Real and Pretend-Real Distinctions'. *Developmental Psychology* 23: 816–22.

Fox, R. (1992), 'Anthropology and the "Teddy Bear" Picnic'. *Society* 30: 47–55.

Goldman, L. (1998), *Child's Play: Myth, Mimesis and Make-believe*. Oxford: Berg.

Groos, K. (1901), *The Play of Man*. New York: Appleton.

Herzog, H. and S. Galvin (1992), 'Animals, Archetypes, and Popular Culture: Tales from the Tabloid Press'. *Anthrozöos* 5: 77–92.

Hoffner, C. (1996), 'Children's Wishful Identification and Parasocial Interaction with Favourite Television Characters'. *Journal of Broadcasting and Electronic Media* 40: 389–402.

Howard, S. (1994), 'Real Bunnies Don't Stand on Two Legs: Five-, Six- and Seven-year-old Children's Perceptions of Television "Reality"'. *Australian Journal of Early Childhood* 19: 35–43.

Howard, S. (1996), 'Bananas Can't Talk: Young Children Judging the Reality of Big Bird, Bugs and the Bananas'. *Australian Journal of Early Childhood*, 21: 25–30.

Kinder, M. (1991), *Playing with Power in Movies, Television, and Video Games*. Berkeley: University of California Press.

Kline, S. (1993), *Out of the Garden: Toys and Children's Culture in the Age of TV marketing*. London: Verso.

Kline, S. and D. Pentecost (1990), 'The Characterization of Play: Marketing Children's Toys'. *Play and Culture* 3: 235–55.

Lerner, J. and L. Kalof (1999), 'The Animal Text: Message and Meaning in Television Advertisements', *The Sociological Quarterly* 40: 544–65.

McCrindle, M. E. and S. J. Odendaal (1994), 'Animals in Books Used for Preschool Children'. *Anthrozöos* 7: 135–46.

Mead, G. H. (1934), *Mind, Self and Society*. Chicago: University of Chicago Press.

Mullin, M. (1999), 'Mirrors and Windows: Sociocultural Studies of Human–Animal Relationships'. *Annual Review of Anthropology* 28: 201–24.

Paul, E. S. (1996), 'The Representation of Animals on Children's Television'. *Anthrozöos* 9: 169–81.

Piaget, J. (1962), *Play, Dreams and Imitation in Childhood*. New York: Norton.

Rapp, U. (1984), 'Simulation and Imagination: Mimesis as Play'. In M. Spariosu (ed.), *Mimesis in Contemporary Theory*. Philadelphia: John Benjamins.

Ryle, G. (1949), *The Concept of Mind*. London: Hutchinson.

Shanklin, E. (1985), 'Sustenance and Symbol: Anthropological Studies of Domesticated Animals'. *Annual Review of Anthropology* 14: 375–403.

Shepard, P. (1998), *The Others: How Animals Made Us Human*. Washington, DC: Island Press.

Smith, C., C. Forrest, L. Goldman, and M. Emmison (2001), 'The Bear (Ir)Realities: Media Technology and the Pretend–Real Distinction on a Television Puppet Show'. In H. Schwartzman (ed.), *Child's Play: Perspectives for the 21st Century*. Westport: Bergin and Garvey.

Szarkowicz, D. L. (1998), 'Are You Thinking What I'm Thinking? Bananas in Pyjamas as a Medium for Exploring Young Children's Understanding of Mind'. *Australian Journal of Early Childhood* 23: 1–5.

Tate, J. (1983), 'Human–Bear Interactions: Profile and Perspective', in A. H. Katcher and A. M. Beck (eds), *New Perspectives on Our Lives with Companion*

*Animals*. Philadelphia: University of Pennsylvania Press.

Teddy Bear UK (2000a), 'How the Teddy Bear got its Name' [online]. Available at: http: //www.teddy-bear-UK.com/lerfram2.htm (accessed 30 April 2001).

Teddy Bear UK (2000b), 'How to ID Your Bear' and 'Bears at Play' [online]. Available at: http: //www.teddy-bear-UK.com/lerfram2.htm (accessed 30 April 2001).

Thompson, E. and T. Johnson (1977), 'The Imaginary Playmate and Other Imaginary Figures of Childhood'. In P. Stevens (ed.), *Studies in the Anthropology of Play: Papers in Memory of B. Allan Tindall*. Proceedings from the Second Annual Meeting of The Association for the Anthropological Study of Play. New York: Leisure Press.

Vygotsky, L. (1966), 'Play and Its Role in the Mental Development of the Child'. *Soviet Psychology* 5: 6–18.

Warner, M. (1995), *From the Beast to the Blonde: On Fairy Tales and Their Tellers*. New York: Farrar, Strauss and Giroux.

Warner, M. (1998), *No Go the Bogeyman: Scaring, Lulling and Making Mock*. London: Chatto and Windus.

Winnicott, D. W. (1971), *Playing and Reality*. London: Tavistock Publications Ltd.

# –8–

# The Elephant–Mahout Relationship in India and Nepal: A Tourist Attraction

## *Lynette A. Hart*

## Introduction

The lifelong relationship of mahouts with their elephants has ancient origins. Preserved artefacts from the Indus Valley civilizations depict elephants, sometimes with a cloth on their backs (Clutton-Brock 1999: 144), revealing they were tamed around 2000 BC. The earlier significance of elephants is evidenced by the numerous artistic carvings in ivory, as found at sites in the Ukraine, for example, yielding evidence that palaeolithic people in the Pleistocene over 10,000 years ago used ivory for artefacts, carvings, and as building material (ibid.: 146). Pressures for acquiring ivory, hunting elephants, and the remarkable training of elephants for warfare (Spinage 1994: 269) seem to have developed along with the traditions of a human caregiver relationship and the mastery of elephants.

In India the role of elephants in society and the maintenance of elephants have changed in recent times. When elephants were owned by kings and chiefs, the prestigious role of mahout was passed down within certain families. A young boy would learn the skills from his father and grow up with a young elephant. In India today it is sometimes said that anybody who can mount and ride an elephant can become a mahout for his livelihood (Basappanavar 1998: 222). Royalty in Asia of the type where elephants were kept in the palace and used on royal ceremonial occasions has virtually disappeared. Owning elephants, which formerly lent prestige to royalty or provided power for work, is now a costly risk. The practical need for elephant power to move and haul logs in the forests has shrunk with the loss of forests and the increasing use of machines. Only someone with free access to a forest jungle and a steady source of salaries for mahouts, such as in tourist areas, now finds it feasible to retain elephants. In former days, special forest tracts were designated as elephant preserves where elephants could live and be captured as needed; these forests were managed by trackers, hunters and tamers in the employ of the king (Basham 1981: 197–8). The fragile fragments of the ancient mahout–elephant tradition, which lasted thousands of years, now barely remain and continue to be eroded by the economic challenges and change in status mahouts face and by the loss of work for elephants.

Although human–elephant relationships encompass engaging positive emotions and rewards, significant problems and conflicts are now inherent in their complex living situations. Conflict with wild elephants in southern India is evident in 'elephant-proof' trenches, grass shacks in high trees that overlook favourite crossing points over the trenches into the farms (Figure 8.1), damaged telegraph poles, and

**Figure 8.1** Lookout Point for Protecting Fields against Elephants.

trees that have been debarked or uprooted by wild elephants. Elephants' cognitive capability can prove extremely frustrating. In one case, 'Herds of wild elephants … had taken it into their heads to demolish all the telegraph poles, bridges, and isolated forestry stations they could find … As fast as the repair-gangs repaired the system it was damaged again' (Baze 1950, in Williams 1989: 127). Domesticated elephants in India and some other Asian countries are commonly co-located in forests alongside villages and farms. Mahouts caring for domesticated elephants, or the elephants themselves, are sometimes confronted with wild elephants causing injury or death to humans or elephants, or damage to crops and villages (Datye and Bhagwat 1995: 340).

Elephants today retain a mythic importance throughout their range in Asia. The Hindu elephant god for overcoming obstacles, Ganesh, is deeply revered in India and elsewhere in Asia. A Hindu begins every serious undertaking by seeking to propitiate him (Dubois [1906]1994: 714). Elephants continue to be an obligatory centrepiece of processions for major festivals (Figures 8.2–8.5), and reside at many temples in India. Pictures and images of Ganesh and elephants are ubiquitous throughout India. In some areas, the traditional role of elephants working in the forest is continued in a token manner in tourism as they provide rides or transport tourists through the forest serving as a focal point for special activities for tourists. As discussed in this chapter, swimming with or climbing onto an elephant,

**Figure 8.2** The Onam Festival in Trivandrum, Kerala, India.

**Figure 8.3** A Decorated Elephant.

or feeding one treats, can be a highlight of a tourist's visit to a national park, and is itself a tourist attraction.

This chapter describes current relationships of mahouts with elephants in two national parks located in southern India and Nepal. With the establishment of Nagarahole National Park in the southern Indian state of Karnataka, ownership of elephants was transferred from the maharajah to the government, with management by the Forest Department. Of interest here are elephants associated with two villages: with a few elephant females and bulls, Bale is at the site of a former logging camp that tourists can visit; Sunkadakatte has several female elephants that are used to provide half-hour rides to tourists. The ethnographic observations presented here are drawn from five visits to Nagarahole National Park, comprising nine weeks during the period 1995 to 2001. Three visits to Royal Chitwan National Park in Nepal between 1989 and 1992 comprised five weeks. Here the elephants were owned by two tourist lodges, Chitwan Jungle Lodge and Gaida Jungle Lodge, and were used to carry tourists on longer rides into the jungle to view rhinoceroses and other wildlife.

**Figure 8.4 and 8.5** Elephants in the Festival.

## Emerging Models for Tourism Involving Domesticated Elephants

Although tourists adopt the rhetoric of adventure, they are never independent of a social arrangement wherein a host organizes the experiences of a sightseeing guest.

D. MacCannell *The Tourist: A New Theory of the Leisure Class*

The relationships of mahouts with elephants in the national parks of India and Nepal described here provide an interface among elephants, mahouts and tourists. Although the two parks differ with respect to the elephants' histories and the mahouts' traditions, they have a shared history in their development of tourism. Some of the same individuals provided the leadership for initiating tourism in these two parks, creating the tourist lodges and methods for shaping tourists' experiences. Tourism offered at the Royal Chitwan National Park, initially at Tiger Tops, was developed by Jim Edwards in the early 1970s (Gurung 1983). Contrasting with wildlife visitation in East Africa, where tourists simply drove or were driven through wildlife parks, Tiger Tops sought to educate and tantalize the tourist's mind with intriguing information, viewing, and demonstrations with plants, animals and birds. They presented the park to their tourist guests, offering a programme with a menu of scheduled activities. Edwards recruited a team of naturalists to serve as informative partners in the experience of the tourists, accompanying them, and describing and interpreting the wildlife and plants. For example, Sundar was a charismatic and knowledgeable young man recruited from southern India as a naturalist and to teach others. By the late 1970s, Colonel John Wakefield, working with Edwards, began planning Kabini Lodge to develop similar tourism for the Nagarahole National Park in southern India; he became resident director of Kabini Lodge in 1986. Wakefield hired Sundar as head naturalist for taking tourists from Kabini Lodge into the Nagarahole National Park, and for teaching other locals to be naturalists in the park. Thus, a coherent philosophy and practice of providing knowledgeable naturalists to accompany tourists in the forest, presenting the park's features, was implemented by both of these national parks. Assuming a strong and informative role at the tourist lodges, the naturalists for both parks offered the tourists bird walks, explanations of elephant behaviour, and descriptions of the trees in the forest. Other tourist lodges in Nepal adopted a similar philosophy. Thus, in the Royal Chitwan National Park, Gaida Jungle Lodge and Chitwan Jungle Lodge opened and offered wildlife activities enhanced by expert naturalists who managed and escorted each safari.

This approach of 'staging tourism' within national parks resembles examples for other touristic contexts presented by Desmond (1999) in *Staging Tourism: Bodies on Display from Waikiki to Sea World*, such as marine parks, zoos, or Hawaiian *luaus*. Tourists receive rehearsed presentations to enhance their viewing and to help them learn more about what they see.

With respect to the elephants and tourists, however, the Nagarahole and Chitwan parks are in sharp contrast to each other. Kakankote, in Nagarahole National Park, is the historic site of successful kheddahs, where close to 2,000 elephants were rounded up and captured over a period of years, from 1874 until 1971 (Sukumar 1994: 19). Nagarahole (Snake River) has a curved shape that was used to trap the elephants and facilitate the captures. Over almost 100 years twenty-four major operations occurred at Kakankote, some with multiple drives, until the final spectacle capturing forty-seven elephants (Basappanavar 1998: Appendix). Interviews with mahouts revealed that, except for a handful of births, the domesticated elephants remaining in the area date from these kheddahs. Mahouts know the individual elephants and can tell their histories, the years of their capture, who has worked with them, their behaviours with other wild or domesticated elephants, and the specific injuries they may have caused to people. Wild elephants in Nagarahole, especially bulls, interact with the domesticated ones, fighting with the bulls and mating with the females. In contrast, wild elephants are gone from Nepal, except for about fifty remaining that are seldom seen. The domesticated elephants of Chitwan were purchased in India with no known history or identity, and without accompanying mahouts.

Thousands of tourists pour into Kathmandu each year from around the world, many scheduled for trekking in the Himalayas; it is a major tourist destination. Royal Chitwan National Park offered an attractive add-on providing an experience with wildlife; tourists could easily see rhino from elephant-back. Typically, tourists added three or four days to their itinerary for this experience of the low-lying Chitwan. Tourism easily expanded to fill a growing number of tourist lodges featuring Royal Chitwan National Park; these lodges operate as concessions that can transport tourists through the park on elephant-back. In contrast, Nagarahole National Park in southern India is far from the big tourist centres in India's golden triangle of Delhi, Agra and Jaipur; it lacks the visibility of a major destination community (Singh *et al.* 2003). Travelling to Nagarahole from other continents is arduous; only recently have there been direct flights to Bangalore, somewhat simplifying the journey. About half of the tourists visiting Nagarahole are Indians from Mysore or Bangalore who know the area. Among other tourists, some are regulars with special interests – for example, those associated with bird-watching groups from England, or other wildlife devotees. Tourists stay at Kabini Lodge, but access to Nagarahole Park for Kabini vehicles is regulated by the Forest Department.

## Southern India

Before the democratic state of Karnataka was established in 1973, domesticated elephants and mahouts were part of the maharajah's retinue, residing either at the palace or within the royal hunting grounds. Elephants were acquired by trapping, or during hunts or kheddahs, after which the maharajah would typically continue to own the elephants. Ownership of the elephants and royal hunting grounds reverted to the government at independence, with the gazetting of the Karnataka National Park. Thereafter, the Forest Department assumed responsibility for the domesticated elephants and hired accompanying mahouts. Many of these new jobs were offered to tribals, just as efforts were underway to encourage tribals to move outside the new park boundaries.

Care of elephants has been continuous since the changeover of ownership. At the time of these interviews, two original mahouts remained from the maharajah period, one at each village. They had fifty-six and fifty-one years of experience respectively; one of them, Chikarama, estimated he had trained seventy elephants. These two senior mahouts had the role of *jamadar*, serving as the head mahout. At Bale, each elephant was cared for by three men, whereas at Sunkadakatte the female elephants were managed only by two men. The twelve head mahouts of the two villages averaged twenty-seven years of experience, ten years with their current elephants (Hart and Sundar 2000). Whether Hindu, Muslim or tribal, mahouts had learned about elephants from their fathers, and sometimes grandfathers, and their sons were planning to become mahouts.

The two camps where elephants are taken each day after spending the night browsing in the forest are near the villages where the mahouts reside with their families. Structured interviews were conducted at these two villages with sixteen mahouts and four young assistants, with a collaborating translator. Many hours of conversations took place with various other individuals associated with the elephants, including tourist lodge director Colonel John Wakefield and naturalists Sundar, Sarath and Sajan of Kabini Lodge. Attending the Oman Festival in Kerala provided experience with a major annual celebration involving elephants. Partial accounts of work from these sites have been published (Hart and Sundar 2000).

Elephants of both villages appear to be at the centre of life. The daily schedule for mahouts includes feeding and bathing the elephants. With relatively little work to do, these elephants are semi-retired. Logging is now illegal, but they are sometimes recruited to assist in moving fallen or poached trees, and female elephants at the riding camp give short rides to tourists as arranged through Kabini Lodge. These various activities occur while the elephants are within the camp during the morning and afternoon, after which they are released unsupervised into the forest to forage on native trees and bushes. The elephants are somewhat hobbled and drag a long chain to restrict them from moving a great distance and to assist in relocating them in the mid-afternoon and again the next morning.

The village of about 350 people that originated as a logging camp, Bale, is located on a two-lane road between the states of Karnataka and Kerala. While there is not a steady flow of traffic, some buses and trucks pass along the road throughout the day and they are required to stop at a guard station before proceeding further west towards Kerala. The village is on one side of the road where a small Hindu shrine to the elephants is found. The elephant yard is a short distance away from the village homes on the opposite side of the road. Mahouts can conveniently walk between the elephant area and their homes in just a few minutes.

The care for each bull elephant is provided by two adult men, the mahout himself and an assistant, plus sometimes a third man assisting with clean-up. Female elephants usually have two men assigned to provide care.

Several bull elephants reside at Bale, and there are one or two female elephants, comprising fewer than a dozen elephants in all. The number fluctuates slightly as elephants are sometimes temporarily relocated to another area if they are required for some work. Mahouts consistently maintain a high level of vigilance around the bull elephants, ensuring that the young boys and other passers-by remain at a suitable distance from the bulls; this appears effective, as no injuries by elephants to mahouts' children were reported (Hart and Sundar 2000). For human safety during *musth*, some bulls are kept under greater restraint than at other times. Mahouts are well aware of fatalities associated with elephants, usually bulls. All have known mahouts, often family members, who have been killed or injured by elephants. They often face risks in encounters with wild elephants and must seek a quick path to safety: as Kumara said: 'I climb trees so many times it's natural.'

The village of about 200 people where the riding elephants are cared for, Sunkadakatte, is located deep with the park near a historic hunting lodge of maharajahs. Several female elephants, usually including one or two young elephants under five years of age, are the focal point of this village. Young elephants are sired by wild bulls who sequester the domesticated female for a couple of days when she is in œstrus. Elephants are retrieved each morning, and brought back to the camp for supplementary feeding and a bath. Following additional free foraging in the forest, another provisioned feeding is given in the afternoon.

Although mahouts were in a lower caste in pre-independence times, they were granted considerable respect for their association with the venerated elephant, the Hindu god Ganesh, and for their ability to manage such awesome animals. Mahouts still speak with great pride about appearing on their bull elephants in full regalia for processions. The tradition no longer involves walking several days to Mysore for the procession; rather, it is a long truck ride. Most mahouts in these two villages expressed pride and satisfaction in their jobs, but two questioned the wisdom of working at such a dangerous job and preferred their sons to get an education instead.

## Nepal

The domesticated elephants in Nepal associated with this study were owned by the two tourist lodges within or beside the Royal Chitwan National Park: Chitwan

Jungle Lodge and Gaida Jungle Lodge. Elephants resided at stables in the vicinity of the lodges. A number of rhinoceroses reside in the park, but no wild elephants can be seen. The domesticated elephants were owned by the tourist lodge at which they were housed, and generally had been purchased at an elephant market in India or from a trader for the specific purpose of transporting tourists to view rhinoceroses in the jungle. Mahouts were employees hired by the lodge. Seventeen mahouts had an average of thirteen years of experience, but only four years with their current elephants. Thus, the Chitwan mahouts had less than half the experience as a mahout, and with the current elephant, as compared with the Nagarahole mahouts. A senior mahout was the head manager who co-ordinated the group of mahouts

Elephants were closely managed, always being either staked in the elephant yard (out of reach of each other) or accompanied by a mahout. The daily schedule included providing rides to tourists for about an hour each morning and afternoon. Around mid-day elephants were taken into the forest by their mahouts to forage on foods of their choice, and then carried back a supply of food gathered by the mahout and elephant. During the relaxed mid-day period, it was common to see mahouts sleeping on their elephants' backs, under an umbrella for shade. Elephants were staked overnight in the elephant yard with a supply of food within reach to last through the night. Mahouts' sleeping quarters adjoined the elephant yard such that the elephants' activities could easily be heard. The very early morning before rides was a special time for the saddled elephants, standing in a circle with their trunks in reach of each other. Otherwise, throughout the day, they typically were not in tactile contact. Elephants also welcomed their daily baths, in which they were allowed playfulness, except if tourists were joining them.

Chitwan Jungle Lodge is located deep within the park; the mahouts reside at the elephant camp adjacent to the lodge, taking periodic leaves of several days to visit their families who live in towns outside the park. Gaida Jungle Lodge is along a boundary of the park, close enough to a nearby village that mahouts went home whenever off duty, though one mahout always remained overnight at the lodge for each elephant. Thus, all mahouts were employees spending long periods of time in the elephant yard. Family members of the mahouts resided off-site and were never present at the lodges. However, when driving through the villages, women were seen doing laundry and carrying water and other supplies as they walked along the roads, accompanied by small children.

In addition to the wild rhinoceroses, the domesticated elephants themselves were a major attraction for tourists. Throughout a variety of special activities, mahouts assumed full responsibility for assuring the safety of tourists in the presence of their elephants, despite not speaking the tourists' languages. Tourists were encouraged to interact with elephants and learn about them. Naturalists who spoke English facilitated demonstrations involving the elephants. For this project, structured interviews were conducted at the two lodges with seventeen mahouts, with two naturalists assisting as translators. Partial previous accounts provide additional detailed information (Hart 1994, 1997).

## Managing the Mahout–Elephant Relationship

Until 1971, elephants were captured and trained in a harrowing process that left many elephants dead. Since then, a few have been acquired as orphans and then trained one at a time by a mahout as they grew up. Some rogue elephants have been captured and brought into domestication. There now is a somewhat systematic process of breeding elephants with an expectation of waiting for young elephants to grow up and become useful as domesticated elephants.

### Southern India
Even today, the relationship with elephants remains standardized. The commands used are fairly consistent across Asia. By about the age of three, the still-small baby elephants have mastered the commands that are basic for their handling (Dinerstein 1988: 75). Table 8.1 shows a sample list of commands as gathered from the Indian mahouts in this study. The lifestyle, procedures for handling elephants, and the schedules are often similar across locations, and were consistent across these Muslim, Hindu and tribal mahouts. Rarely, mahouts will teach special

**Table 8.1.** *Basic Commands Used by Mahouts*

| Commands | |
|---|---|
| *Hindi* | *English* |
| Bite | Lie down |
| Hutte | Get up |
| Dare | Lift timber |
| Dare | Drink water |
| Dare ka mar | Grab and carry chain |
| Dare mar | Break branches, bring |
| Math | Walk forward |
| Say | Walk backward |
| Thole | Lift front leg |
| Are | Stop |
| Lage | Load timber |
| Kule | Sit on two hind legs |
| Salam | Salute |

tricks: one had his elephant pumping water with a lever; another's elephant would place a garland over someone's head during a ceremony. One might think that mahouts are interchangeable for their elephants; however, elephants respond preferentially to their particular mahouts and may ignore commands from others. Young boys who spend their time with elephants retrieve female elephants in the mornings and take them for bathing (Figure 8.6). Girls were never seen performing these activities, although small girls occasionally accompanied their mahout fathers. Young boys often provide a substantial proportion of the effort, assisting their fathers or uncles in working the elephants – the elephant is seen as a family project. The boys take pride in having learned all the commands and being able to manage a particular female elephant, but would not command the same respect as the elephant's official mahout.

Becoming a mahout at Nagarahole for most meant following a long family tradition of several generations, whether for a Hindu, Muslim or tribal mahout. Mahouts knew about the various brothers, uncles, sons, and fathers of mahouts who were also mahouts, and also the stories about injuries these mahouts had experienced in their lifetimes. Ten of the twelve head mahouts were at least second generation, and three were third generation, plus nine had sons expecting to become mahouts. Some of them were waiting for a Forest Department job to open up for them.

**Figure 8.6** Small Boy Learning to Ride an Elephant.

Spending much time with elephants makes a person deeply attached to them, as reflected in the common saying 'You never get enough of an elephant.' Time together provides opportunities to experience the individuality of the elephant, recognize its personality traits, and build up a knowledge of unique episodes. This interchange of intimacy and positive feelings is enhanced with the elephant by a number of positive experiences throughout each day. The mahout gives a soothing bath to the elephant, which involves carefully rubbing the entire body of the elephant, using a rock for scrubbing. Unlike the frolicking baths of Chitwan, elephants are lined up in an orderly row for this systematic process that proceeds by command. As another treat, mahouts cook a pot of a highly favoured, grain-based dish, *ragi,* that is rolled into elephant-bite-size balls after cooling, and then placed into the elephant's mouth (Figures 8.7, 8.8). This practice is similar to one used in eighteenth-century Thailand, where mahouts cooked cereal and placed the balls inside the elephant's mouth (Delort 1992: 63).

## Nepal

The elephants in Nepal were given few opportunities to misbehave seriously; both their schedules and their locations were closely managed. Even their interactions with each other were limited, since they were staked just out of reach of each other. Early each morning, just before giving rides, the elephants were arranged in a circle, each one saddled with a howdah and ridden by a mahout. This appeared to be a special time of day for the elephants, as well as for the mahouts, as the elephants all were within tactile reach of each other during these few minutes of quiet time.

Becoming a mahout in Chitwan seldom reflected a family tradition, though most had yearned as young boys to work with elephants. As in southern India, the Nepalese mahouts offered special care to their elephants, especially in preparing food and bathing the elephants. At the tourist lodges in Nepal, where elephants spend the night in camp, the mahout sits on the ground wrapping some molasses-based food treats in straw, and later feeds these packets, *kuchi,* to the elephant. Food brought for the evening feeding is cut into bite-size pieces, even though the elephant could easily break it apart himself. Tourists are given great latitude in interacting with elephants, and those who make their way to the elephant stables are allowed to feed treats to docile elephants (Figure 8.9).

The bathing tradition for the elephant goes back to the initial training, where the elephant was scrubbed down in the head, back, rump, and hind leg regions, avoiding the ventral regions and the trunk for safety (Fernando 1990: 107). The scrubbing and washing is said to make the animal lose its suspicions of man and also allows the mahouts to gauge the temperament of the animal. In Nepal, the elephants appeared joyful as they were running to the river to bathe. And in the water they were given considerable recreational freedom to enjoy themselves, while also attending to verbal instructions of the mahouts. Tourists, many from Australia and

**Figure 8.7 and 8.8** *Ragi* Balls for Elephants.

**Figure 8.9** Tourists in Nepal.

the United States, jostled around the elephants during the bathing, relishing this unusual experience. Only the more gentle elephants were used for these interactive encounters with the tourists.

In their emerging role of interacting with and protecting tourists in their experiences with elephants, mahouts sometimes face conflicting requirements. For example, in Nepal, most mahouts preferred to avoid close encounters with rhinoceroses that would be uncomfortable for them and their elephants, but felt that many tourists wanted to get closer than they liked (Hart 1997: 47–8). Older tourists, and those with cameras with a long lens, were less likely to urge mahouts to get too close.

## Sentiments of Mahouts Concerning their Elephants

The context of mahouts and elephants includes a spiritual world with many gods. Frequent offerings are made to evoke good fortune and ward off harm.

### *Southern India*
Throughout India, Hindus regularly make offerings to Lord Ganesh, the man–elephant god. Special shrines for Ganesh are available in the national park near where the elephants are cared for, as well as in cities. At the Nagarahole villages, the forest goddess Mastiama was worshipped every Tuesday. Temples associated with elephants contained elephant bells and were the sites of village celebrations (Figures 8.10 and 8.11). Similar shrines to Ganesh are common along small country roads (Figure 8.12). Historically, a stone Ganesh shrine was placed on the meadow at Kakankote, where wild elephants were coralled, and remains today in Nagarahole National Park at the site of the kheddahs (Figure 8.13).

As has been implied, the details of elephants' lives and behaviour are significant to mahouts. Indian mahouts seemed almost more aware of details of the elephants' lives than their own, easily recalling the history of births for each female elephant, and the behaviours and specific behavioural problems of individuals. Certain elephants command almost mythic respect, even years after they have died. Considerable grief among mahouts followed the death of one especially noble bull elephant, Mahendra, who was killed by another domestic bull when a favoured female was in heat. An extremely large bull, Rajendra, was so revered that he was given a full burial in 1977 with a marked grave near the logging camp. He had been the royal elephant until being killed by a wild bull. The royal elephant has responsibility each year to carry the golden howdah during the procession of the Duessarah festival in Mysore. This special status commands respect that continues and precludes selling the elephant to another state, even if the elephant becomes more and more difficult to manage.

The Nagarahole elephants are brought in from the forest twice a day where they are taken for baths and given special foods. They are an inevitable attraction for people nearby. The mahouts' families lived near the elephant camps and their sons and other young boys spent much of their time being with the elephants.

While best known by their mahouts, the domesticated elephants today also have special significance to people throughout the society, as well as to the tourists who come to see them. Most of these local people have not experienced an extensive

**Figure 8.10 and 8.11** Village Temple in Nagarahole.

**Figure 8.12 and 8.13** Shrines to Ganesh in Nagarahole.

relationship with an elephant and lack any special knowledge of them. Some people in Asia live near a village or tourist lodge where they routinely see elephants, and elephants may appear to be just ordinary. For the annual festival, people of Sunkadakatte decorate their elephants for the circuitous village procession that lasts a couple hours, with one elephant carrying a decorated platform with a goddess (see Figures 8.3 and 8.4). Sunkadakatte generally has one or two baby elephants under two years of age; even the children and adults who see these babies daily continue to be attracted to them.

### Nepal

Protection from adversity is sought from the forest goddess, as indicated by daily offerings in the elephant camp. During one visit of this study, rainfall was low, tigers had not been spotted, and an elephant had caused a fatality, all suggesting displeasure of the forest goddess. A special sacrifice was scheduled to rectify this problem, a goat and several chickens forming the offering.

The mahout speaks soft comforting words to the elephant. When queried about this and the reciprocation of feelings, the mahout may say he feels the elephant loves him. At the same time, the mahout knows the elephant would leave forever, walking into the woods and not returning, if permitted (Hart 1994: 308). If the elephant were free, the mahout would not have a job.

Most Nepali mahouts claimed their elephants never got angry with them. Obedience with only voice control at a distance (particularly to the mahout's voice), co-operation, trusting the mahout, and reaching out to touch him were taken as signs of love. One mahout, Resham, was sure that his elephant, Raj Kali, loved him because she had a twinkle in her eye when she saw him, and trusted him (Hart 1994: 309). She tried to touch him, was gentle, and would never run away. He carefully scrubbed her tusklet with sand during her bath. During extreme misbehaviour, the mahout may talk to an elephant about the need to improve. Mahouts retain interest in this work despite their grandfathers or fathers having been killed by wild or domesticated elephants.

Establishing intimate relationships with elephants predisposes mahouts to experience profound grief at the loss of a significant relationship. In the past, capturing wild elephants resulted in a high mortality that sometimes caused considerable grief to mahouts (Basappanavar 1998: xxxiii). Several Nepali mahouts talked about missing favourite elephants that they had worked with in the past. For example, Ramlakhan felt sad when losing a gentle female who never ran away. Maji, the jamadar at Chitwan Jungle Lodge, had worked about thirty elephants in his forty-eight years with them, but felt grief for Ganga Prasad, a bull he worked with for just two years: he had a good temperament and walked well. His current elephant, Appu Kali, was a small, gentle elephant rated second best for him. Kheru missed an obedient female that he had worked with for five years, but then she was sold. Kheru, as one of the most effective mahouts, was often assigned a new challenging elephant.

In Nepal at the elephant camp near one tourist lodge, a stone on the ground served as a Hindu shrine to the jungle goddess; it was regularly decorated with flowers and other offerings. In the Nepali context of tourism, where elephants are owned by tourist lodges, working with elephants is becoming more like a conventional job rather than an interrelationship with an elephant; both elephants and mahouts come and go from the facility (Hart 1994: 300). Even so, I observed that when a group of government-owned elephants, including a baby, appeared unexpectedly at a tourist lodge in Nepal, a crowd of Nepalis working at the lodge excitedly materialized to see the baby.

The elephants used in Nepal have no oral or recorded history. Elephants often are relocated, and no one has long-term knowledge of an elephant's life in captivity. If an elephant becomes too difficult, his name may be changed and he might be sold to someone else who is unaware of the elephant's dangerous behaviour in the past. For instance, an elephant at the study site that became difficult and killed an assistant mahout was sold soon after the fatality.

In a survey I carried out the Nepalese mahouts were asked to describe what they thought elephants wanted. Most mentioned that elephants like to eat. Elephants were said to want love and affection and to obey the mahout because of love for him. Being assigned a new mahout made elephants angry. Many described that elephants would rather be free or wild than live in the company of humans.

## Consistent Sentiments of Mahouts

Despite some contrasts in the details of how they managed their elephants, mahouts in Nepal and India were remarkably consistent in describing the way of life and the qualities associated with being a good mahout. Putting in a lot of effort, treating the elephant well, providing good food, having good experience in caring for and training elephants, and working well with the employer were considered to be essential characteristics of a good mahout, as similarly described by mahouts and their very young assistants.

The mahouts' perception of a good elephant included good behaviour, walking well, listening to each command, not joining with wild elephants, never getting angry, not panicking, not fighting with elephants, coming quickly when called, and having a tolerant character. Some mahouts most admired the strength and power of bull elephants and wanted to be tough and in control of a strong bull, while others preferred the more consistent temperament of female elephants that is easier to control. Traditionally, male elephants were highly favoured over the tuskless females – for example, in processions.

## Possible Sentiments of Elephants

Although elephants have not systematically been studied, animal behaviourists and biologists, including even Darwin, have alluded to the capacities of elephants to experience human-like emotions. According to Darwin ([1872]1965: 165–6). 'The Indian elephant is said sometimes to weep ... Sir E. Tennent ... says, "no other indication of suffering than the tears which suffused their eyes and flowed incessantly ... He lay on the ground, uttering choking cries, with tears trickling down his cheeks".' Many accounts describe elephants weeping and otherwise being emotional. Early accounts by Pliny and Plutarch of the Roman spectacles told of a circus elephant who was slow in understanding instructions and subsequently received frequent beatings; he was discovered practising his lessons in solitary at night in order to avoid the beatings (Shelton 2001: 5). The famous slaughter of elephants in 55 BC arranged by Pompey culminated with elephants supplicating the crowd and bewailing their fate with a kind of lamentation that in turn created grief among the people (ibid.: 4). From her long-term experience in a Nairobi elephant sanctuary, Daphne Sheldrick describes that African elephant babies suffer psychological trauma during experiences when their families are poached, and claimed they subsequently might have nightmares, waking up at night screaming (see Chadwick 1992: 327).

There also are many accounts of elephants exhibiting joyous emotions. They 'quite seemed to enjoy the excitement of climbing and descending the steep acclivities. And sliding down-hill on their bellies, with their forelegs spread straight out in front, and their hind-legs behind' (Bock [1884]1986: 189). I have observed that adult African elephants also can be exuberant and playful, especially when bathing. Once one accepts that elephants have emotions, the question arises as to how they emotionally respond to humans, as well as to other elephants. We might expect that the widely hunted, wild elephants would make great efforts to elude humans, and there is in fact both ancient and modern evidence that wild elephants seek to avoid humans. 'Finding any grass that betrays the presence of man, pulls it up and gives it to the one behind to smell ... They all turn aside to safe ground, always avoiding land that has been trodden by men' (Aelian, *De Natura Animalium*, IX, 56 in Williams 1989: 94–5).

On the other hand, the long-term elephant–mahout relationship seems likely to lead to attachment to a mahout, and anecdotes abound confirming this. Megasthenes, in fourth-century BC Greece, wrote that elephants whose drivers were killed in battle would lift them up and carry them to burial, and that one elephant slew his driver in passion and then died from remorse and grief (Chadwick 1992: 326–7). Elephants have been reported to weep after being scolded, or upon a reunion with a mahout after twenty years (ibid.: 327). Two scientists who systematically trained an elephant visually to differentiate specific figures visited her after an absence of thirty-two years. The reunion was an extremely emotional event, with embraces and touching with the trunk (Altevogt 1990: 480). Mahouts that I interviewed gave consistent reports of the temperaments of the elephants in their group, including the elephants' responses to other elephants and people. One Nepali, Ratan, described actually seeing a female elephant, Bahadur Kali, pick up a drunk assistant mahout and carry him home on her trunk. Drona's mahout mentioned that when a wild *musth* bull was threatening, Drona ran back to the village to save the mahout. Kanthi's mahout described that if he gave commands to other elephants, Kanthi felt bad.

While we have no ultimate knowledge of the feelings of elephants, it does appear that, in particular, the female elephants at the riding camps in India lead a somewhat tranquil life. The female elephants appear to maintain a rich social life within their elephant group, including mating with wild bulls, as well as socially interacting with people in the village. There are frequent births, other females serving in an assisting role, and good survival of young. Elephants in camps at the Nepal lodges spent their nights restrained in the camp, generally out of reach of each other. Thus, their social interaction with each other was limited, nor were they able to forage freely during the night. Lacking wild bulls, they did not get pregnant. Their interactions with humans were limited to the mahouts, since elephants were not housed beside the village.

An indicator of the emotional well-being of elephants is the frequency of stereotypies. For example, in one study of elephants in zoos and circuses, all performed stereotypies (Kiley-Worthington 1990: 78). Although quantified observations were not made, in hundreds of hours of observations I have not seen any stereotypies among the female elephants at the two camps in India, though two males appeared less contented than the others. In my studies of elephants in both India and Nepal mahouts described the strong emotions of their elephants. In Nepal, the elephant, Chancil Kali, for example, was said to like no one, and would only tolerate three people. In particular, she hated two elephants, and would hit them if provided with an opportunity. Ratan Kali was an elephant afraid of all but two of the other elephants in the group. Several mahouts described how their elephants showed their affection by putting their trunks on the mahout.

## The Touristic Experience of Mahouts and Elephants

A tourist attraction … an empirical relationship between a *tourist*, a *sight*, and a *marker* (a piece of information about a sight).

The *information* about the tree (its marker) … is the object of touristic interest and the tree is the mere carrier of that information.

D. MacCannell, *The Tourist: A New Theory of the Leisure Class*

Tourists are an emerging group of advocates for elephants, focused individuals who visit these areas specifically to see the elephants and learn about them. They appreciate close contact with the elephants. How better to enjoy tourism than to experience a sumptuous mode of conveyance that treats riders as royalty (MacCannell 1992: 5). For visitors to the Chitwan lodges, swimming with the elephants and climbing up the trunk to mount an elephant were highlights of their visit, as well as riding alone on an elephant or to feed it *kuchis*. Studies of tourists feeding wild mountain goats suggest that the unfamiliar animal's taking of food conveys an acceptance and regard that is very rewarding for the person (Lott 1988). Tourists visiting the goats were highly motivated to photograph the experience; their distance to the animal was affected by the length of their camera lens (Lott 1992). In Chitwan and Nagarahole, tourists photographed the elephants, and thus retained a marker of the experience.

Tourists riding elephants are able to experience the most intense human–animal relationship vicariously by seeing the mahout interacting with his elephant. They witness the dynamic tension between giving correction to the elephant, with a follow-up reward to assure affection. The process of saddling the elephant with the howdah to carry passengers and bathing the elephant continues; as it has done for hundreds of years. Tourists can get a sense of stepping into an earlier century, not just into another culture and animal world.

Visitors to both Chitwan and Nagarahole dream of seeing a tiger; occasionally this happens. Thus, the tiger is the ultimate tourist attraction, though an unlikely one. The domesticated elephants with their mahouts comprise a major tourist attraction, one that can be guaranteed in both parks.

## *India*

> Although the tourist need not be consciously aware of this, the thing he goes to see is society and its works.
>
> D. MacCannell, *The Tourist: A New Theory of the Leisure Class*

The historic continuity of the elephant–mahout relationship in Nagarahole, and the strong involvement of family tradition, provides tourists with a view of an ancient culture. The Nagarahole villages are much as they were, and only incidentally serve tourists. They approach that ideal touristic place existing outside of history, comprising 'unspoiled nature and savagery' (MacCannell 1992: 26). Visiting the elephant yard at Bale, tourists can sense the danger of working with bulls and respect the courage and skill of mahouts who manage the bulls each day. The mahouts' concern regarding the safety of being around some of the bulls is always evident.

At Sunkadakatte, the elephant yard is virtually in the centre of the village, offering a close-up view of life in a village where transport is by foot or elephant.

Seeing the baby elephants, and hearing about the 'auntie' behaviour of the females lacking babies, personalizes the experience of meeting the female elephants. Nagarahole tourists visit the domesticated elephants in the park on the same circuit as their drive to see wild elephants, so they can experience the boundary between wild and tamed elephants.

### Nepal

Tourists to Chitwan face no prospect of seeing wild elephants, but they can count on enjoying a rich experience with the domesticated elephants. The naturalists provide extensive interesting information about elephants. On the other hand, the mahouts are hired and work away from their family setting. Thus, except for the care and handling of elephants, tourists gain no insight into the lives of the families of mahouts or their culture (nor the naturalists, for that matter). Interviews with the tourists revealed that more than 90 per cent of them were generally satisfied with their experience, finding it exciting and producing a sense of contentment (Lott and McCoy 1993). The experience elicited three affective dimensions, including activity, adventure, and a spiritual feeling. Only a few found it anxiety-provoking or felt remorse about their intrusion on the rhinos.

## Conclusion

It perhaps seems paradoxical to offer extreme reverence to an animal that for most of its history has been brutally captured, and then trained and sometimes extremely restrained. One explanation for the human propensity for domesticating dogs, cats and other tamed species is that the process itself is rewarding to people as an evidence of their own ability to dominate and control nature (Tuan 1984). Viewed in this perspective, taming a huge, intelligent elephant would be the greatest and most rewarding accomplishment. Indeed, audiences in ancient Rome found the displaying of elephants to be humorous, enjoying the illusion that a wild and dangerous animal had been civilized and learned behaviours such as wearing clothes, appreciating music and adopting dining etiquette (Shelton 2001: 5). The process of training an elephant inevitably continues to be challenging for a mahout, as an elephant never completely defers to a person and continues in small ways to test limits, and would still be inclined to wander away into the forest and not return, despite the favoured food and nice baths that are always available at the stable (Hart 1994: 309).

An advanced stage of an object becoming sacred is '*mechanical reproduction of the sacred object*: the creation of prints, photographs, models or effigies of the object which are themselves valued and displayed ... setting the tourist in motion on his journey to find the true object ... Alongside the copies ... The Real Thing' (MacCannell [1976]1999: 45). Whether through tradition or as a recent job, mahouts spend most hours of their days with elephants in the presence of real elephants. Tourists who visit elephants are awestruck by them, and gather up various images of elephants, underlining their status as a compelling tourist attraction.

The emergence of domesticated elephants as a tourist attraction in the context of new tourist destinations enhances the economic viability of the mahout–elephant relationship, while also assuring improved welfare for the elephants on account of the way tourists scrutinize the quality of care offered to the elephants. Such an option is attractive to the tourist lodges, to the extent that the Jungle Lodges and Resorts, the company sponsoring Kabini Lodge at Nagarahole, has announced a two-phased plan to offer in-depth exposure of tourists to domesticated elephants and their mahouts at Dubare Elephant Camp (Jungle Lodges and Resorts 2003). Phase One will offer three-hour visits to observe elephant bathing, feeding and commands, with explanations by a naturalist. In Phase Two a tented accommodation will be created with longer elephant rides, bird-watching from elephant back, and nature walks, with an available elephant interpretation centre and visits to a tribal hamlet. With this project, Jungle Lodges and Resorts 'seeks to be a trend-setter in this niche area and create an eco-tourism product', enhancing interest in conservation.

The classical relationship of mahouts with elephants existed for thousands of years, and represents a unique connection with the largest-brained terrestrial mammal (Hart *et al.* 2001). Human relationships with many other animals are gaining in involvement and importance, such as with dogs, cats and whales, but the long-standing relationship with elephants is now deteriorating. Asian elephants are universally loved by a significant proportion of people, yet we could be approaching a time when they will only survive in zoos. The extent to which they are valued in Indian society – viewed with affection, and worshipped as Ganesh – has played a role in their survival to this point. Tourism is one avenue for continuing their role in India and providing a new veneration for them in a modern world that offers them and their mahouts work in the future.

## Acknowledgements

In India, great help was provided by tourist camp director Colonel John Wakefield, naturalist Sajan, naturalist and collaborator Sundar, the management staffs at Nagarahole National Park and Kabini River Lodge, and the mahouts and their young assistants who conversed with me. Similarly in Nepal, the study was made possible by help from the management at Chitwan Jungle Lodge and Gaida Wildlife Camp, the translation assistance of Uddhav Bhatta, Bishnu Gurung, and Baburam Regmi, and the conversations with the seventeen drivers. David Anderson has offered bibliographic assistance. Michael McCoy made the local research arrangements and through Research Expeditions International, Winters,

California, in association with Wilderness Travel, also provided financial assistance. John and Anne Dickens provided the photograph of the decorated elephant (Figure 8.3).

# References

Altevogt, R. (1990), 'Proboscideans', in *Grzimek's Encyclopedia of Mammals,* Vol. 4. New York: McGraw-Hill Publishing Company.

Basappanavar, C. H. (1998), *Elephant – The Lady Boss*. Bangalore: Vanasuma Prakashana.

Basham, A. L. (1981), *The Wonder That Was India: A Survey of the History and Culture of the Indian Sub-Continent Before the Coming of the Muslims*. New Delhi: Rupa and Co.

Bock, C. ([1884]1986), *Temples and Elephants: Travels in Siam in 1881–1882*. Singapore: Oxford University Press.

Chadwick, D. H. (1992), *The Fate of the Elephant*. San Francisco: Sierra Club Books.

Clutton-Brock, J. (1999), *A Natural History of Domesticated Mammals*. Cambridge: Cambridge University Press.

Darwin, C. ([1872]1965), *The Expression of the Emotions in Man and Animals*. Chicago: University of Chicago Press.

Datye, H. S. and A. M. Bhagwat (1995), 'Man–Elephant Conflict: A Case Study of Human Deaths Caused by Elephants in Parts of Central India', in J. C. Daniel and H. S. Datye (eds), *A Week with Elephants*. Bombay: Bombay Natural History Society/Oxford University Press.

Delort, R. (1992), *The Life and Lore of the Elephant*. New York: Harry N. Abrams.

Desmond, J. C. (1999), *Staging Tourism: Bodies on Display from Waikiki to Sea World*. Chicago: University of Chicago Press.

Dinerstein, E. (1988), 'Elephants, the Original All-Terrain Vehicles'. *Smithsonian* 19(6): 70–81.

Dubois, J. A. ([1906]1994), *Hindu Manners, Customs and Ceremonies*. New Delhi: Rupa and Co.

Fernando, S. B. U. (1990), 'Training Working Elephants', in *Animal Training: A Review and Commentary on Current Practice*. Potters Bar: Universities Federation for Animal Welfare.

Gurung, K. K. (1983), *Heart of the Jungle: The Wildlife of Chitwan*. London: Andre Deutsch Limited.

Hart, B. L., L. A. Hart, M. McCoy and C. R. Sarath (2001), 'Cognitive Behavior in Asian Elephants: Use and Modification of Branches for Fly Switching'. *Animal Behavior* 62: 839–47.

Hart, L. (1994), 'The Asian Elephant–Driver Partnership: The Drivers'

Perspective'. *Applied Animal Behaviour Science* 40: 297–312.

Hart, L. A. (1997), 'Tourists' Effects on Drivers of Working Asian Elephants'. *Anthrozöos* 10: 47–9.

Hart, L. and Sundar (2000), 'Family Traditions for Mahouts of Asian Elephants'. *Anthrozöos* 13: 34–42.

Jungle Lodges and Resorts (2003), 'Dubare Elephant Camp', June 18 (http://www.junglelodges.com/dubare.htm).

Kiley-Worthington, M. (1990), *Animals in Circuses and Zoos: Chiron's World?* Harlow: Little Eco-Farms Publishing.

Lott, D. F. (1988), ' Feeding Wild Animals: The Urge, the Interaction, and the Consequences', *Anthrozöos* 1: 255–7.

Lott, D. F. (1992), 'Lens Length Predicts Mountain Goat Disturbance'. *Anthrozöos* 5: 254–5.

Lott, D. F. and M. McCoy (1993), 'Tourist Impact on Asian Rhinos', *International Society for Anthrozoology* (abstract).

MacCannell, D. ([1976]1999), *The Tourist: A New Theory of the Leisure Class.* Berkeley: University of California Press.

MacCannell, D. (1992), *Empty Meeting Grounds: The Tourist Papers.* London: Routledge.

Shelton, J. (2001), 'The Display of Elephants in Ancient Roman Arenas'. *ISAZ Newsletter* 21: 2–6.

Singh, S., D. J. Timothy and R. K. Dowling (2003), *Tourism in Destination Communities.* Wallingford: CABI Publishing.

Spinage, E. (1994), *Elephants.* London: T. and A. D. Poyser Natural History, Limited.

Sukumar, R. (1994), *Elephant Days and Nights: Ten Years with the Indian Elephant.* Oxford: Oxford University Press.

Tuan, Y.-F. (1984), *Dominance and Affection: The Making of Pets.* New Haven: Yale University Press.

Williams, H. (1989), *Sacred Elephant.* New York: Harmony Books.

# –9–

# Loving Leviathan: The Discourse of Whale-watching in Australian Ecotourism

## *Adrian Peace*

It is a commonplace that whales and whaling have together become the object of intense and complex emotions in Western society. The fact that this has been the case for at least a couple of decades has been examined in a wide range of litera-ture for lay audiences, and social anthropologists too have made some contribution to explaining how this has come about. Popular films, nature programmes, coffee table volumes and mass media coverage generally (Day 1992; Rose 1989) have all been held to play a significant part in generating strong emotions where whales and whaling are concerned. From an anthropological vantage point, Kalland (1992, 1993a, 1993b) has argued in several places that the more prominent environmental organizations in the West (Greenpeace International especially) have constructed the 'super whale', a symbolic ensemble which they have extensively manipulated in their efforts to bring virtually all whaling to an end. Kalland writes: 'Environmental and animal rights groups have skilfully played on our susceptibility towards whales and created the image of a "super whale" by lumping together traits found in a number of species, thereby masking the great variety that exists in size, behaviour and abundance among the 75 or so species of cetaceans' (1993a: 4).

In this chapter, I want to show how whale-watching in an Australian context is also geared to exploiting this broadly based susceptibility to whales, most espe-cially through a richly embellished anthropomorphic discourse. Anthropologists (e.g. Ingold 1997) and other social scientists (e.g. Evernden 1992; Katz 1997) fre-quently query or lament Western anthropomorphism, but its specific qualities are rarely detailed; so this is one goal for what follows. It involves unpacking in some detail the speech acts (Hymes 1986) of professional skippers and guides on whale-watch vessels. In total I will here draw on the details of half-a-dozen day long trips, and it is appropriate to emphasize at the outset that, whilst it is select and common features with which I am concerned at present, each skipper's individual perform-ance also differs markedly on other counts from those of his peers and rivals.

By way of conclusion, I will briefly indicate some of the costs which result from this profoundly skewed way of talking about whales and other sea creatures. My main concern, however, is to show how the production of emotion in the course of whale-watching is achieved through precisely the reverse discursive process to that itemized by Kalland. Whereas the super whale is constituted through the erasure of differences between whale species, in the course of whale-watching the discourse frequently and distinctively moves from the general to the particular, to the point at which quite specific human qualities are attributed to individual whales with which skippers and guides claim some familiarity.[1]

### 'Worth More to Us Alive than Dead'

Ever since the closure of the country's last whaling station at Albany on the west coast in 1978, Australia has been a significant player in the constitution of a global discourse about whales and whale-watching. The institutional contribution has been varied, ranging from the substantial Federal resources committed to the International Whaling Commission (IWC), through the work of diverse environmental non-governmental organizations (ENGOs), to financial investments made by regional state and private enterprises. Diversity has also been the order of the day in policy terms with some authorities urging the setting up of whale sanctuaries in territorial waters and further afield, some looking to phase out most commercial whaling whilst allocating quotas to designated aboriginal communities, and yet others demanding a complete ban on whaling whatever its provenance.

Setting aside the fact that by the late 1970s whaling was an insignificant part of the national economy, the commitment which Australia has shown to promoting a protective regime for whales in the southern hemisphere has been striking. It has to be explained in substantial part by reference to the country's ongoing assessment of its own status within the modern world order over the past twenty years or so. For being at the forefront of the international campaign over whales and whaling has been part and parcel of Australia's still ongoing attempt to constitute itself as a civilized and cultivated place in the world, thus consistently distinguishing itself from the frequently illiberal and conflict-ridden South-East Asian region of which it is an often much-qualified part.

Time and again, what have often proved to be extremely costly measures of caring for whales have been justified on the grounds that this is what civilized people do in the late twentieth century, and no doubt through into the twenty-first century as well. Taking this high moral ground generates its own problems in a highly integrated global economy. In that Australia's chief trading partner is also the most prominent practitioner of what is, by prevalent definition, a quite barbaric practice, considerable linguistic agility is required in political circles to avoid giving offence. Not only do diplomatic niceties occasionally escape government officials but also other strident voices, the more popular tabloid newspapers and magazines for example, are notably less restrained. There is no question but that a racist dimension (McGuinness 1994 Peace n.d.) runs through many of the attacks on the continuation of Japanese whaling. Be that as it may, Australia's international stance on the conservation of whales has become both internally and externally a regularly cited indicator of its cultural status as a civilized place and a morally responsible member of the global community.

Relatively recently, this commitment has taken a substantial step forward as whale-watching has been incorporated into the hugely important Australian tourist industry. But in addition to whale-watching becoming one of the fastest growing components of that industry over the past decade – it is said to be already worth over $10 million per annum – it is also a form of economic development which has received open plaudits from a wide range of powerful institutions. Some of the recurrent words and phrases applied to whale-watching have been 'rational', 'logical', 'forward looking' and 'intelligent', and these labels of unqualified approval have emanated from government circles, IWC representatives, the spokespersons from ENGOs, as well as state authorities and private industry. It is difficult to recall any other type of development which has generated such an unqualified consensus.

Above all, however, whale-watching has achieved considerable public promi-nence over the last decade or so because it resonates so effectively, not only with the image of Australia as a civilized society but also as a continent distinguished by an exceptional environment which can be exploited for tourist purposes yet kept fully intact and properly protected at the same time. The mantra of sustainability has been sung long and hard throughout the 1990s across this purportedly envi-ronmentally conscious country. Claims about sustainable development play espe-cially well in a society which is demographically small and globally peripheral, and so has to become and remain, as one previous prime minister memorably dubbed it, 'the clever country'. Whale-watching has become part and parcel of this ideological emphasis on the intelligent use of natural resources. Its outstanding merit is summarized in the technical claim that it involves 'the non-consumptive use of cetaceans', or, put more prosaically, that 'whales are worth more to us alive than dead'.

Both of these phrases are frequently encountered in the rhetorical pronounce-ments of economic and political policy-makers. Their significance is rooted in the common recognition that contemporary consumption almost inevitably involves the physical destruction of the natural resource involved. To use, to consume, is to physically destroy – and that for the most part is an end to the matter. Accordingly, the great merit of whale-watching is that its raw resource remains untouched and intact. It remains perpetually recyclable, as it were, and this is why, more tellingly still, the rhetorical possibilities have been seized upon to hold up whale-watching as a shining example of how the country can 'rationally', 'intelligently', and so forth, utilize its environmental resources for economic development and, indeed, social progress.[2] It is what the management of natural resources in the post-industrial era should be all about. Whale-watching is seen as sustainable development exemplified.

From an anthropological perspective, of course, this notion of consumption is too narrow by half. Most important for current purposes, it belies the fact that whale-watching involves the extensive consumption of the symbolism or the totemism of the whale, and it is the specifics of the way this is done that are most significant. Phrases like the 'non-consumptive use of cetaceans' can prove quite misleading in failing to acknowledge (as Baudrillard and others would insist) the multi-faceted nature of most, if not all, forms of consumption in late capitalist society. They can effectively disguise the fact that there are substantial costs involved in the non-physical modes of consumption which have proliferated so extensively in the late capitalist epoch (see Appadurai 1986; Moeran 1992). It is these costs which will be addressed by way of conclusion. For the moment what is required is to draw out and detail the anthropocentric threads which run through and connect together the different, discursive contributions which aim to encourage and inform the apparently common experience of watching whales.

## Anthropomorphism in Action

Hervey Bay, a small town on the south-central coastline of Queensland, is billed as 'the whale-watch capital of Australia', and there is considerable justification for this. Substantial numbers of whales – some claim as many as 3,000, the majority of which originate in Antarctica – migrate from the south in the summer months and breed in the warmer waters north of Hervey Bay, before returning to Antarctic waters once again. One result of this vast annual migration is the strong likelihood that a whale-watch boat will deliver the goods daily during the season, to the extent that tourists are generally guaranteed a 'free trip' if their initial attempt proves unsuccessful.

The more important upshot of this predictability is that the typical whale-watch tour can be highly orchestrated, and to achieve maximum impact this means its being carried off in culturally specific ways. It is organized visually and linguistically to theatrically climax in the encounter with a pod of whales, a dramatic accomplishment which is substantially dependent on the way the universe of cetaceans is talked about by boat skippers and guides on the fifteen licensed vessels operating from the large and modern Hervey Bay marina.

The initial point to emphasize is the extent to which the symbol of the whale is commodified in this location. A commercial mall comprising tour companies, souvenir shops, and drink and fast-food outlets, is the sole point of entry for all visitors to the marina. Assailed by continuous-play videos of whales in spectacular

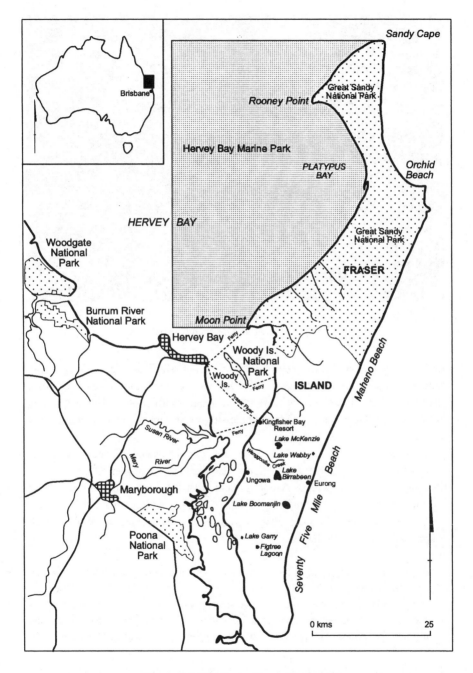

**Figure 9.1** The Fraser Coast, Queensland.

**Figure 9.2** A Whale-watching Boat.

action sequences, and surrounded by whale songs from hidden speakers, it is possible to buy jewellery, clothing, coffee mugs, welcome mats, pens, posters, books, T-shirts, and much else besides bearing some whale motif or other. The peak to this parade of kitsch is a huge (and hugely garish) polystyrene model of a whale hung in the marina waters directly below the mall.

The second point is that in this same milieu the visitor directly accesses dozens of brochures and pamphlets in which is inscribed the anthropomorphic mode of thinking which will be extensively elaborated in the course of the tour. These inscriptions are the tour's chief stage-setting devices, and their discursive detail is epitomized in the following extract from the brochure for a 'Whale-watch Experience' on the MV Islander:

> Hervey Bay is recognized as the best area in the world to see the humpback whales. They are taking a break in the southern migration from their Barrier Reef breeding grounds, so they are not in a hurry. The most energetic of all whales, they put on incredible displays, often hurling their 40 tonne bodies right out of the water, waving and slapping the surface with their huge tails and flippers and performing their barrel rolls.

Evidently, the underlying metaphor here is that of the circus where animals also 'put on incredible displays' for the entertainment of a paying audience. But the significant feature is the way the whales begin to be metaphorically presented as complexly sentient creatures, 'taking a break', 'not in a hurry', 'hurling their bodies', 'slapping the surface', and so on.

In the brochure for a 'Whale-watch Safari' – the concept of the safari being another revealing appropriation – on the MV Mikat, the element which is added is the prospect of this sentience being the basis for social relations eventuating between whales and watchers:

> There are more whales to see and more behaviour patterns to enjoy. Breaching, spy-hopping, tail and pec-slapping, and the very popular 'socializing', when some animals become as inquisitive about us as we are about these gentle giants from Antarctica ... *Socialising with whales!* ... Seldom in a lifetime is anyone offered an opportunity to come face-to-face with the fifth largest animal that has ever lived on this planet. The most playful of the big whales and the most acrobatic ... but also the most gentlest [*sic*] as they approach our vessel in a gesture of friendship and trust (emphasis in the original).

So even before one gets on board a boat, the prospect of social relationships being established with the whales is being held out. As boats depart from the marina, the largest provide slide shows below deck in order to fulfil the 'educational function' which is a recurrent part of whale-watch advertising. This is an important advertising pitch: it is possible to be entertained by and educated about 'the marine environment' at one and the same time; and these shows are generally well attended. Conducted by younger crew members dressed in ranger outfits, maps, slides, photographs and posters are deployed to establish the differences between whale species, their migratory patterns, their eating and procreation habits, and so on. None of this goes further than the kind of elementary information routinely available in magazine articles. What is notable about them, though, is their concentration on the physical properties of whales *tout court* – this at the manifest expense of situating them in the intricate and changing regional ecology, both in relation to other sea creatures or to the human populations which have exploited them by different means over time.

Out of the public gaze, various reasons are given by skippers and guides for not addressing at length the past or ongoing killing of whales. One reason is that the whale-watch tour is a leisure experience and 'people don't want to talk about that kind of heavy stuff when they're on holiday'. Another, and likely more important one, is that skippers are exceedingly careful to avoid giving offence to Japanese visitors who comprise a substantial proportion of the tourist population in this part of Australia; and 'you can never tell which of them (i.e. holiday-makers of Asian appearance) are ours (i.e. born in Australia) and which are foreigners'. Whatever the rationale, however, the result is a distinctly non-environmentalist aspect to this unfolding discourse. The impact of humans, past and present, in constituting this historically transformed and still dynamically developing ecological niche is quite systematically understated.

This feature is further compounded in the otherwise entertaining patter of the skipper. It is most immediately evident from the outset in the way a hierarchy of cetaceans is articulated in terms of their presumed sociability. The cetaceans are accorded different degrees of human sensibility, as in the following commentary from one of Hervey Bay's most prominent boat owners when only about fifteen minutes out to sea:

> I'm just going to slow down a bit because we're at the edge of the reef where there's often a group of dolphins which are pretty co-operative and ready to come to play under our bows ... [at which point, as if on cue, half a dozen dolphins appear to starboard] ... They're really friendly these guys. They are bottle-noseds [i.e. bottle-nosed dolphins] and ... they'll always play with us. The others [i.e. other species of dolphin] are always grazing so they'll never get interested in us.

This commentary has been prefaced by speculation about the reasonable prospects for encountering whales close up on this early season trip by contrast with the distinct improbability of encountering dugongs in Platypus Bay, which lies between the Hervey Bay settlement and Fraser Island, one of Australia's leading eco-tourist destinations. After warning that dugongs 'aren't all that much sociable anyway', what the skipper had established was: 'We can pretty much rule out dugongs today because it's choppy and when it's choppy they don't get interactive with the boat.'

So what is being constituted here is a ranking of different cetaceans in terms of their exhibiting 'recognizable' human traits and human characteristics. At other times, comparisons are further established between different species of whale (as is the case with dolphins in the preceding quotation) according to the extent of their sociability, and thus their purported talents for relating to people. On another boat at this stage, the skipper talked at some length about the merits of whale-watching in this particular region because of the frequency of humpbacked whales: 'The thing about humpbacks is that they like being seen, and they like to see people as well. They're kind of people-oriented. They're much better that way than the whales you get down in Tassie [Tasmania] where they aren't interested in people at all.'

The chief purpose of these commentaries is to set the stage properly for the encounter with either single whales or a pod of them, a prospect which all on board are encouraged to facilitate. All whale-watching out of Hervey Bay is presented as a predominantly visual experience (even on the boats, videotapes of whales in spectacular 'action sequences' are constantly played in observation lounges), and in the run up to the first encounter everyone is put on watch: 'lots of pairs of eyes are better than a few, there's a lot of water out there'.

Invariably it is the skipper or another crew member who makes the first siting, but this is often announced as the result of a co-operative effort. On the trip mainly referred to above, the skipper quietly announced: 'And look what we've found!

Your patience has been rewarded. We have to slow down now and play patience some more [with the whale].' And at this point, as is quite customary, the anthropomorphic emphasis became all the more intense as the skipper entered into a sustained translation of the meaning of whale conduct into human behavioural terms. This is how the skipper or the guide generally functions from this point onwards: the organization of whale pods and the performance of individual creatures are consistently and expansively talked through in terms of their being variations on what is assumed to be characteristic human conduct.

## Establishing Meanings and Identifying Individuals

In the case of a whale pod, the terminology most recurrently deployed is that of 'caring', 'mothering', 'connecting', 'loving', and so on, in order to privilege the relation between a female and her offspring. Male whales are generally cast in the role of 'macho' defender of their variously vulnerable dependants, so that on one occasion a large male situated about a kilometre from the female and one offspring was described as 'riding shotgun on them', prepared to ward off any other humpback in the vicinity and eventually looking 'to protect his family against killer whales' as the pod returned to Antarctica.

Only an extended extract can capture how marked this anthropomorphism is. This one is taken from a trip which encountered a sole male after about 75 minutes 'scouting' at the northern end of Platypus Bay. The whale had lived up to the expectations carefully contrived previously by engaging in what is usually described (see p. 197) as 'tail and pec-slapping'. Most of the thirty-five people on board had been shifting back and forth to get a good view, but this was followed by a lengthy respite as the whale disappeared below the surface:

The period they're underneath is called 'downtime' so it may be half an hour before he comes up again. The whale moves very much as an individual so we have to be patient. They're very much individuals, these Leviathans, you can't really predict ... [at which point the whale surfaces again to many loud cheers; timing is all at this stage] ... Here comes the fluke as he goes for a deep dive, it's a bit like us kicking our legs out of the water before we go for a dive under, so now he's busy down there, we won't see him for some time. [This proves to be accurate, and the skipper fills in the time by recalling with evident pleasure how intensely sociable this whale and its 'partner' were the previous year. Then the whale breaches once more.] This is a really, really good whale, because he's close in and headed south ... which suits us just fine. His tail is very clean so you can recognise him but that's unusual. With a lot of them, they have scars because they're hunted by killer whales which catch the pectoral fin. The pectoral is very sensitive which is why you get older ones and babies touching each other there.

[For over 15 minutes little is said, until the whale begins to move southwards with the boat in close attendance.] One of the advantages of Hervey Bay is that they're relaxing here rather than migrating ... But when it's like this, although he might just take off away, at other times they'll be all over you. Just now, he's just motoring along which is fantastic. It's pretty obvious this guy's steaming to the end of the bay which suits us fine. He certainly knows where he's going. But we'll give him a bit of room because it's possible that when he was slapping back there, he was warning off the boat ... This guy's pretty aloof, but sometimes we have incredible interaction, you wouldn't believe the intensity. [The whale now surfaces and breaches splendidly.] He seems to be putting on a bit of a show for us before we go home. He might feel threatened by two boats, but I don't think so. He wouldn't have presented his tail to us like that if he felt threatened. We'll pull away now anyway ...

There are several points to extract from this much-abbreviated commentary, the first being how at this climactic stage the skipper enlarges on his role as interlocutor between the whale and its observers. On a number of counts, he provides a definitive interpretation on what the whale is 'really up to', what is 'really going on'. Inasmuch as the whale spends a good deal of time below the surface, or seemingly idling on it, so the skipper marshals all his interpretive skills in order to extract the significance with which his clients might effectively identify. Even when an elementary physiological point is made (for example, about the pectoral fin), he slips with ease into the attribution of human qualities.

One of the conversational gambits often deployed is to identify an area of uncertainty or ambiguity in the whale's conduct, to weigh up the different interpretive possibilities, and then to plumb for one over the rest. This acknowledgement of interpretive latitude makes the skipper's final comprehension all the more impressive and somehow plausible. In this instance, the skipper himself proposes that the whale's surface slapping might indicate a sense of being threatened now that a second vessel has joined his own: it was clearly not a suggestion already in the minds of the watchers; but it was the skipper too who finally set that possibility to one side whilst nevertheless manoeuvring his boat some distance away.

The second feature is the proliferation at this later stage of social attributes and social qualities which are accorded to the whale. It can take on the character of an anthropomorphic avalanche as the whale assumes the status of a fully sentient, even socially complex, being – including here the prospect of 'the whale being all over you'. In the initial instance, modest parallels with humans are proposed: the whale's deep dive is 'like us kicking out our legs'. But this is followed by much stronger claims as the whale assumes a range of human attributes, from having direction, motivation and purpose, as in 'motoring and steaming along', through to the public display of markedly human sentiments, as in the sense of 'feeling threatened' – as would, naturally enough, any other sentient creature being crowded in on his own territory by unwarranted intruders.

Lastly, and most important in light of this escalating attribution of human qualities, the skipper also opens up the prospect of a meaningful social encounter. It now becomes possible to conceive of whales and those who are observing them as mutually and emotionally responding to one another. The essential ingredients are, so to speak, all present in light of the narrative threads woven by the interpreting, mediating skipper. What is required is the right catalyst or the appropriate chemistry, so imperative to any social encounter taking off and assuming significance on both sides.

In this instance, the prospect was only modestly realized, as the skipper explicitly acknowledges. On the one hand, he generalizes from past experience about the possibility of 'incredible interaction ... you wouldn't believe the intensity'. But on the other, he produces an explanation as to why something akin to that now fails to eventuate; it is to be found in the whale's individual personality. 'This guy's pretty aloof', he opines, and all present can well appreciate the difficulties of properly engaging with something/someone who is 'aloof'. Having articulated an elaborate anthropomorphism to indicate the promise which the encounter generally holds out, the same register of interpretation is sustained to explain why it does not now specifically eventuate; it lies in the psychological make up of this particular Leviathan.

A couple of days later on the same vessel, a different set of circumstances appropriately emphasized that chance factors continue to play a significant part in the final outcome of a whale tour. On this occasion, the boat encountered a female humpback whale accompanied by one offspring with a couple of males of quite different size standing off at some distance. The changing positions of the two males – changes which were quite impossible to see with an unpractised eye – were translated by the skipper into a narrative of 'male rivalry'. He explained that the larger, older Leviathan was in the process of being driven off by a younger, virile upstart which was, in true Darwinian style, better equipped to protect the pod as it undertook 'that hazardous journey southwards ... It's the survival of the species and all that. That's what we're seeing out there in action.' For about twenty minutes, the behaviour of the two males was the subject of intermittent speculation on much the same lines: 'the old one's tired, he's got no fight left in him, you can see that by his sluggish movements. But the young fellar, he's getting agitated, he's ready for a bit of a fight, I reckon, if the other [one] doesn't recognize that his time's up and pull away.'

The skipper then shifted quite seamlessly into an account of how very similar the social organization of a large pod of whales is to an extended human family – for him, apparently, an unequivocally co-operative and unceasingly caring social unit – at which point the female humpback and her offspring swam right up to the boat, no more than 3 or 4 metres from the thirty-four tourists on board. Many of these became quite conspicuously emotional as the distance between themselves and the whales narrowed. The skipper immediately cut the engine for 'fear of scaring them off', and the boat began to roll as the two whales circled close round it, at times only a metre or so from the vessel's hull:

It doesn't get much better than this folks, you've just been mugged by a humpback, so it's a pretty unique experience for all of us ... Next time they come up, make a lot of noise, plenty of noisy 'hellos', because their hearing is good, their sight is good, so why not? They're as interested in us as we are in them, so make plenty of noise to attract their attention. [At this, the whales surface immediately alongside the boat, and most people do exactly as instructed – calling, whistling, shouting, clapping, in some cases very loudly.] So they're getting interested in you again, so you've got to show them that you're really interested in them. You really love them, right? [Whereupon some shout back: Yeh right!] Now's the time to act like real clowns, let your hair down, you can make real idiots of yourselves, and they'll show they're interested back in us. [Except for a couple of older people who remain seated, everyone continues to rush from starboard to port, and then from stern to bow, to get the best view.]

[As the whales circle the boat and disappear beneath it, virtually everyone shouts and claps, especially as the mature whale rolls on the surface exposing her white belly, and then swoops underneath the boat to the other side, with the juvenile in close attendance.] ... This is really exceptional, usually mum tries to shepherd her baby away from the boat because she wants to be cautious, cautious about the danger, but this one doesn't seem to mind at all. She seems to be encouraging the baby to take an interest in the boat. So this is really very special folks, even for us [i.e. the whale-watch crew], this is special.

For many people on the tour, this was beyond question a highly emotional experience: expressions of joy, amazement, delight, and even a few tears were evident on all sides.[3] As I talked with some in the group on the long return trip to Hervey Bay, they were content to summarize the experience in just a word or two: 'wonderful', 'just awesome', 'out of this world', 'really, really moving', 'the most exciting experience imaginable', and so on. What was striking about more extended comments, however, was the way they followed the skipper's example in talking of members of the pod as having not just distinctive physical markings but also personality characteristics as well, just like humans. In other words, by this stage the cetaceans had been effectively made to take on individual identities.

The skipper had begun this on the previous occasion by reference to the 'aloof' nature of the sole male. But on this one, which proved to be more emotionally intense all round, the description of the whales as individuals was far more pronounced. From the rivalry between the two males through to the conduct of the female, particular traits and specified attributes were made explicit in order to differentiate these creatures from one another. The most conspicuous case was the mother who was, by the skipper's account, not just caring, affectionate, and loving towards her offspring, but was also variously described as curious, intelligent, nosy, and accommodating. Above all, she was depicted as setting aside her 'natural caution' in favour of 'encouraging her baby' to relate to, even connect with, those on the boat in whom she had an evident 'trust'.

On the return trip to the marina, several people talked to me in terms similar to this, one of whom was a middle-aged housewife and divorcee from Sydney, in the company of her two small children, who explained what had 'really moved' her in the following way:

> I thought that was just fantastic because I could really relate to the mother, I could really feel for her. What was incredible about it – y'know, it was like [the skipper] said – was that she trusted the little one with us. Despite everything we've done to the whales, all that time of killing them, slaughtering them to the point of extinction and all that, she didn't seem to be afraid of us at all. To me, I mean, that's just incredible. We can't even trust each other nowadays to that extent.

Another, somewhat younger woman travelling alone with whom the first had struck up a friendship during the course of the trip, expressed her reaction like this:

> It's like, y'know, they've got all these qualities that we've kind of lost on the way through. They're all devoted to one another, and they're caring, so that if one gets into trouble, apparently the rest go in to help out. With us nowadays, it's everybody for himself, isn't it, a real cut-throat world, so I reckon we have a lot to learn from the whales. But that's probably – how do we put it? – [*my prompt* : 'sort of wishful thinking?'] yeh, that's it, just wishful thinking, which makes it real sad. Still that was a wonderful experience, wasn't it just? It was really, really moving, the best thing. I wouldn't have missed it for quids, no way.

## Whale-watching and Myth-making

The first point I want to extract from these commentaries is the critical one that the meanings which derive from the common experience of whale-watching are varied. There are some which I have not recorded – at least not yet, for this chapter presents ongoing work – for example, the 'cult-like seances' mentioned by Kalland (1992: 28). But for some people the whale-watch tour constitutes the realization of a long-held ambition extensively fuelled by nature programmes, films and other simulations; usually the experience far exceeds individual expectations. With other visitors, the Queensland experience is to be added to and compared with whale-watch trips elsewhere in Australia or overseas, including locations along the west coast of North America. Alternatively, these trips onto the ocean are often compared most favourably with visits to Sea World-type contexts (see Davis 1997; Desmond 1995) which are considered – if only in retrospect – quite inauthentic and unsatisfactory.

Whale-watching is, of course, most often undertaken in family groups, and parents talk of inculcating a sense of respect and responsibility for animals, attitudes which they consider distinctly lacking in their own generation. There are whale-watchers for whom taking a trip is an act of redemption for past slaughter. For rather more, the trip is itself part of the conservation effort: since ENGOs allow no active role for lay people other than the handing over of subscriptions, to go on a whale tour can express one's disassociation from the past and an identification with current conservation policy. Finally, by no means least, and as is the case with both women quoted above, the experience of watching whales generates private reflections on the quality of everyday life, especially its highly competitive, self-centred and morally unimpressive aspects. The idealistically constructed world of whales throws into even sharper relief the harshly experienced world of ordinary folk.

Having emphasized these variations in meaning, it is important to balance the account by underscoring the persistence and pervasiveness of the anthropocentric mentality articulated by skippers and guides alike. It is, of course, quite possible – although in my experience thus far, quite rare – that tour clients have misgivings about how readily the behaviour of whales is translated into human terms. What has to be added here, though, is that the same or somewhat similar anthropocentric emphases are readily detected in many other sources: whale conduct is widely interpreted on just the same lines in popular films and nature documentaries.[4] Furthermore, skippers and guides generally appear as experienced and assured figures who have been around this area for many years and claim intimate acquaintance with it.

Under the circumstances, there is no ostensible reason for doubting their interpretive expertise, and this includes the ways in which they make sense of what is for most of their clients a wholly novel experience, an encounter with nature at sea that has no precedent. Indeed this points to an important difference between the more commonly experienced visit to a zoo and the whale-watch trip. As John Berger (1980) points out, the zoo is an expression of our collective distance from nature: by bringing its animals into physical proximity, we confirm our enormous separation from them; yet in the artificial setting of the zoo, where captive animals are conspicuously listless, there is relatively little left to explain. By contrast, the real significance of whale-watching lies precisely in its involving penetration, even an invasion, of their natural environment. That makes the role of the experienced guide all the more necessary and the more authoritative. Again, there is rather little warrant for believing that the terms and the framework which the guide deploys might be at all questionable.

It is precisely on this count that the unfolding, developing character of the anthropocentric discourse is important, especially in the generation of emotional response. The extent to which the discourse of whale-watching in this setting is the reverse of the process which Kalland specifies behind the construction of the super whale should be quite clear by this juncture. Whilst in the case of the latter even differences between species are obliterated, in the case of the former it is differences between individual whales which are finally constituted and embellished. The discursive trajectory is from degrees of sociability between cetaceans in general to the identities of whales in particular.

To this extent, the whale-watch trip peaks, so to speak, in such a way that observers can identify with particular whales and experience a variety of emotions. It is not just a matter finally of the whales being generally 'like us': it is rather that 'he' or 'she' is specifically like 'you' or 'me'. I am not of course suggesting that those who embark on whale-watch tours come to identify fully with individual whales. The important point is rather that the whale-watcher is led and encouraged by this anthropocentric discourse to think of these creatures as having individual characteristics and specific identities in quite the same way that human populations are internally differentiated; and it is clearly at that point that the strongest emotions are generated.

In certain respects of course, the whale-watch tour stands as testament to the ocularcentric quality of Western culture: it is part of the visual obsession with which the 'spectacularization of nature' (Macnaghten and Urry 1998) proceeds apace; it is imperative to see that the whale is saved, conserved and protected rather than being simply satisfied by the assurances of others. That said, the most telling quality of the whale-watch trip as an orchestrated performance is that it peaks visually and linguistically once the whale pod is finally joined in its natural habitat. The paradox is that it is precisely at that point of visual contact that the linguistic emphasis is on how very similar whale society is to our own, how closely the individual attributes of whales match the differences we recognize and celebrate amongst ourselves.

This anthropocentrism is clearly integral above all to the whale-watch tour as popular entertainment. Its educational value cannot be easily dismissed, but it is assuredly of limited consequence by comparison with the stress on entertainment. Similarly, inasmuch as ENGOs assuredly relegate lay people to mere revenue sources, it is important that such tours represent to increasingly large numbers of people the critical point that whale populations are 'worth more to us alive than dead', that this is a truly 'non-consumptive use of cetaceans'.

On the other hand, it is equally the case that costs are involved in encouraging people to consume the symbolic, iconic properties of whales in this way. This anthropocentric discourse has distinctly problematic aspects to it, and the first is that implicit within this discourse is the idea that whales are worthy of exceptional conservation efforts precisely because they are so like us. As mentioned at the outset, the spelling out of a hierarchy of cetaceans in terms of their human-like sociability is an integral element of the discourse in its opening phase; but that hierarchy is extensively fleshed out in the course of the typical tour. Throughout it is implicitly understood that the whales above all other cetaceans, and indeed most other animals, are worth saving because of their similarity to ourselves, and thus no expense is to be spared in conservation efforts devoted to them. But it is difficult to imagine, in effect, an assumption which runs more contrary to an environmentalist position than this, shot through as it is with the belief that human populations and their qualities are what determines the worth and the value of everything else on the planet.

The second difficulty is that this relentless attribution of human qualities necessarily separates – and indeed extracts – the whales from the complex ecological systems of which they are an integral part. As was previously indicated, the whales under observation in the Hervey Bay location are, in the main, part of a huge migration from Antarctica: they move through and contribute to an exceptionally complex and significantly changing ecological system before arriving north of Hervey Bay and then commencing the return journey. But in that it is their superficial similarities to human populations which is focused upon in whale tour discourse, this has the inevitable consequence of leaving quite unexplored the place of the whale population in this vast macro-ecology, a system which is itself in the process of significant transformation due to global meteorological changes. Crudely put, a sustained concern with how 'similar' whales are to humans renders impossible the informed comprehension of their place in the ecological system of the southern hemisphere; and that may be a high price to pay for an afternoon's entertainment.

The third problem is that consumption of the whale as icon under these circumstances essentially serves to reinforce the pattern of overconsumption in Western societies which lies at the core of global environmental crisis in the first place. The phrasing of the claim that 'the whales are worth more to us alive than dead' in a sense encapsulates the central difficulty here: the whales are still being evaluated *in terms of their worth to us, and no other value*. It is still the significance and the scale of our own consumption patterns which exert full sway: it is still our own volition to consume which is accorded priority; and this means the reproduction, if not indeed a deepening, of the arrogance and the hubris which has underpinned ruthless exploitation of global resources to the point of ecological collapse.[5]

Naturally it is preferable that animals that were killed to the point of extinction are now conserved: of course it is proper that forests which were cut down without limit are now left alone, even that they are 'harvested'; and obviously the move towards solar and wind-powered energy so that fossil fuels might eventually be left in the ground is to be welcomed. But none of these and many other significant changes will be of lasting benefit if it continues to be assumed that these 'natural resources' are of worth and of value exclusively in terms of our own determination, and no other. This is where the whale-watch tour continues to be as emblematic of mankind's early twenty-first century hubris as whale slaughter was expressive of its arrogance in the twentieth century. It is taken for granted that the worth of whales is to be determined according to our consumption-fixated world-view alone, and that may constitute a matter of much greater concern than how superficially similar their behaviour is to ours.

## Acknowledgements

The research for this chapter has been funded by minor Australian Research Council grants from the University of Adelaide to myself and Peter Mühlhäusler. I am obliged to my colleague for the many conversations we have had on the language of eco-tourism and related linguistic issues, both on and off Fraser Island. I am similarly grateful for comments made by other members of the Kraków seminar on an earlier draft of this chapter.

## Notes

1. Previous accounts of whale watching include Kalland (1992), Ris (1991), and Spong (1992), whilst local and regional responses to whales and whale symbolism (both in the context of Iceland) come from Einarsson (1993, 1996) and Bryden (1990, 1996).
2. See, for example, the contribution from Bridgewater and Anderson (1993). By the mid-1990s, Bridgewater was Australia's representative on the IWC and also director of the Federal Environment Department's Australian nature conservancy agency.
3. Having said that, such expressions of emotion are positively downbeat by comparison with those generated by whale beachings which are relatively frequent in some parts of the Australian coastline. Consider, for example, the following extract from Micheli (1992) headed 'Deliverance: touched by the plight of beached whales, hundreds of rescuers rallied to send them to sea':

   Some rescuers, like Susan Clarke, 40, a former registered nurse from nearby Bulahdelah, 'adopted' individual whales and became their ferocious protectors. 'You're a really good boy,' Clarke cooed, gently stroking the whale she named Hope, as it took a gasping breath from its blowhole. 'Hang in there. You'll be in the water soon.' Another young woman, Chris, from Forster, 40km to the north, tended a calf and its mother who watched every move with one huge eye. 'I have a 2–year-old,' said Chris, tears welling in her eyes,' and I just felt for the mother. I told her, 'Don't worry I'll take good care of your baby.'

   The importance of emotion in environmental issues has been most recently explored in detail by Milton (2002).
4. Although by no means in the same optimistic register as is now characteristic of whale watching. In a chapter on environmental narratives, Harré *et al.* write that tragic storylines are extensively informed by anthropomorphic emphases:

The tragic story line, for example, as it appears in narratives concerning the blue whales, is not only bleak but involves another literary device, anthropomorphism. Green cartoons depict whales with human faces. In writings about dolphins, we note the use of expressions like 'mother and baby' rather than 'cow' and 'calf'. In some texts 'seal pup' gives way to 'baby seal'. Framed in the dimensions of humanoid narration, the destruction of the blue whale is not just a disaster but takes on the color of a tragedy. (1999: 80)

Anthropomorphism is by no means restricted to whales in the Hervey Bay–Fraser Island region. Dingoes are another important case in point. See Peace (2002).

5. Escobar makes the general point well here when he writes:

Although ecologists and ecodevelopmentalists recognize environmental limits to production, a large number do not perceive the cultural character of the commercialization of nature and life integral to the Western economy ... It is not surprising that their policies are restricted to promoting the 'rational' management of resources. Environmentalists who accept this proposition also accept imperatives for capital accumulation, material growth, and the disciplining of labor and nature. (1996: 53)

# References

Appadurai, A. (1986), 'Introduction: Commodities and the Politics of Value', in A. Appadurai (ed.), *The Social Life of Things: Commodities in Cultural Perspective*. Cambridge: Cambridge University Press.

Berger, J. (1980), 'Why Look at Animals?', in J. Berger, *On Looking*. New York: Pantheon.

Bridgewater, P. and G. Anderson (1993), 'Whales or Whalers?' *Search* 24(7), August.

Bryden, A. (1990), 'Icelandic Nationalism and the Whaling Issue'. *North Atlantic Studies* 2(1): 185–91.

Bryden, A. (1996), 'Whale-siting: Spatiality in Icelandic Nationalism', in G. Pàlsson and P. Durrenberger (eds), *Images of Contemporary Iceland: Everyday Lives in Global Contexts*. Iowa City: University of Iowa Press.

Davis, S. (1997), *Spectacular Nature: Corporate Culture and the Sea World Experience*. Berkeley: University of California Press.

Day, D. (1992), *The Whale War*. London: Grafton.

Desmond, J. (1995), 'Performing "Nature": Shamu at Sea World', in S.-E. Case, P. Brett and S. Foster (eds), *Crossing the Performative: Interventions into the Representation of Ethnicity, Nationality and Sexuality*. Bloomington: Indiana University Press.

Einarsson, N. (1993), 'All Animals are Equal but Some are Cetaceans,' in K.

Milton (ed.), *Environmentalism: The View from Anthropology*. London: Routledge.

Einarsson, N. (1996), 'A Sea of Images: Fishers, Whalers, and Environmentalists', in G. Palsson and E. P. Durrenberger (eds), *Images of Contemporary Iceland: Everyday Lives and Global Contexts*. Iowa City: University of Iowa Press.

Escobar, A. (1996), 'Constructing Nature: Elements for a Poststructural Political Ecology', in R. Peet and M. Watts (eds), *Liberation Ecologies: Environment, Development, Social Movements*. London: Routledge.

Evernden, N. (1992), *The Social Creation of Nature*. Baltimore, Md.: Johns Hopkins University Press.

Harré, R., J. Brockmeier and P. Mühlhäusler (1999), *Greenspeak: A Study of Environmental Discourse*. London: Sage.

Hymes, D. (1986), 'Models of the Interaction of Language of Social Life', in J. Gumperz and D. Hymes (eds), *Directions in Sociolinguistics: The Ethnography of Communication*. Oxford: Basil Blackwell.

Ingold, T. (1997), 'Life Beyond the Edge of Nature? Or, the Mirage of Society', in J. D. Greenwood (ed.), *The Mark of the Social: Discovery or Invention?* Lanhan, Md.: Rowman and Littlefield.

Kalland, A. (1992), 'Whose Whale is That? Diverting the Commodity Path'. *Maritime Anthropological Studies* 5(2): 16–45.

Kalland, A. (1993a), 'Whale Politics and Green Legitimacy: A Critique of the Anti-Whaling Campaign'. *Anthropology Today* 9(6): 3–7.

Kalland, A. (1993b), 'Management by Totemization: Whale Symbolism and the Anti-Whaling Campaign'. *Arctic* 46(2): 124–33.

Katz, E. (1997), 'A Pragmatic Reconsideration of Anthropocentrism'. *Environmental Ethics* 21(4): 377–90.

Macnaghten, P. and J. Urry (1998), *Contesting Natures*. London: Sage.

McGuinness, P. (1994), 'Racism Surfaces in the Hug-the-Whale Lobby'. *The Australian*, 18 February.

Micheli, R. (1992), 'Deliverance'. *Who Weekly*, 27 July.

Milton, K. (2002), *Loving Nature: Towards an Ecology of Emotion*. London: Routledge.

Moeran, B. (1992), 'The Cultural Construction of Value: "Subsistence", "Communal", and Other Terms in the Debate about Whaling'. *Maritime Anthropological Studies* 2(2): 105–33.

Peace, A. (2002), 'The Cull of the Wild: Dingoes, Development and Death in an Australian Tourist Location'. *Anthropology Today* 18(5): 14–19.

Peace, A. (n.d.), '"No Cultural Aspect to it ...": Modern Japanese Whaling, the 52nd Congress of the International Whaling Commission, and Australian Cultural Imperialism' (xerox).

Ris, M. (1991), 'Why Look at Whales? Reflections on the Meaning of Whale-watching', in G. Blichfeldt (ed.), *Eleven Essays on Whales and Man*. Reine, Norway: High North Alliance.

Rose, T. (1989), *Freeing the Whales: How the Media Created the World's Greatest Non-Event*. New York: Birch Lane Press.

Spong, P. (1992), 'Why We Love To Watch Whales'. *Sonar* 7: 24–5.

# –10–

# Enchanting Dolphins: An Analysis of Human–Dolphin Encounters

## *Véronique Servais*

## Introduction

In the transnational community focused on dolphins that we consider here, the figure of the dolphin is permeated with love. Not only do people love dolphins, but the dolphins' anthropophilia belongs to their natural history as well: they rescue men at sea, play in the bow waves of boats, and sometimes develop enduring 'friendships' with humans. People who have encountered dolphins in the open sea regularly speak about 'falling in love', or feeling 'pure love' from the dolphin; others report telepathy, trance or mystic revelations. The emotions that people might experience in an encounter with a dolphin are very powerful. Although such experiences are clearly embedded in a cultural context (a system of beliefs, representations, tales and wondrous stories that shape the occidental vision of dolphins), they cannot be fully understood as long as we treat them as merely cultural constructs. Of course animals are socially (or culturally) constructed, but the human–animal interactions cannot be described as the mere imposition of symbolic meaning on meaningless organisms (see Ingold 1988). As ethology has stated many times, animals are active organisms in an environment which is significant for them. Consequently, human animal interactions are always double-sided interactions. In this chapter I attempt to describe human–dolphin encounters as an interspecies communication system that forms the interactional context in which the emotional experiences are to be understood.

## Enchanted Encounters

In occidental countries one can find various private associations devoted not so much to the protection of cetaceans as to the promotion of their 'message': a message of love, peace and harmony. For this purpose, formal meetings such as conferences or cultural events are organized and newsletters published and circulated among members. Many marvellous stories about dolphins are told among members; most of them depict dolphins as deliberately *doing* something (good) to the humans and suggest that dolphins are conscious beings. The following story is recorded by Johan A. Bishop in *The Australian Dolphin and Whale Journal*:

> [A] friend of mine was on a camping trip near Mexico and had decided to try catching a sea bass for dinner. After fishing for two hours with no luck, she gave up and was sitting quietly admiring the sea, when she saw a dolphin leaping and jumping, swimming back and forth very excitedly and chattering. It came closer and closer, and finally drove a big red sea bass right into shore at her feet! Amazed and delighted, she lifted the tired fish from the water, and sent her heartfelt thanks to the dolphin, who went off leaping joyfully.[1]

For the most part, people attending those non-scientific conferences about dolphins are already 'touched by the dolphin's magic' and want to hear more about the dolphin's marvellous qualities. Their expectations are usually fulfilled. Most of the associations devoted to the promotion of the dolphin's messages are, to one degree or another, connected with the New Age spirit. Among the people one encounters at the meetings of these associations are people dreaming of building twenty-first century utopias (places in the world where people and dolphins could live together in peace and harmony), an assorted collection of therapists, meditation teachers, authors expounding theories of dolphins as extra-terrestrial angels, and practitioners of water birth in the presence of dolphins. Sometimes one hears about a new human species (*Homo delphinus*) which is said to be shaped by the growing intimacy of the human–dolphin relationships all over the world. Because of its large brain, the dolphin is figured as 'closer to us' than any other animal; but this animal is also *better* than us: 'While we humans have devoted our creativity to the technological achievements possible when one has chosen thumb over flipper, they have devoted their vast intelligence to the realms of the heart: community, pleasure, play, touch', says the program of the association Delphys (New York) which offers seminars and workshops based on human–dolphin communication. The fin and the thumb: a metaphor for the *hubris* of man (contrasted with the grace of the dolphin) that I have often met in the 'marvellous dolphin' associations. In the occidental bestiary, the dolphin is probably the only animal whose animality is not figured as a regression from humanity but as a progression towards better humans.

From this perspective, dolphins should be our guides towards a better life and an opened consciousness. '[Dolphins] are a message for humanity to show man how peaceful and wise an evolved creature should be', says Laurent Pommes, a young biologist, in a letter addressed to *Dolphin*, the newsletter of International Dolphin Watch.[2] He concludes: '[I]f you really love dolphins you should not hesitate to work to become what they implore you to be: a completely realized being

who resonates with higher dimensions of consciousness.' Hence it is not too surprising to observe that the big meetings of associations like the ICERC[3] sometimes closely resemble religious ceremonies devoted to the glory of the dolphin.
On each page of the programme of one such conference, those attending could
read: 'may the spirit of the dolphin be with you'. Undoubtedly, there is religiosity
here, and the figure of the dolphin is sacred: the dolphin is not 'like any of the other
animals' – dolphins and whales are unique creatures in the animal kingdom.[4] This
brief description of some of the ideas that are bound to the image of the dolphin
in occidental countries shows how constructed and cultural the image of the
dolphin is. But I shall argue that this construction is not an arbitrary cultural imposition of meaning on an animal. On the contrary, it must be related to the interactional context of the human–dolphin encounters and to the emotions that are
reported by the people who have met dolphins.

Many human–dolphin encounters may be read under the rhetoric of revelation.
When they meet a dolphin at sea, people seem to experience something totally
new, something they had heard about but that perhaps they did not dare to believe;
they seem to discover a part of themselves they did not know about. Through the
encounter they learn something about themselves – thus the often-held belief that
dolphins 'deliver messages' to human beings; that they 'speak' to them. Such an
encounter with a dolphin – in which some kind of 'revelation' is experienced – is
what I call an enchanted encounter.[5] Of course not all dolphin encounters are
enchanted. From 1989 to 1993 I have attended many conferences and gatherings
of associations devoted to the promotion of the dolphin's message. There I have
gathered data about human–dolphin encounters. Many were first-hand accounts of
encounters, and many referred to personal transformation following the encounter.
But those data proved hard to analyse. As soon as it was taken for granted that the
testimonies should not be considered as 'mere beliefs' – or, worse, as mere anthropomorphic illusions – a particular conceptual framework had to be constructed to
make sense of them. A modernist (or dualistic) point of view that would try to separate the nature ('real' facts) from the social ('constructions') (see Latour 1997) is
clearly inadequate in the analysis of interaction and communication. It is thus necessary to resist any temptation to separate, from the testimonies, what would be
'real facts' from what would be 'beliefs' or 'illusions'. The temptation might be
hard to resist, because of the supernatural flavour of many accounts and because
they are obviously anthropomorphic interpretations of the animal's behaviour. But
the testimonies must be taken at face value and as true transcriptions of the emotions experienced if they are to be used in an ethnography of the emotions that
people experience in their contact with the animals.

The emotions described must then be related to the broader context of the
human–dolphin encounter in which they appeared. There is no conceptual kit
available for the description of human–animal interaction and communication.

Here I tentatively suggest a three-level description: patterns of interaction, etho-logical signals and representations. Note that in any case, no information about the dolphins themselves will be obtained. This is the approach that I shall use in order to provide an ethnographic description of enchanted human–dolphin encounters. Relating the emotions reported to the broad communicational context in which they occurred will allow us to speak about 'enchantment' without assuming super-natural power or telepathy – that is, without adhering to the specific beliefs that sustain it. This will also allow us to understand the many attributes that dolphins are credited with (consciousness, intentionality, intelligence, healing power, and so on), not as pure cultural constructs but as the products of specific communication and interaction patterns as well.

## An Emotionally Powerful Experience

Many first-hand accounts of 'enchanted' dolphin encounters refer emphatically to love. 'Allowing a dolphin to touch your heart is like falling in love', says Joan Ocean, psychotherapist in New York. 'The experience was one of mutual and unconditional love and trust which perhaps only another intelligent species like the dolphin can provide',[6] explains Jemina Biggs, an anorexic girl who has met the solitary dolphin Dorad.[7] The experience is intimate, moving, and unique. Sometimes people find it difficult to translate their experience in words: 'I experi-enced something that cannot be transcribed on paper', says Scott, who works on a taxi-boat in Hawaii. It is 'the feeling of sitting in a boat surrounded by 40–50 dol-phins of all ages, babies to full grown males, happily laying in our bow wave, stern wake and along side, so close you could touch them'.[8] 'There are no words to explain it', says Hall, when he gets out of the water after a swim with wild dol-phins. 'It is so natural. It's like what you're supposed to do.'

Often the encounter is described as a unique, lifetime experience. 'The grace and flow of the ballet they performed in natural harmony will stay with me until I die', concludes Scott. And even if the contact is not as moving as wished, it is still unforgettable. Paul Spies has had such an experience with the solitary dolphin Fungie at Dingle in Ireland. 'He soon came over to me and watched me very intently under water. Unfortunately I couldn't enter wholeheartedly into the exciting mood as my face was burning from the cold.' He nonetheless begins his letter by stating that he 'recently had the experience of a lifetime'.[9] More emphatic is the mother of a handicapped child she took to Eilat (Israel) to meet captive dol-phins. Writing to *Dolphin*, she says that she feels she 'must share the most exhil-arating experience' of her life. 'It has no doubt been said before but I must say it again. Swimming with dolphins has to be one of the most unique experiences in the world', says Karen Steele;[10] 'those few days [in Dingle] are probably the most memorable of our lives' a couple in Brussels told me.

Most enchanted encounters take place at sea, either with solitary or truly wild dolphins. 'Two years ago, I had the great privilege of swimming with a group of bottlenose dolphins near Coffs Harbour', writes Rita to the *Australian Dolphin and Whale Journal*.[11] 'This powerful, yet gentle creature towed me around as I held on his dorsal fin. He then allowed me to stroke and tickle him as I admired his beauty ... I will never forget the feeling of euphoria as I swam and frolicked with these magnificent sea creatures and for this I thank them.' Uncommon euphoria, happiness, beauty and love – these are what the human being sees and feels when meeting friendly dolphins at sea. The experience may be intimate and soft or more active, but it is always embedded in powerful emotions. For Karen Steele, who found herself in the middle of a dolphin pod, the experience was full of sweetness:

There I was with dolphins above me, beneath me and all around me ... I was so exhilarated I felt I could leap as high as the Dusky dolphins, who are renowned for their acrobatics, and I think perhaps I even tried. I felt like a child in a snowstorm of sweets, with dolphins as far as I could see.[12]

When the experience is a success (i.e. when some enchantment is at work), the human being is generally surprised by the upsurge of emotions he had rarely, if ever, experienced before. As a photographer, Michael McIntyre has spent a lot of time travelling and searching for dolphins. On one particular morning on an Ulludulla beach he was contemplating the surf when, to his right, appeared a pod of dolphins:

Without even thinking I was paddling out to them ... What happened in the next 30 minutes reduced me to tears. As they reached me, I was struck by their size and blackness, overwhelmed by their mastery in the water ... The air was alive with activity and love. Two smaller dolphins swam slowly towards me, stopped for what seemed like 10 minutes to check me out, then disappearing at breakneck speed.[13]

Some people feel they will never be the same again after their encounter with a dolphin. 'I am writing to you as a changed person!' These are the words of Aimée Skerrat, who has swum with Freddie. 'Have you swum with a friendly dolphin?' asks Kate Carr in a poem.[14] She has. 'And my life will never – I know full well – be the same again.' For the anorexic girl Jemina Biggs, meeting Dorad proved to be the first step towards recovery. 'I am still fighting to extricate myself from the grasp [of anorexia] but I am convinced that the reason I continue to fight it after nearly seven years, and have not given in to it, is that I have been swimming with a wild dolphin'.[15] This is what happened:

Dorad approached me from behind and below. Slowly and gently he nudged my feet, then my knees, then my stomach, and then he swam up to within six inches of my face.

Turning to the side to look into my face with one eye he then gazed deliberately into my eyes. There was nowhere to hide. This wild creature was looking not at my body nor even at my expression, but right at the pain in my soul ... Dorad taught me how to look at and truly face my pain.

Many people report that their lives have been changed by their encounters with dolphins. 'I have been unwell for 7/8 years', says Wendy Huntingdon, an English woman who has suffered from bouts of depression since her early twenties. 'Last year I sought the help of people in the fields of various natural therapies and the culmination was the dolphin trip this year ... Since my return, I feel lighter, have more energy ... I feel in love with the universe'.[16] In some extreme cases, people divorce, change jobs or go and live abroad. Many associations are indeed set up by individuals who, after their encounter with a dolphin, feel an urge to *do* something. That is what happened to Horace Dobbs.

A former physician, Dobbs once had a great experience with a dolphin at sea. Years later, we find him taking depressed persons to solitary dolphins around Great Britain. The way he tells the story of Bill, an Englishman who has suffered from deep depression for years, is a digest of many dolphin stories:

> The next day, in the company of Tricia Kirkman, who was totally under the spell of the dolphin Simo,[17] we took 52 year old Bill to see the dolphin. Tricia told him of her experiences with Simo and how the dolphin wouldn't harm him if he got in the water. She told him how she experienced a great feeling of what she described as 'pure love' coming from Simo when she was with him. Furthermore, she explained how the dolphin reacted to what people feel inside. It did not matter in physical terms whether they were fat or thin, old or young, ugly or beautiful, rich or poor. If they were gentle and sensitive inside, the dolphin would respond accordingly. The dolphin would not judge them by human standards, but by the standards of an intelligent being without possessions living in harmony with the environment. When Bill goes into the water, 'the dolphin loves him. As we watched the man change from being apprehensive, scared and withdrawn to a smiling, joyous person who became totally involved with the dolphin and forgot everyone and everything around him. 'He has blossomed – just like a sunflower', Tricia commented to me.[18]

Well aware of the impossibility of taking many patients out to sea to meet a dolphin, Horace Dobbs later undertook 'Operation Sunflower', an investigation of how to 'capture the essential emotion-changing quality that dolphins have onto film and music'.

The stories told here are not isolated ones. Many people experienced some kind of 'magical moment' with dolphins. But not all dolphin encounters are enchanted. Some people hunt dolphins, others work with them at aquariums, and many people enter into some form of contact with dolphins when attending shows at sea parks.

**Figure 10.1** Swimming with Dolphins.

Very few of them come back 'changed' after their visit. They have not discovered anything new about themselves, they have not learned anything of profound urgency. Here the figure of the human–animal interaction is a redundant one, as it has been patterned by a century of zoo visits. No revelation at the zoo visit, no elation, no euphoria. But even at sea, many dolphin encounters are not enchanted. One afternoon in November 1996 in Nuweba, a small Bedouin location on the Red Sea in Egypt, a dozen people had the privilege of swimming with Oline, the friendly female dolphin who has stayed there since the early 1990s. There were women, children and men, tourists coming from occidental countries brought there by some local tour operator. Only one of them, a young French man, got out of the water shouting his happiness: 'C'est fabuleux! formidable! …' He did not want it to stop and spent a long, long time in the water. The others were getting impatient with him, waiting for him so that they could go back to their hotel. For me, swimming with Oline had been a nice moment, not much more. She was a nice, indolent animal, but I had not read anything special in her eyes.

As it is obvious that not all dolphin encounters are enchanted, the question arises as to what the ingredients of the enchantment effect are. What must happen if the human being is to learn something about himself or herself from the contact with the animal? What kind of interactional context makes it possible? What kind of signals are emitted by the dolphin and perceived by the human being? What kind of representations help the people to find meaning through the interactional process?

## The Context of the Encounter: Patterns of Participation

### An Inverted Asymmetry

When someone goes to sea to meet a dolphin, he knows that he's going to meet an animal whose anthropophilia has been known since antiquity. One jumps into the water and faces an animal obviously much more powerful than oneself. Even the most accomplished swimmer is a beginner compared to a dolphin. The muscular power of the dolphin, its ease, agility and grace in the water are often underlined by the poor 'splashing around' human beings. 'My senses were fully aware that this dolphin could kill me with one blow – if he had wanted to', said Rita. In a way, the human being is 'at the mercy' of the animal, has no other choice but to leave it up to the dolphin to decide. Moreover, in mammalian communication, the act of showing his/her strength and not using it can function as a signal of appeasement, a message which can be translated as 'I shall not harm you'. In human–dolphin encounters, the whole situation seems to be understood as such a message from the dolphin.

The asymmetry of the interaction (the human being for once the impotent one) is further reinforced by the widely held belief that a dolphin can 'see through us'. As Tricia was telling Bill: 'the dolphin reacts to what you are inside'. Many times I heard that 'thanks to their sonar, dolphins see the emotions of people directly', 'people are transparent to them!' That is what Jemina experienced, and when 'there is no place to hide', as she said, the best action is to let go. Even when the encounter is not as deeply involving as Jemina's, as in the case of Scott, the interaction is the dolphin's, not the human's, choice. This relational asymmetry is echoed in the numerous discourses which say, in one way or another, that 'we must be humble enough to learn' from the dolphins, as was said by Jemina. It is further echoed in most of the (non-scientific) discourses about dolphins (including mass media discourses): dolphins have something to teach us, they have messages for us. It is also in this context that we can understand that solitary dolphins, who stay for a while at the same location near a coast and interact closely with humans, sometimes with one individual in particular, are constructed as 'ambassador' dolphins. When the metaphor is pushed a little bit further, it says that the dolphin people sent ambassadors to the humans because they have important messages to deliver to them. The content of the messages has to do with ecological wisdom and survival.

### A True Social Bond

Another feature of our enchanted human–dolphin encounters is the fact that people succeed in interpreting the dolphin's behaviour as responses to their own behaviour, feelings or emotions. And this is, according to Bateson (1936), the simplest definition of a social bond: 'the response of A to the behaviour of B towards

A'. It is probably in Aimée Skerrat's report that we find the most explicit illustration of a social bond. She is surprised (and delighted) to see that Freddie reacts to her behaviour towards him. She immediately has the feeling of being understood:

> As the shock of the cold water on my bare head and hands subsided I was able to float and look around the water surrounding me. [J]ust then Freddie as if from [nowhere] appeared next to me. I did as Gordon[19] had said and scratched his side. [I noticed] Freddie's enjoyment, as ... *he turned over* on his back right beside me and lay practically motionless *waiting for more* ... The next ten or so minutes were possibly the most wonderful ten minutes of my life. It consisted of me scratching Freddie's back, head, chin and chest and *in return* giving me long rides to and from the boat – pure joy! It was as though he *responded* to my smiles and laughter by flapping his flippers out of the water ... I think also that he understood me as once he gave me a long ride away from the boat and realizing my position I asked him to transport me back and he did![20]

When someone discovers that the dolphin responds to him/herself, (s)he is filled with wonder.

> 'Amazing Freddie', cries out John Nolan. He has seen the dolphin adjusting his behaviour to the cries of the little girl Kara: 'Freddie was having a great time rubbing himself against Dave and the boat, but when Kara started to cry, he instantly stopped all movement and lay perfectly still. No amount of soothing by Dave or myself could calm Kara so Freddie himself decided to have a go. Without moving the rest of his body, Freddie lifted his head clear of the water and tried to reassure Kara with squeaking and clicking sounds. This, too, was to no avail so we lifted Kara back into the boat. Upon doing so, Freddie immediately started his boisterous antics once again, playing ad frolicking with Dave and myself.'[21]

Such bouts of interaction give the human being the feeling that the creature that faces them is a sentient, intelligent and intentional creature. The premise that we are the only conscious creatures on earth is suddenly challenged. This is never as convincing as when the human is surprised by the dolphin, and this can be the case when the animal spontaneously imitates the human being. Wade Doak tells such a story: a male dolphin named Jagged imitated the slow vertical fall of the divers on the sea floor, then their position on the sea floor.[22] Seeing this sequence on film later, a radio astronomer recognized that if such a response had been received from space it would indicate that there were other intelligent creatures in the universe. But for our purpose, the main lesson of this story is elsewhere – because at the time the divers did not notice anything. Ironically, they were installing material for human–dolphin communication (a pneumatic piano, etc.), but as they were busy working the dolphin's behaviour did not mean anything to them. It was simply 'strange'. This means that for the human being to find meaning in the dolphin's behaviour; he must be socially bonded that is, be prepared to see in the dolphin's behaviour a response or a comment to his own behaviour.[23]

When the person who comes to meet a dolphin is convinced that 'a dolphin never does anything by chance', as an Australian seaman told me, and that 'thanks to their sonar, dolphins can read our emotions', the social bond may be constructed (but not perceived) even in the absence of any reaction from the dolphin. When John Bolwell swam out twice for long periods from Amble port, Dougal did not appear. Trying to figure out what could have happened, John Bolwell said that 'maybe he sensed that I wasn't ready to meet yet'. We all know that in an established social bond the absence of a reaction is in itself a response. Inside an interactional frame there is no 'no response', and any behaviour of the dolphin becomes capable of 'telling' us something. The position of a human being in an enchanted encounter with a dolphin is one of deep involvement. Because the encounter is up to the animal (they 'choose' to meet humans), and because human beings are able to perceive the dolphin's behaviour as a response to their own behaviour, feelings or emotions, they cannot escape the conviction that the dolphin is aiming behaviour at them. In the process, people have the strong feeling that they face a conscious, intelligent and intentional animal. The human–animal boundary is subjectively crossed, and suddenly, as in our occidental tales of magic communication with animals, a new world seems to open.

## Play

Another kind of human–dolphin interaction is play. In order for two mammals to play together they need to be able to exchange metacommunicative signals stating that the behaviours framed as play are not 'real', in the sense that a bite is not a real one, for example. In many mammalian species, the signal 'this is play' has evolved by ritualization and has become a fixed display of the body and/or the face. Dogs have a particular posture and display of the face, and monkeys have an unmistakable 'play face'. In humans, metacommunicative signals framing a statement as 'not real' can be very subtle and elusive, but we still have (children at least) the play face of the other primates. We don't know what the 'this is play' signal is in cetaceans. They have lost most of the mammalian means of communication, and we don't even know if they have such a ritualized signal. Nevertheless, it appears that human beings are able to build what they experience as playful interactions with dolphins. As Aimée tells *Dolphin:*

Another of his games was to vanish into the depths for a while and, suddenly from nowhere, spring up behind me nudging me on the way past as if it was a game of hide and seek and [as if] he was teasing me … It was loads of fun though because it seemed we were both laughing about it.

Michael McIntyre was also able to 'feel' play in the behaviour of the dolphins, which 'appeared to take great delight in catching the waves, often surfing straight towards me on collision course only to veer away at the last moment, and often swimming right underneath me to surface 50 feet away'.

## The Pragmatics of Human–Dolphin Communication

In the enchanted encounters, the dolphin 'answers me'; she aims her behaviour 'at myself'. But the self the dolphin is 'talking' to is not a conventional social self: it is a deep emotional self that is only called upon in the most intimate relationships. The emotional involvement of enchanted dolphin encounters cannot be understood outside the pragmatics of communication. Two main functions of non-verbal communication can be retained. First, the interaction could not be sustained without a continuous, two-way communicational process. This kind of communication has been called 'integrative communication' by Birdwhistell (1970: 14). Its function is to maintain the interactional system in operation and to regulate the interactional process according to the timing, spatial structure, intensity and direction of the behaviours. In the case of enchanted human–dolphin interactions, we can assume that messages that maintain the interactional process are exchanged. But one specific feature of human–dolphin interactions should be mentioned: contrary to human interaction, a distant observer does not necessarily perceive the behaviours of the human and the animal as structured in an interactional system. He might merely see a dolphin swimming in the vicinity of a human being, while at the same time this human being is experiencing a close and intimate relationship.

The second kind of signals are ethological signals which can be related to the emotions and feelings experienced by humans. We are here concerned with what the dolphin *does* to the human being, the effect that the dolphin's behaviour has on him. According to Bateson, mammalian communication is first of all concerned with social relationship:

> The wag of the dog's tail which for individual psychology signifies an inner state of the dog becomes something more than this when we ask about the functions of this signal in the relationship between the dog and his master. I want to suggest to you that it becomes an affirmation or a proposal about what shall be the contingencies in that relationship. (1963: 230)

It was Warren McCulloch who pointed out that every message has a report aspect (a report on what previously happened) and a command aspect (a stimulus for the next behaviour). For Bateson, the 'command' aspect of a message is responsible for the creation of order and patterns in interactional systems. It is also linked to the emotions that are released by the stimulus aspect of the message. In fact, Bateson has gone as far as stating that emotions and feelings are the subjective equivalent of patterns of relations:

> In the language describing relationship many words which are commonly used to describe individuals now become technical terms for systems of contingency in the interchange. Such words as dependency, hostility, trust, and even the names of feelings or emotions such as fear and anger, can be translated by the formal characteristics of the sequences in which they occur. (1963: 130)

## Eye contact

'A dolphin looks you in the eye' – this was told me in 1990 by an anonymous attendant at the 2nd ICERC Conference in Australia. Eye-to-eye contact is indeed a powerful ethological signal in humans. In most mammalian species, direct stare is a threat and is linked to aggression and dominance. In humans, a direct stare might be enough to trigger a fight as well, but according to Ellsworth and Langer (1976) it does not release any particular behaviour pattern. The authors suggest that stare has the more general function of acting as a releaser for emotional arousal, which must be interpreted or altered according to its context. The signal still has its mammalian aversive function (think of the stare of an adult who wants to discipline a child), but the frequency and duration of eye contact is correlated with feelings of love in courting couples (Weitz 1979). No other human signal is as closely associated with both negative and positive feelings than the gaze. As a sign and a signal for emotional arousal, gaze and mutual gaze must be carefully patterned by cultural rules in order for the interaction to be sustained. Those are the rules governing involvement, as Erving Goffman has termed it. For example, a certain amount (not more than 30 per cent) of mutual gaze is necessary for a conversation to take place between American subjects. In human interaction in public places, visual contact is also the first necessary step towards the establishment of social interaction (people unwilling to get engaged in an interaction bout simply avoid the gaze of the other).[24] Eye contact is probably a powerful signal in human–dolphin communication as well. Besides its emotionally arousing function, the first eye contact signals the beginning of an interaction bout. Consequently, all the subsequent behaviour of the dolphin is perceived as part of the interaction. 'Almost immediately Fungie swam close to me and gave me a look that has stayed with me ever since – a look of great intensity, knowing and acceptance … It was that first look of unqualified acceptance that will stay with me forever.'[25] 'Eye contact with wild dolphins is magical', according to Kim Rosen, a psychotherapist at the same conference. 'I have often read descriptions of the feeling one has when looking into the eye of a dolphin', says Lisa Sill,[26] 'and it truly is indescribable – like looking deep into one's soul; an understanding of equally intelligent beings.'

When associated with positive emotions, close distance (less than 50 centimetres) and eye contact are the marks of a loving and intimate relationship. Intimacy in human–dolphin encounters is also triggered by touch, as it was for Bill:

**Figure 10.2 and 10.3** Underwater Encounters with a Dolphin.

From the moment I leant over ... and put my hand on Simo's head, I was gone. Out of this world. In the water he never left my side. I felt he wanted to show me his world, that he was as isolated and alone as I was, that he needed me as much as I needed him. It was the same with Dorad. He seemed to be saying: 'Don't worry, I'm with you.' So much love, so much tenderness seemed to be coming from him.[27]

But intimacy does not rely only on close contact. 'Being in the pod' is another kind of intimacy which is sometimes offered to humans. When Scott and Karen Steele find themselves surrounded by dolphins, for a while they are suddenly transported into the intimacy of the dolphins' everyday life – a privilege for which primatologists are ready to fight for years if they have to!

### Appeasement Signals

The message 'I shall not harm you' is clearly perceived by the human being who meets a dolphin. First, the animal is powerful and it is obvious that he could easily seriously harm any swimmer.[28] But instead, the animal comes by, tilts the head, and searches for eye-to-eye contact. Since the work of Blurton-Jones (1972) and Montagner (1978), we know that leaning the head aside, looking in the eye and smiling is an appeasement posture from the non-verbal repertoire of occidental children. We find all those signals on the dolphin's face when he makes contact with a swimmer. Even the picture of a dolphin's head is enough to make us feel that this animal is friendly. Oddly, the famous dolphin smile is never explicitly mentioned in our enchanted encounters, although it is mentioned in more casual contacts. But this purely anatomical smile certainly plays its part in framing the dolphin's face as friendly. Smiling is an appeasement signal of our primate heritage.

### The Dolphin's Impassiveness

Because of their adaptation to sea, cetaceans have lost all the classic mammalian devices for social communication. They have no ears to move, no hair to erect, no arms to wave, no place to deposit odoriferous substances, and very few body postures. Their whole body is encapsulated in a compact hydrodynamic shape. This undoubtedly favours the projection of thoughts, emotions and feelings, and it might be necessary, in order for the human–animal interaction to follow its course, that the human isn't disturbed by the animal's expressions.[29] This in turn favours a very focused interaction in which concentration is high. During the course of the interaction, the human perception is not distracted by the constant flow of gesture, facial expressions and changes of body postures that characterize human interaction. Except for a few postures, the communication system is restricted to the observation of behaviour.

## *A Slight Trance*

Through our reports, we can see some evidence for a slight trance on the human side. Many people lose perception of time, others are so focused on the animal that they forget the world around them. One evening, Helen Kay was walking on the beach with her dog Jess. Suddenly, a pod of dolphins appeared. Then they came closer and Helen felt 'an instinctive urge to try to communicate with these lovely creatures'. She then began singing *Amazing Grace* and

> they came in as far as they could in the white water about 20 feet away … I started walking back up the beach and they all came with me, swimming quietly now, but still surfing into the white water at times. We went about 500 metres like that. I was getting bored with 'Amazing Grace' by now and I'm sure they were too, so I tried something different, but it wasn't right – it just did not sound right. Perhaps it was just a coincidence, but at this point communication stopped. It was a strange thing to know that it had, even though they were still there. Shortly afterwards, they were gone, quietly, with no more leaping … I was so euphoric about the whole thing – I don't know how long they were with me. At least half an hour; probably longer.'[30]

Wade Doak had a similar experience. While he was contemplating the sea from a cliff, a pod of dolphins appeared. 'Then', said Doak, 'began the most accomplished human–dolphin communication I ever experienced. They were leaping and surfing in exact accordance with my thoughts. I don't know how long it lasted, several hours.'[31]

In these two examples human and animals are not engaged in true social communication. But the behaviour of the dolphin is nevertheless timed and spatially structured in a way that fits with a meditation state in the human brain. The contemplation of the sea may also play a role in the establishment of a meditation state, and we can compare it to the relaxing effect that fish tanks have on blood pressure in humans (Katcher *et al.* 1983), although the timing is different.

Taken together, the signals that humans perceive favour a deep involvement and a very focused interaction. Prolonged eye contact is probably responsible for an emotional arousal which is affiliative rather than aggressive, thanks to, among other signals, those of appeasement. The pattern of eye contacts is also very significant: they signal the beginning of the interaction and their duration is more typical of a loving intimacy than of a casual social encounter. The impassiveness of the dolphin might facilitate the interactional process, as might high concentration on the behaviour of the animal. The powerful emotions of love, happiness or euphoria previously mentioned probably originate in these very basic ethological signals. Surprised by the upsurge of emotions they sometimes did not know about, people discover a new side of themselves.

## Occidental Figures of the Dolphin

In occidental discourses about dolphins, the patterns of human–dolphin interaction and communication are constructed as special attributes of the dolphins. What is perceived or experienced during the encounter is ascribed to the dolphin. Dolphins are consequently constructed as having special qualities that in turn 'explain' the experience of the encounter. The first of these qualities is the 'power to heal'[32] – dolphins are said to be miraculous healers. Every newspaper article that I have read about children having 'therapeutic sessions' with dolphins uses, in one way or another, the rhetoric of the miracle. One autistic boy gave a kiss to his father for the first time after a few sessions in Eilat. Recently, a young Belgian girl taken to Panama City to meet dolphins was reported to be 'in a remission for 8 months'. The dolphin is always considered to be the one who triggered the changes observed in the child. The animal must therefore possess some kind of 'healing power'.[33] The second attribute is a will to save mankind from ecological disaster. Many pilot whales are slaughtered each year at the Faeroe Islands. 'Why don't they escape if they are intelligent?' asked an ingenuous attendant at a conference organized by Delphus in Brussels in December 1993. 'It is a sign of intelligence', answered the speaker. 'They could flee if they wanted. But they don't. How could they better deliver a message of love to us? They love us and we kill them in return.' Dolphins offer their life to human beings in order to teach them something about love and respect of animal life. If the dolphin is an intentional animal, then not only do people perceive messages, but the dolphins *want* to deliver them messages as well. Hence the dolphin appears as a saviour for humankind. The last prominent figure of the dolphin in occidental discourses is the telepathic animal. 'The communication process will not be a vocal one; enough is known now already to appreciate that cetacean communication is at a mind level', according to Kamala Hope-Campbell, founder of the ICERC, in her opening address at the 2nd ICERC Conference in Australia. 'If man wants to communicate with dolphins, he certainly is the one who has to change, to engage himself in a transforming personal and transpersonal development to try to reach these creatures' world of telepathy', writes Laurent Pommes to *Dolphin*.[34] These three occidental figures of the dolphin can be read as non-reflexive (in the anthropological sense) transcriptions of what is experienced at contact with the animal. In return, they give shape to the encounter and help to interpret the behaviour of the animal. Belief in the telepathic power of the dolphin, for example, favours the perception of the behaviour of the animal as a response to human's emotions, feelings or thoughts and the establishment of an interactional system on the human part.

## Conclusion

In occidental tales and stories, when human beings are reputed to be able to communicate with the animal world it is because they possess 'special powers' or because some kind of charm or spell is at work. In such stories as in Maeterlinek's *L'oiseau bleu*, the human being suddenly has access to a totally new world, a world which s/he did not previously suspect existed. Our 'enchanted' dolphin encounters share some of the features exhibited in this tale. Outside any arbitrary code or language, humans seem to receive clear messages from the dolphins, and they learn something new about themselves. Having related the emotions experienced during enchanted encounters to some of the signals perceived and to the patterns of human–dolphin interaction, it is now clear that what is experienced in the human–dolphin encounter (love, euphoria, happiness) is both perceived and believed.

## Notes

1. Joan A. Bishop, *Australian Dolphin and Whale Journal* (*ADWJ*), 1990, p. 40.
2. *Dolphin* 27, 1992.
3. International Cetacean Education Research Centre, based in Nambucca Heads, Australia. The last ICERC huge conference was held in Paris, 1998.
4. I first understood that the dolphin is truly sacred when, attending a conference in Brussels, I made a casual remark implying that the dolphin *is* an animal. Instantly I was stared at angrily by my neighbours. In a way I had committed the sin of breaking the charm.
5. The word 'enchanted' has been chosen because it refers at the same time to the positive emotional content of the experience and to the charm which, in occidental tales and legends, is usually at work when animals speak to humans.
6. *Caduceus* 8, 1989, p. 13.
7. Solitary dolphins are dolphins who stay for a while (a few months, a few years) at the same location near the coast, and usually interact closely with humans. All of them are given one or several names. They are called 'ambassadors' by the people who believe that dolphins send us messages.
8. *Dolphin* 26, 1992.
9. *Dolphin* 18, 1988, p. 6.
10. *Dolphin* 24, 1991.
11. *ADWJ* 1990, 11.
12. *Dolphin* 24, 1991.
13. *ADWJ* 1990, 36.
14. *Dolphin* 22, 1990.

15. *Caduceus* 8, 1989, p. 13.
16. *Dolphin* 25, 1992.
17. Another solitary dolphin.
18. *Caduceus* 4, 1988.
19. Gordon is the fisherman who accompanies people on his boat.
21. *Dolphin* 25, 1992.
21. *ADWJ* 1990, 42.
22. Wade Doak 1993. *Ambassadeur des dauphins*. Paris: Jean-Claude Lattes.
23. It should be noted that the feeling of facing an alien consciousness might happen to dolphin trainers as well, when animals use the communication system of operant conditioning to 'question' the trainer about what they are exactly supposed to do. Karen Pryor (1986) gives several examples of such two-way human–animal communication.
24. For a review of visual interaction see Cook (1979).
25. Sarah Anderson, *ADWJ* 1990, p. 7.
26. *ADWJ* 1990, p. 40.
27. *Caduceus* 4, 1988.
28. It happens sometimes. We know of three recent reports. One in captivity where an orca forced one of her trainers to stay beneath the surface, resulting in drowning; another one at the Canary Islands, where a pilot whale almost did the same to a woman being filmed by her husband; a third one in Mexico, where a man was killed by a solitary dolphin he had tormented.
29. The projection goes, of course, as far as gross perceptive distortions. Many people see a joyous welcome when a dolphin opens his jaws at them, a signal which is in fact a threat.
30. *ADWJ* 1990, p. 19.
31. Doak (1993: 187).
32. Cf. Cochrane and Callen (1992).
33. Cf. Servais (1999a, 1999b).
34. *Dolphin* 27, 1992.

# References

Bateson, G. (1936), *Naven: A Survey of the Problems Suggested by a Composite Picture of the Culture of a New Guinea Tribe Drawn from Three Points of View*. Cambridge: Cambridge University Press.

Bateson, G. (1963), 'A Social Scientist Views the Emotions', in P. H. Knapp (ed.), *Expression of the Emotions in Man*. New York. International Universities Press.

Birdwhistell, R. (1970), 'The Age of a Baby', in *Kinesics and Context*. Philadelphia: University of Pennsylvania Press, 11–23.

Blurton-Jones, N. G. (1972), 'Non-Verbal Communication in Children', in R.

Hinde (ed.), *Non-Verbal Communication*. Cambridge: Cambridge University Press.

Cochrane, A. and K. Callen (1992), *Dolphins and Their Power to Heal*. London: Bloomsbury Publishing Limited.

Cook, M. (1979), 'Gaze and Mutual Gaze in Social Encounters', in S. Weitz (ed.), *Nonverbal Communication*. New York. Oxford University Press.

Ellsworth, P. and E. T. Langer (1976), 'Staring and Approach: An Interpretation of the Stare as a Nonspecific Activator'. *Journal of Personality and Social Psychology* 21: 302–11.

Ingold, T. (ed.) (1988), *What is an Animal?* London: Unwin Hyman.

Katcher A., E. Friedman, A. Beck and J. Lynch (1983), 'Looking, Talking and Blood Pressure: The Physiological Consequences of Interaction with the Living Environment', in A. H. Katcher and A. M. Beck (eds), *New Perspectives on Our Lives with Companion Animals*. Philadelphia: University of Pennsylvania Press.

Latour, B. (1997), *Nous n'avons jamais été modernes*. Paris: La découverte.

Montagner, H. (1978), *L'enfant et la communication*. Paris: Stock.

Pryor, K. (1986). 'Reinforcement Training as Interspecies Communication', in R. J. Shusterman, J. A. Thomas and F. G. Woods (eds), *Dolphin Cognition and Behavior: A Comparative Approach*. Hillsdale, NJ: Lawrence Erlbaum Associates.

Servais, V. (1999a), 'Context Embodiment in Zootherapy: The Case of the Autidolfijn Project'. *Anthrozöos* 12(1): 5–15.

Servais, V. (1999b), 'Enquête sur le "pouvoir thérapeutique" du dauphin'. *Gradhiva* 25: 92–105.

Weitz, S. (1979), 'Facial Expression and Visual Interaction', in S. Weitz (ed.), *Nonverbal Communication*. New York: Oxford University Press.

# –11–

## Feeding Mr Monkey: Cross-species Food 'Exchange' in Japanese Monkey Parks

### *John Knight*

### Introduction

*Saruyama* or 'monkey mountains' are popular visitor attractions in Japan. These parks are open areas, often scenically located, where free-ranging troops of indigenous macaques (*Macaca fuscata*) can be viewed by the paying public. Many of the parks are formally known as *shizen dōbutsuen* or 'natural zoos' (as well as *yaen kōen* or 'wild monkey parks'), but they do not 'keep' the animals in the way that zoos keep animals. Instead of physical confinement, the park authorities control the movements of the monkeys by means of regular provisioning at a fixed site within the park where the monkeys can be easily observed. The parks do not own the monkeys, but simply take advantage of their presence, which is manipulated by the use of the food handouts made at a number of set feeding times during the day. In addition to these feeding times, when the whole monkey troop is fed en masse by the park staff, the parks allow the public to feed the monkeys, a practice known as *esayari*. In many respects, *esayari* is the main attraction of the *saruyama*, advertised as an opportunity for visitors to interact directly and intimately with the monkeys. The feeding of animals is widespread in Japan, and is directed to a range of animals including pigeons, carp and deer, as well as monkeys. But what is said to give *esayari* in the monkey park a special appeal is that when visitors give food to them the monkeys receive this food by hand. In other words, in contrast to the distanced observation of the zoo, the *saruyama* offers visitors the chance to enter into a kind of food exchange with monkeys.

This chapter focuses on visitor feeding of monkeys as the principal form of claimed human–monkey intimacy in the *saruyama*. I examine the *esayari* interaction by tracing the different perspectives of the two parties – human and monkey – to it. First, I consider why *esayari* is understood as intimacy on the human side. After looking at some of the social anthropological literature on the symbolism of food exchange, I describe actual *esayari* interactions, using my own ethnographic observations from a number of the parks. I then draw on the work of primatologists to trace the monkey perspective on this interaction in an effort to account for the discrepancy between the ideal of *esayari* as a kind of cross-species contact and the actuality of monkey aggression and violence. The following discussion is based on visits to monkey parks between 1997 and 2003, including Hagachizaki in Izu, Shizuoka Prefecture; Iwatayama in Arashiyama, Kyoto Prefecture; Isegatani in Tsubaki, Wakayama Prefecture; Funakoshiyama in Hyōgo Prefecture; Awajishima in Hyōgo Prefecture; Chōshikei on Shōdoshima, and Takasakiyama in Oita Prefecture.

## Food Exchange and Personhood

Anthropologists have long recognized the importance of exchange and reciprocity to full human status. For Claude Lévi-Strauss, exchange behaviour was a critical part of the transition from a nature to culture and the emergence of a full human status (Lévi-Strauss 1970: Ch. 5). The ability to engage in exchange behaviour is often seen as a condition of inclusion in the moral community of persons. Food exchange tends to have a special character in this context because of the symbolic value of food. The giving of food to others can take on strong nurturant associations:

> Food is life-giving, urgent, ordinarily symbolic of hearth and home, if not of mother. By comparison with other stuff, food is more readily, or more necessarily shared … Food dealings are a delicate barometer, a ritual statement as it were, of social relations, and food is thus employed instrumentally as a starting, a sustaining, or a destroying mechanism of sociability … (Sahlins 1974: 215)

The giving and receiving of food is an important symbolic act. As an expression of generosity or hospitality, food-giving may be deemed a key attribute of moral personhood (Munn 1986: Ch. 3). Food exchanges 'develop and express bonds of solidarity and alliance' and are often 'parallel to exchanges of sociality' (Meigs 1997: 103). Food-giving thus creates obligations between giver and receiver and serves to demarcate social boundaries (Young 1971: 40–1; Dietler 2001: 88–90). The offering of food is an important means of creating amicable relations with strangers or outsiders, and a means of forging social alliances (Sahlins 1974: 216; Carsten 1997: 128).

In Japan, as elsewhere, food-giving is an important medium of communication and the food gift a key symbol of social intimacy. Three motifs of food-giving or sharing can be identified in Japanese society. First and foremost, food-sharing is associated with the family. The daily commensality of the family meal – conventionally, a rice-based meal – is an important expression of family unity. A second kind of food-giving in Japan has to do with the management of social relationships and networks through consecutive exchanges. Food gifts help to maintain good relations with relatives, friends, and neighbours. There are many different kinds of food gifts and occasions of food-giving, including the twice-yearly gift-giving seasons of *ochūgen* (mid-year) and *oseibo* (end of year), the *miyage* souvenir one buys on holiday for friends and neighbours back home (which is usually a food gift), and the regular offerings of home-grown fruit and vegetables or home-made pickles among neighbours and friends. A third kind of food-giving is what might be called compassionate food-giving, which is directed at those in need or in a state of dependence, such as monks, beggars, or those who are handicapped in some way. It is a pure gift in the sense that, in contrast to gifts to social equals, this kind of gift carries little or no expectation of a return. The offering of food to the hungry is also an expression of the normative moral qualities of the social person such as kindness and generosity. The act of compassionate giving to the needy is important in Japanese Buddhism, representing virtuous behaviour for which the giver acquires *kudoku* or merit.

These exchanges are morally predicated with respect both to the giver and the receiver. The recognition and acceptance of one's obligations to benefactors is a basic feature of moral personhood in Japan. A variety of Japanese words express this notion of obligation or indebtedness to others, including *giri* and *on*. *On* is of particular importance. '*On* is a debt intrinsically beyond repayment, but which the debtor must nonetheless repay as much as possible, by gratitude (*kansha*) at the least. *On*, as much as seniority, characterizes the relation of child to parent, from whom he had received existence' (Guthrie 1988: 43). But it also extends to ancestors. 'The unrepayable *on* of children to parents transcends death and is owed by all descendants to all household ancestors' (ibid.: 43). In Japan people who lack a sense of *on* – who are *onshirazu* or 'ignorant of obligation' – are deemed to be morally defective. But the morality of *on* is not confined to interactions with other people. 'There is also a Buddhist idea of the *on* that one owes to all beings of the six planes of existence – *shujo no on*' (Smith 1974: 132). The source of *on*, while centred on the family and ancestors, potentially extends 'to a countless number of benefactors' (Lebra 1986: 359). Gratitude for existence should be directed to those other sentient beings which give up their lives in the course of human existence. Now the moral capacity of accepting or recognizing *on* is sometimes seen as exclusive to humans. Humans incur *on*, but animals do not. Guthrie writes that '[t]he gratitude associated with it [*on*] is sometimes said to separate humans from animals' (Guthrie 1988: 43). However, the situation is not quite as clear cut as this suggests because there is also a long-standing tendency for people to attribute feelings of *on* indebtedness and gratitude to animals.

Folklore is one area in which this is evident. In Japanese folktales animals are often depicted as grateful and dutiful and as reciprocating human kindness or compassion shown to them. The theme of reciprocity between people and animals is prominent in Japanese myths and folktales, featuring a variety of animals including wolves, dogs and cats (Nomoto 1990: 65–6; Saitō 1983; Hiraiwa 1983: 88–96).[1] The monkey too appears as a grateful animal in Japanese folklore. A monkey suffering from severe stomach pains is cured by the medicine offered by a traveller on a mountain path; later that night the traveller, sleeping in a mountain shrine, is saved from a snake by the monkey (Inada 1994: 395). Another example of this grateful monkey motif is the tale of the poor man who saves a monkey from the hunter's bullet and is rewarded by becoming wealthy (ibid.). Other variants include the monkey being stuck between the branches of a tree, having his hand caught in a clam-shell, or suffering from burns – for which monkeys show their gratitude by making some sort of return to the people who help them (Seki 1966: 66; Tokuyama 1975: 122–3). These tales should be understood, first and foremost, as instruments of human edification, which serve to remind people of the proper way to behave towards one other.

Monkey parks have gone one step further than this and suggest to their visitors that monkeys are persons able to engage in morally infused exchange behaviour with people. Visitors have been offered the opportunity to 'play' with monkeys by feeding them, and are assured that the monkeys will accept the food by hand. Herein lies the special character of *esayari* in the monkey park. The visitors would not simply *put out food for* the monkeys, but *give food to* them, food which would be duly *received by* the monkeys. As we shall see, the parks are sites of a pervasive anthropomorphism, whereby human dispositions and capacities are widely projected onto the monkeys (in the form of images of talking monkeys, monkeys walking on two legs, monkeys wearing human clothes, etc.); but the parks also provide an opportunity for visitors to interact directly with the monkeys and to experience the humanlike character of monkeys for themselves. In other words, what is special about the *saruyama* is that the claimed monkey personhood is based not simply on *projection* (representations) but also on *interaction* – direct contact with monkeys. The monkeys are supposed to behave like persons in the context of visitor hand-feeding. There is a sense in which the *saruyama* represents itself to visitors as a place where they can encounter the grateful monkey of Japanese folklore.

## Monkey Parks in Japan

Most Japanese people have visited a monkey park at least once in their lives, usually in childhood on a family trip with their parents or on a school trip with classmates and teacher. But even Japanese people who have never visited a monkey park know of their existence. An indication of the cultural familiarity of the *saruyama* in Japan is that it is the source of a variety of metaphors applied to

**Figure 11.1** The Chōshikei Monkey Park on Shōdoshima.

human society. A prime example is *saruyama no bosu* or 'boss of the monkey mountain', a common metaphor applied to people who are proud to the point of arrogance of their status in their own narrow circle, but have little status in the wider world (roughly equivalent to the English expression, 'big fish in a small pond'). The *saruyama* is also familiar from the media. Monkey parks are regularly featured on television, in magazines and in newspapers. In a survey of newspaper articles between 1985 and 1997, the primatologist Watanabe Kunio found that nearly one-tenth (that is, 130 out of 1,470) of the articles on the theme of Japanese monkeys referred to monkey parks (Watanabe 1999: 200). These articles tended to cover new developments in the park troops, such as the appearance of newborn monkeys in the summer or the 'succession' of a new 'boss' monkey.

Many of Japan's monkey parks were established by, or in collaboration with, primatologists who initiated or supervised the provisioning process, and the main parks continue to be places of scientific observation of monkeys. The provisioning of wild monkey troops for scientific purposes has taken place in many different sites across Japan. The practice of regularly feeding free-roaming monkeys in special clearings allows for systematic scientific observation of a monkey troop to take place and forms the methodological basis of modern Japanese primatology. Provisioning makes possible the individual identification of troop members and the fine-grained research on social relations between monkeys for which Japanese primatology is renowned. But the parks are not just places of science. Most of them are, in the first instance, visitor attractions where the emphasis is on entertainment more than education. The parks are run by local authorities, by tourist companies, by transport companies (rail and bus), or by individual entrepreneurs. The parks are located on mountainsides, in valleys surrounded by mountains, or even near the sea, and many parks are near existing holiday destinations such as hot-spring resorts, from which they draw many of their visitors. Typically, the parks offer overnight visitors to nearby hot-spring resorts the chance of an enjoyable outing the following morning (perhaps in conjunction with a visit to a scenic shrine or temple), before the coach ride or car ride back to the city.

## Visitors and Monkeys

Monkey parks in Japan attract large numbers of visitors each year. For example, Iwatayama attracts around 40,000 annual visitors, Jigokudani attracts around 100,000 visitors, and Takasakiyama attracts up to a million visitors (in July 2001 Takasakiyama recorded its 50 millionth visitor)! Many of these visitors are children, young children accompanied by parents (occasionally grandparents) and parties of schoolchildren. There is a good number of regular visitors among the thousands of visitors to the parks. Long-standing visitors develop an impressive knowledge of the park monkeys, to the point where they are able to distinguish a significant number of individual monkeys and identify monkey lineages. They also tend to have their individual favourites among the monkeys. The visit of a regular tends to last that much longer than the visit of a first-timer. While first-timers tend to stay for up to half an hour, or at most an hour, it is not unusual for regulars to stay for hours on end and even the whole day in some cases, spending their time observing and photographing favourite monkeys or (as we shall see in the case of Iwatayama regulars) waiting patiently at the feeding window for their favourites to come and feed.

When ordinary, first-time visitors arrive at the park and see a monkey, they may well exclaim (especially when accompanied by children) *Osaru-san* or 'Mr Monkey' (though the suffix '-*san*' is actually gender-neutral), a reference to the generic monkey with which they are familiar from the mass media, children's books, and so on. Visitors go on to make certain basic distinctions among the monkeys of the park. First, visitors distinguish between the *bosu* or 'boss' monkey and the rest. *Bosu* is the English loanword which is used to denote the alpha male of the troop. Much of the keeper's time spent talking to visitors is on the subject of the boss. Typically, on arrival at the park, visitors point to a large monkey and identify it as the 'boss', or ask the keeper to verify it or to tell them where the 'boss' is. Sometimes, when the boss is not present, the keeper will try and make the boss appear by suddenly dispensing a large amount of food. Many parks reinforce this popular preoccupation with the boss monkey by highlighting the name of the boss on noticeboards and in publicity pamphlets.

**Figure 11.2** An Anthropomorphic Monkey Sign in the Takasakiyama Monkey Park.

Another elementary distinction made by visitors is between young or small monkeys and the rest. Young monkeys are commonly referred to as 'children', with a variety of Japanese terms being used, including *akachan*, *kodomo*, and *bebii* (English loanword). The words *kawaii* and *kawaiirashii*, both of which can be translated as 'cute', are routinely applied to park monkeys by visitors. Monkeys are also addressed by visitors as children (the suffixes '*-chan*' and '*-kun*' are commonly applied to them). The parks are complicit in this representation of monkeys as child-like. Visual images of the monkeys on billboards or in pamphlets usually show them in children's clothes, give them a childish demeanour, or portray them playing child-like games. Park monkeys are anthropomorphized in a variety of other ways as well. Visitors try to communicate verbally with the monkeys, as when they greet monkeys on arrival and again when leaving. This may be a general greeting of the kind *ohayō gozaimasu*, or 'good morning', and *baibai osarusan*, or 'goodbye Mr Monkey'. Mothers with young children are especially prone to do this. The monkeys are also given human names such as the standard birth-order names normally received by human children: Ichirō/Tarō (First Son), Jirō (Second Son) and Saburō (Third Son), or are named after famous people whom they facially resemble.

## *Esayari*

A key distinction in monkey feeding behaviour in the park is between the regular feeding times when keepers put out food for the whole troop and the visitor hand-feeding of individual monkeys that occurs between these times. The keepers feed the park monkeys a number of times each day at set feeding times. In Takasakiyama monkeys are fed wheat every half-hour, except at 2 p.m. and 5 p.m., when they are fed potatoes. The Iwatayama park has four set feeding times at 10.30 a.m., 1 p.m., 3.30 p.m. and 5 p.m. In Isegatani monkeys are fed by the elderly keeper Itani Kosaburō three times a day, in the morning at around 8 a.m., at noon and at around 4 p.m., when the monkeys are fed with wheat (sometimes soya beans). The Isegatani keeper fills a bucket with feed from the storeroom, and then walks around the park scattering the feed widely and in equal amounts, as many monkeys follow him. In his feeding round the keeper covers a wide area of the park. Monkey feeding times are popular among visitors who can witness the spectacle of the whole troop suddenly assembling at the *esaba* and following the keeper as he scatters the feed. Feeding time creates a frenzy among the monkeys, with monkeys fiercely competing with each other for the food handouts.

*Esayari* occurs between these feeding times. In the early days of the monkey parks *esayari* was an integral part of the visit, unlike the visit to the zoo where feeding, while it occurs to some extent, is officially prohibited. The monkey park was not a place for passive observation of monkeys, but of active engagement with the monkeys through hand-feeding:

> Usually in zoos visitors are forbidden from freely feeding the animals. The reasons for this include that caged animals would overeat and that it would interfere with providing the animals with a proper diet. But despite this, one often sees people at the zoo totally absorbed in feeding animals right in front of a sign reading 'Please don't feed'. But in wild monkey parks where there is freedom [for the animals] to come and go, such warnings would have made no sense. It can be said that feeding by hand is an indispensable condition of people playing with monkeys. (Mizuhara 1966: 7)

**Figure 11.3** A Keeper Scattering Feed in Iwatayama Park.

In Isegatani, after buying the bag of *esa* or 'feed' – usually a choice between peanuts or oranges, for ¥300– at the entrance, the visitor proceeds to walk around the park, giving oranges or peanuts to the monkeys. The observant monkeys readily distinguish between people with bags of feed and other people, and people with feed soon find themselves followed by solicitous monkeys.

Nowadays, it is common for visitor feeding of monkeys to be subject to some degree of restriction or even to be discontinued altogether. One form that this restriction of *esayari* takes is the confinement of the feeding area to a particular zone in the park, usually one that is faraway from the entrance and exit of the park. This is the case in Isegatani, though in practice most visitors seem to ignore it and continue to feed monkeys throughout the park. Another restricted form of visitor feeding of monkeys is where it is confined to an indoor setting, entering what is in effect a feeding hut from inside which visitors dispense feed to clamouring monkeys outside. Nowadays, this 'feeding hut' arrangement, whereby visitors on the inside feed monkeys on the outside, is found in many parks, including Iwatayama, Funakoshiyama, Awajishima and Hagachizaki. The arrangement allows visitors to continue to have the thrill of feeding monkeys by hand, while maintaining public safety in the park. The rationale for these restrictions on *esayari* is to limit the monkeys' tendency to associate visitors with food to a particular feeding area, and therefore to dissociate visitors from food outside this area in order to stop them from being pestered by monkeys.

Where it is allowed, many visitors take the opportunity to do *esayari*. Usually, people buy only one or two bags of feed, though it is not uncommon for visitors to

**Figure 11.4** *Esayari* in the Isegatani Park.

**Figure 11.5** *Esayari* at the Feeding Window in the Iwatayama Park.

end up buying extra bags of feed. One example of this is the family of four – father, mother, and two children – who come to feed the monkeys but find that their feed quickly disappears. The children, desperate to feed the monkeys more, demand extra feed – and they or one of the parents buy another couple of packets. The regulars, whose visits tend to last much longer, give a lot more feed in the course of an afternoon or a day. I noticed this in Iwatayama. For example, there is a middle-aged Osaka man who visits at weekends, on Saturday, on Sunday or even on both days. This man, who spends up to five or six hours in the park, told me that he usually buys ten bags of feed (at a total cost of ¥1,000) a day. Another weekend regular at Iwatayama is a middle-aged man from Nagoya who makes the long journey from Nagoya to Kyoto every weekend. This man, whose time in the park is even longer (up to nine hours a day), told me that on average he spends ¥1,500 a day for the fifteen bags of feed he gets through. One of the biggest spending visitors at Iwatayama is a middle-aged woman from the nearby town of Takatsuki, who spends between ¥2,000 and ¥3,000 per day on feed (20–30 bags a day!) during her monthly visits to the park.

*Esayari* is often a child-centred activity. Parents encourage and help their children to feed the monkeys. They may physically hold up or support small children to allow them to feed the monkeys. Some parents provide a running commentary as the child feeds the monkeys, with comments such as 'He is waiting for it', 'He's staring at you', 'The boss has come for the food', 'The baby wants some too', 'He is asking for it', 'He took it by hand', 'He is so quick', 'Now that monkey there wants some too', and so on. Mothers often 'translate' the gestures of the monkeys into words for their children. For example, in the case of the monkey with its arm outstretched through the window mesh at Iwatayama, one mother repeated the word *chōdaitte* ('he is saying "please"') to her young son as he was holding the feed in his hand. Some parents fulsomely praise their children for successfully feeding the monkeys – 'Well done', 'They must have been hungry', 'They have now had something delicious to eat', and 'They ate everything up for us' – indicating to the children that they have done a good thing. The achievement is often recorded by the parent with a photograph (sometimes a home video). Occasionally, the feeding goes a little wrong, and the monkey pinches or scratches the fingers of the child in the process of taking the food, reducing the child to tears and requiring the parent (usually the mother) to offer comfort. Sometimes, especially with very young children, the parents carry out the *esayari* themselves in front of the watching child, who is also likely to be treated to a running commentary. *Esayari* can lead to disputes between children over who gets to give what – such as when a younger brother complained that his older brother did not let him have his proper share of the food to give to the monkeys – and parents have to respond by buying extra packets of feed to pacify the aggrieved child.

Park visitors distribute their feed in a number of different ways. First, some offer their feed randomly to the monkeys they come across. This may extend to a feeding strategy of what might be called *equal distribution* whereby, surrounded by five or six begging monkeys, the visitor tries to give oranges or peanuts to *each* of them. There is often an implicit assumption of normative sharing among the monkeys on the part of the visitor: that the monkey recipient of an orange will move away to let the other monkeys have their share. But what usually happens is that the recipient of the first orange stays around for another orange, and then another, and so on. In other words, the feeding strategy of equal distribution is undermined by the existence of monkey hierarchy – because the senior monkey present has priority, with other monkeys either deferring to this monkey or, if they do not defer, being driven away or attacked by this monkey. It is not uncommon for a visitor, feeling sorry for smaller monkeys that appear meek and reserved in the background, to throw them oranges, only to see the oranges snatched by the dominant monkey, or the intended recipient attacked by this monkey. There are ways around this, but the visitor only learns of these with experience. Most first-time visitors feed one or two peanuts or one orange at a time, and this sequential or piecemeal pattern of feeding inadvertently leads to the dominant monkey monopolizing the feed of the visitor and minimizes the chances of the lower-ranking monkeys getting fed. In time regular visitors learn to scatter-feed – to throw a handful of peanuts in different directions at the same time – and thereby ensure that monkeys other than the dominant monkey present also get a share of the *esa*. This may still not succeed totally – for the intended recipient can still end up empty-handed. Moreover, such scatter-feeding, while more successful than piecemeal feeding in distributing food more widely, becomes expensive as one's bagful of feed is soon used up so that, in order to continue, the visitor has to keep buying more feed. The pursuit of equal distribution may well mean that visitors end up spending many times more money on feed than they anticipated.

Second, visitors engage in a kind of charitable or redistributive form of monkey feeding, in which they attempt to feed those monkeys that appear in greatest need. One form this takes is what we might call the *small-monkey preference*, whereby visitors pick out small or young monkeys to feed. This goes against the principle of dominance rank in connection with monkey feeding, according to which dominant monkeys feed first. Mindful of this, park staff may advise visitors to 'please feed the monkeys in turn, starting from the largest ones' (Mizuhara 1966: 6). But in practice visitors tend to opt for the opposite strategy. Thus, faced with a row of clamouring monkeys outside the window of the feeding hut, visitors to Iwatayama are likely to give food to the smallest monkey first – often with words such as 'let's give to the baby'. This quasi-parental disposition to park monkeys among visitors becomes all the more marked where a young monkey is orphaned, following the death of its mother (or, as occasionally happens, has been disowned by its mother). In Iwatayama I noticed that orphaned monkeys attract the attention of regular visitors, who may well endeavour to get to it the food that its lowly status usually prevents it from getting. Other categories of apparently disadvantaged or helpless monkeys – such as those monkeys which have some obvious physical handicap due to congenital deformity or extreme injury – also elicit the sympathy of visitors. But the attempt to feed these low-ranking or disadvantaged monkeys can be frustrating, as it is likely either to fail (the peanut or orange instead being snatched by another monkey) or to have unintended negative consequences for the chosen recipient (getting attacked by other monkeys).

A third feeding strategy involves picking out favourite monkeys. Here we can recall the Takatsuki woman who spends a lot of money at Iwatayama on monkey feed (and who first started visiting the park in 1995). I observed this woman closely on one of her visits to the park in December 2000. Her favourite monkey is a peripheral male called Guransu. As one of the largest monkeys in the troop, Guransu is well-known to the keepers and much talked about, both among keepers and among regular visitors, because despite his size he is very low-ranked and submissive to most of the other prominent males. One keeper, referring to Guransu as *donkusai* or 'slow-witted', told me that 'although his body is big, his spirit is small' (*karada ga ōkii kedo ki ga chiisai*). Because of Guransu's low rank, the Takatsuki woman must wait a long time for him to appear at the feeding window. For example, on Wednesday, 6 December 2000, I noticed that she arrived at the park at around 11 o'clock in the morning, but only got to see Guransu at half-past-three in the afternoon. When Guransu finally made his appearance at the feeding window, she jumped up from her seat, pulled out a packet of peanuts from her bag, ran over to the window and planted the packet through the mesh directly into his mouth, after which he fled to find somewhere safe to eat the offering. She felt great relief that her favourite had finally appeared and she now prepared other bags of feed, expecting him to return for more. Sure enough, a short while later he appeared again, and she made another offering, and a little later he appeared once more. The Takatsuki woman had successfully seized her chance and had managed to get three packets to him. She could now return home, having achieved the main aim of her visit.

As these examples show, *esayari* can take on a moral significance, as visitors try to get *esa* to those monkeys that appear to be in greatest need of it. The offering of food to monkeys may serve as an expression of the proper moral qualities of the social person such as kindness and generosity. Mizuhara Hiroki has suggested that after people carry out *esayari* in a monkey park they feel like they have *hodokoshi o shita* or 'performed a charitable act' (Mizuhara 1977: 17). *Hodokoshi* is a Buddhist term that can be translated as 'alms' or almsgiving' and is used in contexts such as the offering of food to monks or to beggars, a virtuous act from which the food offerer gains *kudoku* or 'merit'. This kind of virtuous conduct is set out in Buddhist sutras which extol the act of giving to the poor and needy as an expression of the ideal of Buddhist compassion. One also recalls Buddhist customs such as *kansegyō* or 'the cold [season] offering rite' (also known as *kitsunesegyō* or 'fox offering rite') whereby villagers put out food for wild animals such as foxes in mid-winter, a time when the natural food supply is at its lowest (Nomoto 1996: 223–4). This 'compassion' motif has also been identified in reports of the feeding of wild monkeys in other parts of Asia such as India (Southwick *et al.* 1965: 133), Thailand (Aggimarangsee 1993: 120, 125) and China (Zhao 1994: 260).

## Monkeys 'Receiving' Food

It is common for park monkeys to 'beg' for food, both from keepers and from visitors. The primatologist Kawai Masao has described the appearance of this form of learned behaviour in Kōshima as follows:

> When the observer puts his hand into [his] pocket to take out peanuts, the monkeys wait, sitting in front of him, taking [up] the posture of let-me-have-some-please; that is, with his arm raised a little, his forearm held out, and [his] flexed fingers pointing upwards. This behavior [closely] resembles that of a human child when he is given sweets or cookies. (Kawai 1965a: 20)

Kawai goes on to describe some of the variations of this gesture in the Kōshima troop: some monkeys keep their upper arm close to the side of the body and extend the forearm out horizontally towards the human observer, while others extend both arms outwards; some always put out their right hand, some always put out their left hand, and others alternate hands (ibid.). Kawai refers to this kind of solicitatory gesture as 'give-me-some-behavior'. He points out that the hand put out is done so as a 'symbolic' gesture rather than a practical attempt at food-getting because the Kōshima monkeys actually receive the food given to them by humans with the *other* hand (ibid.). He sees this begging behaviour as an instance of 'cultural' or 'precultural' learned behaviour and suggests that the 'give-me-some-behavior' manifested in the Kōshima troop is an expression of the monkeys' 'gentle, friendly attitude towards men' (ibid.: 22).

This favourable interpretation of monkey 'begging' behaviour tends to be shared by recreational visitors to the park when they first encounter it. 'Give-me-some-behavior' makes it possible for park visitors to feed monkeys from hand-to-hand, an interaction known as *tewatashi* or 'hand-passing', rather than just throw feed to them. This is important because *tewatashi* is seen as a much more intimate method of *esayari*. In their appeal to the Japanese public, many parks have high-lighted the opportunity for visitors to engage in *tewatashi* with monkeys. In the 1960s the Takasakiyama park lured visitors with the catchphrase, *yaseizaru ga anata no te kara esa o torimasu*, or 'Wild monkeys will take food from your hand' (Sugiyama 1999: 112). The website of the Kawaguchikō monkey park in Yamanashi Prefecture carries a picture of monkeys extending out their arms for food, along with a caption that reads: 'In the land of the monkeys you can give food to Mr Monkey by hand-passing [*tewatashi*]. He extends his hand to say "please"' (Kawaguchiko 1999). A website advertising the Ōdōyama park similarly shows pictures of *tewatashi* behaviour, and even a picture of a monkey eating directly out of the palm of a visitor's hand (with the caption, 'the monkeys here eat out of your hand') (Ōdōyama n.d.).

The special appeal of *tewatashi* has to do with its ability to symbolize a con-nection or relationship between the human giver and the monkey. 'When you feed a wild monkey not by simply throwing it food but by handing the food into the monkey's hand so that the monkey, which can skillfully use its hands, becomes a partner, you can experience a definite pleasure that you have never had before' (Mizuhara 1967: 20). *Tewatashi* is therefore 'one of the greatest attractions in the wild monkey park' (ibid.). Visitors often respond to this monkey gesture with a smile and may well spontaneously translate the gesture as *chōdai o suru* or 'saying please' – that is, 'he is saying please'. When monkeys slowly and gently take the peanuts offered to them, they seem to *receive*. This relative passivity on the part of the monkey appears to the human feeder as though the monkey is *waiting to be fed* or *accepting what is offered*.

However, this 'give-me-some-behavior' is not always as passive and gentle as the above description suggests. In the Isegatani park, for example, some monkeys pinch the feeder's hand as they take food from it, or even hold the visitor's hand or wrist in order to check to see if there is any more food concealed in the palm of the hand. In some cases, monkeys *snatch* food from the giver, seizing the orange or peanut as soon as it is within their reach. The vigour of the monkeys' actions suggests that they are oblivious to the fact that the *esa* is being *handed to* them. Sometimes the snatch is clumsily – almost violently – performed such that the hand of the visitor is scratched in the process, causing the visitor to wince or shout out in pain. Some monkeys attempt to snatch the whole bag of feed. Many visitors have their bags of feed snatched away, creating a frantic free-for-all among the monkeys and leaving the visitors annoyed and upset, not least because they must buy extra bags of feed and start again. The propensity for some monkeys to snatch feed is why, when selling the *esa*, park staff usually make a point of warning visitors to keep it out of the reach of the monkeys. Monkey snatching of food subverts the human act of *giving*, which instead is transformed into an act of *taking* or even a kind of theft (visitors may well call such monkeys *dorobō* or 'thieves').

In some cases, as in Isegatani, hand-fed monkeys actually search the visitors' pockets for any remaining food. These monkeys may well stand upright on two legs to reach up to the coat pockets of visitors. I have seen monkeys pull out a visitor's hand from his or her coat pocket in order to inspect the pocket themselves! Young monkeys even climb up the legs of visitors in order to reach food they suspect is in their jacket pockets. Visitors often react to such behaviour with amusement, seeing it as further evidence of the 'clever', humanlike behaviour of the monkeys. But because of their persistence, monkey 'thieves' can and do offend and upset some park visitors. The following complaint about the behaviour of a particular monkey by a 12-year-old boy (which appeared in the Iwatayama newsletter in October 1985) refers to an example of such offensive behaviour. The monkey 'puts his hand right into the pockets of people. He doesn't let go however much you hit him or kick him' (*Hōbukuro* 1/10/1985)! Some observers refer to the existence of *oihagizaru* or 'highwaymen monkeys' in the *saruyama* that accost and frighten visitors into giving up any food they are carrying (Kawai 1964: 6–7). Instead of *accepting what is being given*, these monkeys seem to be *taking what has become available*. Although visitors may seek to *give* feed to the monkey, the monkey does not *receive* or *accept* it from the human feeder, but *takes* it.

Another way in which monkeys appear to breach etiquette during *esayari* is by constantly demanding more. The feeder, when faced with the outstretched hand of the monkey, offers the monkey a peanut, but then discovers that immediately after taking the peanut and putting it in its mouth (cheek pouch) the monkey puts out its arm again for another. This manifestly 'greedy' behaviour elicits different reactions among visitors. Some refuse to give any more and try instead to offer peanuts to other begging monkeys nearby. Others may give two or three peanuts in succession to the monkey, before they get annoyed with the monkey's relentlessly importunate behaviour. The receiving monkey never seems to be satisfied with what it has got and always demands more. Indeed, the monkey's desperate demeanour is such that it is as though those earlier offerings from the visitors had never happened. The visitor soon becomes aware that feeding monkeys arouses little in the way of obvious gratitude among the monkeys, but instead just an intensified anticipation of further food. In this sense, *esayari* is an interaction that has no natural ending in the way that human-to-human gift-giving does, when the receiver gratefully accepts what has been offered. The gift of a piece of food to monkeys cannot end with the monkey receiving the food; the act of receiving food just seems to trigger the demand for more food. Instead of a passive receiver reacting to the active giver, the giver ends up reacting to the receiver. The initiative lies with the receiver and the giver is reduced to passivity. There is an asymmetry in the feeding transaction: on the human side it is seen as a social act of giving, while on the monkey side it is an extension of asocial foraging behaviour.

Some people respond to monkey snatching by refusing to offer any more food to the monkey: *ja mō agenai yo* or 'right, I won't give you any more!', as though reprimanding a child for its rude behaviour. In this way, people respond to their loss of agency as food-givers by refusing to give any more, thereby reasserting human will in the food transaction. The behaviour of the monkey in this transaction recalls the behaviour of a child who has not been raised properly – and who fails to show proper gratitude on receiving food. Here one recalls the Japanese practice of saying *itadakimasu* before each meal – the word meaning literally 'I receive', and serving as a public recognition of the efforts of the food preparer. In Japan, eating and gratitude should go together, and gratitude for food is one of the elements of *shitsuke* or proper upbringing that parents should instil in their children. Viewed in terms of such norms, food-snatching monkeys resemble poorly raised children in need of corrective socialization. Hence snatching behaviour readily invites the human riposte of refusing to give the monkeys any more food, thereby informing them that they will not benefit from their misbehaviour.

*Esayari* can degenerate still further and lead to violence against visitors. Monkey threats to and attacks on visitors are common occurrences in monkey parks. The monkeys find that aggressive behaviour towards visitors is a successful means of obtaining food from them:

> [W]hen visitors are solicited by monkeys for food, and suddenly see the monkey bare its teeth at them, they tend to be startled, and, unable to refuse, immediately give all of the monkey food to the monkey. Even visitors without monkey food come to be threatened – and when they [the monkeys] do not receive any food they may jump up at the person and even try to bite him or her. (Wada 1991: 96–7)

For one wild monkey park in Japan, it has been estimated that there were, on average, some 300 monkey attacks on visitors each year between 1967 and 1974 (ibid.: 97). These attacks take the form of displays of aggression (mouth-pouting, baring of teeth), aggressive pulling and tugging of clothing (skirt hems, trouser-legs, jackets), snatching objects (cameras, bags, spectacles, etc.), as well as biting incidents (typically, hands and arms). Some people have been knocked over by monkeys – in one park '[a monkey] pushed over an old woman clinging onto her bag' (Sugiyama 1999: 113), while in another park a man was thrown into a pond by a monkey (Ōta *et al.* 1984: 14)! This rise in monkey aggression and violence towards visitors (as well as between the monkeys themselves) is the background to the trend towards greater restriction and regulation of *esayari*.

## Dissonant Socialities

To account for these problems in the *esayari* interaction we need to examine the divergence of human and monkey perspectives. Parks explicitly offer visitors the opportunity for intimate interactions with monkeys through *esayari*. The park presents itself as a kind of playground where people can 'play' intimately with monkeys using food. But the monkey perspective on *esayari* is rather different. To appreciate this, we should recall the social intelligence of monkeys. Interactions between monkeys are informed by an awareness on the part of each monkey of the likely consequences of its own actions as well as anticipations of the actions and reactions of other monkeys (Humphrey 1976: 309). Moreoever, apparently dyadic interactions between monkeys are in fact based on a 'triadic' sociality, 'with a third party crucially affecting what happens in the dyad' (Byrne 1995: 41). Thus when two monkeys interact, their mutual actions are informed by precalculations of the likely reactions of nearby third parties.

This pattern of social interaction has been well documented by Japanese prima-tologists, most notably by Kawai Masao in his notion of 'dependent rank', according to which the rank of a monkey derives from that of its mother and other kin rather than its individual attributes (Kawai 1965b: 70–3). As with many other primatological findings, 'dependent rank' was discovered on the feeding grounds of a monkey park. Primatologists devised feeding tests whereby an orange or sweet potato is rolled between two monkeys to determine which one of them takes it (Itani 1961: 424–5; Kawai 1965b: 68). The relative rankings are sufficiently clear-cut for one monkey to defer to the other, without the need for overt aggression. At first, this food test was considered a simple but powerful field technique for deter-mining the hierarchy of the troop. However, it soon became apparent that monkey ranking with respect to food was rather more complicated than this 'dyadic' test suggested. Although the food test appeared to be an efficient means of establishing the relative statuses of the two monkeys involved, primatologists discovered situa-tions where the presence of other monkeys had a bearing on the test (Kawai 1965b: 69–70). The outcome of the food test tended to vary depending on which other monkeys were nearby.[2] This same principle of dependent rank emerges in the *esayari* context where monkey are faced with a desirable food held in the hands of a human. The begging monkey does not see *esayari* as a discrete, one-to-one encounter with the human visitor, but must take into account the possible presence of a monkey third party. For the monkey, *esayari* is a food-getting opportunity for which it is, willy-nilly, in competition with other monkeys, even if these other monkeys are not immediately present.

In fact, as a human–monkey interaction, *esayari* becomes even more complicated, as there are *two* kinds of third party – monkey *and* human. At times of *esayari*, monkeys must anticipate the responses both of surrounding humans and of surrounding monkeys to their food-getting behaviour. Thus monkey behaviour towards visitors is likely to differ depending on whether keepers are nearby or not. Where keepers are out of sight, a monkey may well act more boldly than where keepers are present. This is because the monkey knows that aggression against the visitor in front of the keeper could lead to retaliation by the keeper (who usually carries a catapult or a stick to use against the monkeys). The keeper, in short, is one of the important third parties in the visitor–monkey interaction – and usually the most important human third party, even if the visitor is unaware of this.

As is the case with most other primates, feeding among Japanese macaques is competitive and hierarchical in nature, with dominant individuals using their status to claim access to food. Agonistic behaviour in connection with feeding has been documented even among non-provisioned monkeys in the course of foraging (Nakagawa 1990: 27; Saito 1996: 977). But research findings suggest that over time provisioning exacerbates the tendency in Japanese macaques towards agonistic and aggressive behaviour and increases the influence of dominance rank on feeding behaviour (Mori 1977; Furuichi 1984: 115–17; Sugiyama 1992). This is because of the greater spatial concentration of provisioned monkeys. The pattern of mutual avoidance through inter-individual spacing that obtains under conditions of natural foraging breaks down in the provisioning site where the density of monkeys greatly increases (Imakawa 1988: 493). It is widely recognized that provisioning, by concentrating monkeys around a food source, intensifies feeding competition and is a source of 'social stress' (Lyles and Dobson 1988: 168), and that provisioned monkey populations experience significant 'crowding effects' (Paul and Kuester 1988: 219). Indeed, in his Kōshima study Mori concludes that '[t]he high frequencies of aggressive interactions ... were caused by the overcrowding of monkeys in the feeding area' (1977: 346). In the feeding station the nearby presence of higher-ranking monkeys requires a monkey to forgo a food-getting opportunity.

Thus one cause of monkey aggression derives from the concentrated conditions of the monkey park. But on top of this, there are reasons to believe that *esayari* itself can also lead to greater monkey aggression. One reason has to do with the provocative character of visitors' proximity to the monkeys. In many cases, visitors stare at the monkeys as they hold out food for them, something that tends to elicit monkey mouth-pouting and the baring of teeth. Other provocations that arise during *esayari* are when visitors attempt to touch the monkey or when visitors tease monkeys by pretending to offer the food, but then withdraw it. But perhaps the main reason for increased aggression has to do with the way that visitor *esayari* tends to exacerbate monkey crowding. When keepers dispense feed at feeding time, they scatter large amounts of feed over a wide area (in a conscious effort – albeit not always that successful – to mitigate the crowding effect). But when a single visitor with a single bag of feed attracts the attention of a large number of monkeys, the concentration effect becomes much more extreme.

Among Japanese macaques there is an efficient avoidance mechanism whereby subordinate monkeys leave when dominant monkeys approach (Chaffin *et al*. 1995: 109–11). The approach of a dominant individual triggers the withdrawal of the subordinate individual, resulting in spatial displacement rather than overt aggression (Aureli *et al*. 1992: 150). But where, for one reason or another, this withdrawal of the subordinate monkey does not occur, the dominant monkey may opt to 'escalate' the interaction into aggression (ibid.: 153). The dynamics of *esayari* tend to undermine this avoidance mechanism. One reason for this has to do with the food offered. It has been reported that aggression tends to be greater among Japanese macaques in feeding situations involving 'competition over a very desirable food item distributed in small quantities and therefore rapidly exhausted', such as provisioned foods as opposed to natural forage (ibid.: 151–3). The question arises as to why a subordinate monkey would not withdraw. One factor is where it attaches great value to the food in question (ibid.). Another factor may be the apparent ease of obtaining the food. When, in the context of *esayari*, a visitor *offers* the food to a subordinate monkey, or in some other way draws out the interaction with that monkey, one would expect the mechanism of spatial displacement to be hindered. Moreover, violence between monkeys can occur even after the food has been obtained by a low-ranking monkey. Aureli *et al*. point out that in a situation where a subordinate monkey obtains a highly desirable but scarce food (as is the case with *esayari*, where a visitor soon gets through a limited bag of feed), it becomes worthwhile for a dominant monkey to chase and threaten the subordinate monkey as a means of getting this food itself (ibid.: 153).

## Conclusion

The *saruyama* is an institution which sells intimate contact with 'wild monkeys' to the visiting public. Visitors learn the names, ages, and relationships of the park monkeys. Over time regular visitors learn to differentiate the monkeys physically and to identify their different temperaments and personalities. Visitors can observe monkeys grooming each other, and some visitors are directly groomed by monkeys. Above all, visitors can 'play with monkeys' by hand-feeding them through *esayari*. *Esayari* is represented as an intimate interaction across the species barrier. However, in practice *esayari* proves to be problematic because the monkey behaviour that emerges is at odds with this expectation of intimacy. Instead, it tends to become aggressive and violent, distressing many visitors and creating a major management problem in the park. This discrepancy between the ideal of *esayari* and its reality is in part explained in terms of the anthropomorphic misrecognition of the 'receiving' monkeys as exchange partners, when in fact monkeys approach *esayari* as socially competitive foragers. Visitors are misled by the park's rhetoric about intimacy with monkeys into believing that they are going to have an unmediated encounter with park monkeys through *esayari*, when actually they are getting caught up in the intense social rivalry for food between the monkeys of the troop.

## Notes

1. However, the cat is often represented in contrast to the loyal dog as an ungrateful animal which forgets its moral debts (Hayakawa 1982: 249, 264).
2. This was confirmed in another kind of test – the wheat box test – the results of which also varied according to which monkeys were present (Kawai 1965c).

## References

Aggimarangsee, N. (1993), 'Survey for Semi-Tame Colonies of Macaques in Thailand'. *Natural History Bulletin of the Siam Society* 40: 103–66.

Aureli, F. *et al.* (1992), 'Agonistic Tactics in Competition for Grooming and Feeding among Japanese Macaques'. *Folia Promatologica* 58: 150–4.

Byrne, R. W. (1995), 'The Ape Legacy: The Evolution of Machiavellian Intelligence and Anticipatory Interactive Planning', in E. N. Goody (ed.), *Social Intelligence and Interaction: Expressions and Implications of the Social Bias in Human Intelligence*. Cambridge: Cambridge University Press.

Carsten, J. (1997), *The Heat of the Hearth: The Process of Kinship in a Malay Fishing Community*. Oxford: Clarendon Press.

Chaffin, C. L., K. Friedlen and F. B. M. de Waal (1995), 'Dominance Style of Japanese Macaques Compared with Rhesus and Stumptail Macaques'. *American Journal of Primatology* 35: 103–16.

Dietler, M. (2001), 'Theorizing the Feast: Rituals of Consumption, Commensal Politics, and Power in African Contexts', in M. Dietler and B. Hayden (eds), *Feasts: Archaeological and Ethnographic Perspectives on Food, Politics, and Power*. Washington and London: Smithsonian Institution Press.

Furuichi, T. (1984), 'Symmetrical Patterns in Non-Agonistic Social Interactions Found in Unprovisioned Japanese Macaques'. *Journal of Ethology* 2: 109–19.

Guthrie, S. (1988), *A Japanese New Religion: Rissho Kosei-kai in a Mountain Hamlet*. Ann Arbor: Center for Japanese Studies, University of Michigan.

Hayakawa, K. (1982), *Hayakawa Kōtarō zenshū 4 Collected Works of Hayakawa Kōtarō, Volume 4*. Edited by T. Miyamoto and N. Miyata. Tokyo: Miraisha.

Hiraiwa, Y. (1983), 'Watashi no inu' [My Dogs], in Y. Hiraiwa *et al.* (eds), *Zenshū nihon dōbutsushi 9 [Record of Japanese Animals Vol. 9]*. Tokyo: Kōdansha.

*Hōbukuro* (1/10/1985), 'Saru no miryoku' [TheAppeal of Monkeys]. Iwatayama.

Humphrey, N. K. (1976), 'The Social Function of Intellect', in P. P. G. Bateson and R. A. Hinde (eds), *Growing Points in Ethology*. Cambridge: Cambridge University Press.

Imakawa, S. (1988), 'Development of Co-Feeding Relationships in Immature Free-ranging Japanese Monkeys (*Macaca fuscata fuscata*)'. *Primates* 29(4): 493–504.

Inada, K. (1994), 'Saru hōon' [Monkey Gratitude], in K. Inada *et al.* (eds), *Nihon mukashibanashi jiten [Dictionary of Japanese Old Tales]*. Tokyo: Kōbundō.

Itani, J. (1961), 'The Society of Japanese Monkeys'. *Japan Quarterly* 8(4): 421–30.

Kawaguchikō [Kawaguchikō Yaen Kōen] (1999), *Kawaguchikō yaen kōen [Kawaguchikō Wild Monkey Park]*. Available at: http: //www.ne.jp/asahi/mar/ nuts-garden/chipmun.../yaen1.html (accessed 22 September, 2000).

Kawai, M. (1964), 'Engai taisaku ni tsuite' [On Countermeasures for Monkey Damage]. *Yaen* 18: 6–7.

Kawai, M. (1965a), 'Newly Acquired Pre-Cultural Behavior of a Natural Troop Of Japanese Monkeys on Koshima Islet'. *Primates* 6(1): 1–30.

Kawai, M. (1965b), 'On the System of Social Ranks in a Natural Troop of Japanese Monkeys (I)', in K. Imanishi and S. A. Altmann (eds), *Japanese Monkeys: A Collection of Translations*. Published by the Editors (University of Alberta).

Kawai, M. (1965c), 'On the System of Social Ranks in a Natural Troop of Japanese Monkeys (II)', in K. Imanishi and S. A. Altmann (eds), *Japanese Monkeys: A Collection of Translations*. Published by the Editors (University of Alberta).

Lebra, T. S. (1986), 'Self-reconstruction in Japanese Religious Psychotherapy', in T. S. Lebra and W. P. Lebra (eds), *Japanese Culture and Behavior: Selected Readings*. Honolulu: University of Hawaii Press.

Lévi-Strauss, C. (1970), *The Elementary Structures of Kinship*. London: Tavistock.

Lyles, A. M. and A. P. Dobson (1988), 'Dynamics of Provisioned and Unprovisioned Primate Populations', in J. E. F. and C. H. Southwick (eds), *Ecology and Behavior of Food-Enhanced Primate Groups*. New York: Alan R. Liss.

Meigs, A. (1997), 'Food as a Cultural Construction', in C. Counihan and P. Van

Esterik (eds), *Food and Culture: A Reader*. New York and London: Routledge.

Mizuhara, H. (1966), 'Yaen kōennai ni okeru engai to sono taisaku – 5' ['Monkey Problems Inside Monkey Parks and Countermeasures – No. 5]. *Yaen* 24: 5–7.

Mizuhara, H. (1967), 'Tewatashi' [Hand-to-Hand Feeding]. *Yaen* 29: 20.

Mizuhara, H. (1977), 'Jigokudani – 3' [Hell Valley – No. 3]. *Monkey* 21(6): 16–17.

Mori, A. (1977), 'Intra-Troop Spacing Mechanism of the Wild Japanese Monkeys of the Koshima Troop'. *Primates* 18(2): 331–57.

Munn, N. D. (1986), *The Fame of Gawa: A Symbolic Study of Value Transformation in a Massim (Papua New Guinea) Society*. Durham (N.C.) and London: Duke University Press.

Nakagawa, N. (1990), 'Choices of Food Patches by Japanese Monkeys (*Macaca fuscata*)'. *American Journal of Primatology* 21: 17–29.

Nomoto, K. (1990), *Kumano sankai minzokukō [A Treatise on the Mountain and Coastal Folk Customs of Kumano]*. Kyoto: Jinbun Shoin.

Nomoto, K. (1996), 'Shini no naka no dōbutsu' [Animals in Folk Consciousness], in M. Akada, Y. Katsuki, K. Komatsu, K. Nomoto and A. Fukuda (eds), *Kankyō no minzoku [Folklore of the Environment]*. Tokyo: Yūzankaku.

Ōdōyama (n.d.), *Ōdōyama – osaru kōen [Ōdōyama: Monkey Park]*. Available at: http://www.geocities.co.jp/HeartLand-Suzuran/5009/koti/koti.html (accessed 11 August, 2003).

Ōta, E. *et al.* (1984), 'Arashiyamagun – sanjūnen o furikaette' [The Arashiyama Troop – Looking Back Over Thirty Years], in *Arashiyama no nihonzaru [The Japanese Monkeys of Arashiyama]*. Kyōto: Arashiyama Shizenshi Kenkyūsho Hōkoku 3, 5–14.

Paul, A. and J. Kuester (1988), 'Life-History Patterns of Barbary Macaques (*Macaca sylvanus*) at Affenberg Salem', in J. E. Fa and C. H. Southwick (eds), *Ecology and Behavior of Food-Enhanced Primate Groups*. New York: Alan R. Liss.

Sahlins, M. (1974), *Stone Age Economics*. London: Tavistock.

Saito, C. (1996), 'Dominance and Feeding Success in Female Japanese Macaques, *Macaca fuscata*: Effects of Food Patch Size and Inter-Patch Distance'. *Animal Behaviour* 51: 967–80.

Saitō, H. (1983), 'Aiken monogatari' [Tales of Favourite Dogs], in *Zenshū nihon dōbutsushi 12 [Record of Japanese Animals Vol. 12]*. Tokyo: Kōdansha.

Seki, K. (1966), 'Types of Japanese Folktales'. *Asian Folklore Studies* 25(1): 1–211 (Special Issue).

Smith, R. J. (1974), *Ancestor Worship in Contemporary Japan*. Stanford: Stanford University Press.

Southwick, C. H., M. A. Beg and M. R. Siddiqi (1965), 'Rhesus Monkeys in North India', in I. DeVore (ed.), *Primate Behavior: Field Studies of Monkeys and Apes*. New York: Holt, Rinehart and Winston.

Sugiyama, Y. (1992), 'Behavioral Studies of Japanese Monkeys in Artificial Feeding and Natural Environments', in N. Itoigawa *et al.* (eds), *Topics in Primatology. Volume 2: Behavior, Ecology, and Conservation.* Tokyo: University of Tokyo Press.

Sugiyama, Y. (1999), *Saru no ikikata, hito no ikikata [The Way Monkeys Live, the Way People Live].* Tokyo: Nōbunkyō.

Tokuyama, S. (1975), *Kishū no minwa [The Folktales of Kishū]).* Tokyo: Miraisha.

Wada, K. (1991), 'Ezuke, kyūji no mondaiten' [Problems Arising from Provisioning], in NACS-J (ed.), *Yasei dōbutsu hogo – 21 seiki e no teigen [Wild Animal Protection: A Proposal for the Twenty-First Century].* Tokyo: Nihon Shizen Hogo Kyōkai.

Watanabe, K. (1999), 'Dainibu: gendai no saru – engai mondai to sono hogo o megutte' [Part II. Present-Day Monkeys: On Monkey Pestilence and Conservation], in Y. Mito and K. Watanabe (joint authors) *Hito to saru no shakaishi [A Social History of People and Monkeys].* Tokyo: Tōkai Daigaku Shuppankai.

Young, M. W. (1971), *Fighting with Food: Leadership, Values and Social Control in a Massim Society.* Cambridge: Cambridge University Press.

Zhao, Q.-K. (1994), 'A Study on Semi-commensalism of Tibetan Macaques at Mt. Emei, China'. *Revue d'Ecologie* 49: 259–71.

# –12–

# Anthropomorphism or Egomorphism?
# The Perception of Non-human Persons
# by Human Ones

## *Kay Milton*

In this chapter I raise objections to the concept of 'anthropomorphism' as a tool for analysing how human animals understand non-human ones, and suggest that an alternative model, which I call 'egomorphism', might be more appropriate. 'Anthropomorphism' is commonly defined as the attribution of human characteristics to non-human things (Regan 1988: 6; Guthrie 1993: 3). As an analytical concept in social science, it is used most frequently in the study of religion, to describe representations of gods and spirits. Guthrie (1993) based his theory of religion on what he sees as a 'natural' tendency for humans to anthropomorphize their environment – to see human-like forms in it. The concept is also used, particularly by anthropologists and psychologists, to describe how people understand or represent non-human animals. Here, I am concerned with understanding rather than representation, with the way people think about non-human animals rather than the way they represent them in discourse. This is a subtle distinction between closely related phenomena. I shall assume, as other anthropologists have done, that understanding and representation are distinct moments in the single dialectical process often referred to as cultural construction; but their relationship is problematic, and I shall return to it below.

I shall argue that to use the term 'anthropomorphic' to describe human understandings of non-human animals can be misleading in three ways. First, it is based on assumptions made by the analyst about non-human animals, for which there is often little evidence in the actions and verbal statements of the people whose understanding is supposedly being described. Second, it assumes that 'humanness' is the primary point of reference for understanding non-human things; a more reasonable assumption, I suggest, is that the 'self' or 'ego' (in the general rather than the Freudian sense) is the primary point of reference for understanding both human and non-human things. Third, it implies that people understand things by *attributing* characteristics *to* them. I shall suggest, as others have done (notably

Ingold 1992), that we understand things by *perceiving* characteristics *in* them. This third point locates the argument within the wider debate in anthropology about the relationship between cultural construction and direct perception; I shall return to this point towards the end of the chapter. My main tasks are to explain why I consider 'anthropomorphism' to be a misleading label in the ways outlined above, and to develop an alternative model. I begin by showing how anthropomorphism is used as an analytical concept, in order to clarify the object of my critique.

## 'Anthropomorphism' as an Analytical Concept

Social scientists writing about human–animal relations tend to apply the label 'anthropomorphism' in three main ways. First, they use it to describe the way some animals are represented in myths, fables, stories, cartoons, television commercials, and so on. Thus the characters in Beatrix Potter's stories, in Kenneth Grahame's *The Wind in the Willows*, and in George Orwell's *Animal Farm* are anthropomorphic, as are Snoopy, Tom and Jerry, Mickey Mouse, Sooty and Sweep (see Forrest *et al.*, this volume). Such characters variably think human-like thoughts, wear clothes and use spoken language. I am not concerned here with these instances, since they are not attempts to understand or represent 'real' animals. They are characters created with specific purposes in mind – entertainment, education, propaganda, satire – and in many cases are human stereotypes cast in animal form: zoomorphic humans rather than anthropomorphic animals. This is not to say that they bear no relation at all to the way real non-human animals are understood. Wily Coyote's wild counterparts might really be seen as wily. Many symbolic representations of animals, familiar to anthropologists through the work of Douglas (1957), Leach (1964), Willis (1975, 1990) and others, are based, at some point, on observations of what the animals represented are 'really like' (Richards 1993).

Second, the term 'anthropomorphism' is used in social science to describe some of the ways in which people act towards non-human animals. The treatment of pets is often described as anthropomorphic, for instance, when they are dressed up (Edelman, this volume), talked to, given their own special furnishings (chair, bed or rug) and incorporated into family rituals such as Christmas and birthday celebrations (Belk 1996). Knight (this volume) describes the treatment of monkeys in Japanese monkey parks as anthropomorphic; they are given names, played with and talked to by visitors. Perhaps the most literal form of this kind of anthropomorphism was found in the trials of 'criminal' animals which took place over a long period of European history (Evans [1906]1987; Beirnes 1994). Animals were tried, convicted and punished for crimes against human beings; punishments included excommunication and public execution.

Anthropomorphism as represented by the treatment of non-human animals by humans is also not my main focus – not because it is irrelevant but because its interpretation is problematic. Does someone who talks to their pet, or a Japanese visitor who talks to the monkeys in the park, really believe that the animals possess a human-like ability to understand language? Some appear to claim that they do (Belk 1996: 132–3), but we clearly cannot assume that they do. I talk to my cats a great deal, but it would never occur to me that they understand my words; I take whatever powers of understanding they display to be feline in character. Even the apparently 'literal anthropomorphism' (Mullan and Marvin 1999: 14) of the animal trials may not be what it seems. Beirnes drew attention to the importance of religion as a context for understanding the supposed criminality of animals, and pointed out that 'there is no solid evidence of a general belief that the volition and intent of animals was of the same order as those of humans' (Beirnes 1994: 29). It is possible, perhaps probable, that animals were punished, not because they were held morally and legally responsible for their crimes, but because they were assumed to be agents of Satan, or instruments of witchcraft, or, in the case of animal 'murderers', because they had violated the divine order according to which higher animals can kill lower ones but not vice versa.

The third sense in which the label 'anthropomorphism' is used in the study of human–animal relations is to describe some of the ways in which non-human animals are quite explicitly understood. In particular, it is used when non-human animals are spoken of as if they had motives, emotions and individual personalities, characteristics which I take to be diagnostic of 'personhood' (see Milton 2002). It is this use of the concept that interests me most, precisely because it appears to be saying something useful and informative about the way real animals are perceived and thought about. It suggests that we come to think of non-human animals as 'persons' (intentional, emotional, individual beings) by attributing human characteristics to them. For instance, in two psychological studies, Rasmussen and Rajecki (1995) and Morris et al. (2000) described as 'anthropomorphic' the tendency to ascribe degrees of 'mindedness' to dogs.[1] The first study explored students' views of the comparative mental capacities of a boy and a dog, and concluded that 'the dog and boy were seen as *quantitatively different*, but *qualitatively similar*' (Rasmussen and Rajecki 1995: 131, emphasis in original). In other words, while the boy was seen as having greater mental capacity than the dog, their mentalities were of the same kind. This was described as 'an essentially anthropomorphic picture of students' views of dog mindedness' (ibid.: 132).

In the second study, participants, who again were students, were shown video footage of a man interacting with his dog, and were asked to describe what was happening. Their descriptions were classed as 'anthropomorphic' if they ascribed emotions and intentions to the dog; for instance, 'Dog raised paw to encourage further stroking', 'Dog enjoys petting from owner' and 'Dog is confused by owner's tone of voice' (Morris et al. 2000: 157–9). The authors noted that anthropomorphic descriptions of the dog's behaviour heavily outnumbered non-anthropomorphic descriptions, and that the anthropomorphic descriptions were remarkably consistent; in other words, most participants agreed on what the dog was thinking and feeling.

For an anthropological example we need look no further than this volume, and Peace's analysis of whale-watching off the coast of Queensland. Peace draws attention to the language used to describe whales, both in the literature promoting whale-watching and by the skippers and guides on whale-watch boats. Descriptions of the whales as friendly, trusting, caring, loving, and so on, create the impression that tourists can experience social relationships with them. Not only are whales in general described in these emotional terms, but individual whales encountered on whale-watch trips are described as having distinctive personalities – one whale was described as 'aloof' – and their behaviour is explained in terms of particular desires and purposes. All this is described by Peace as 'anthropomorphic'.

In fact, whales have received considerable attention from anthropologists and other social scientists, largely because of their iconic status in environmental discourse. People who take it upon themselves to represent whales – not only environmentalists, who have an interest in conserving them, but also presenters of captive whale shows and, as we have seen, whale-watch guides – are often accused of anthropomorphism. According to Einarsson, 'One of the most powerful metaphors', in environmentalist discourse about whales, 'is that of anthropomorphism' (Einarsson 1993: 78). He argued:

> an important part of the explanation of why whales are so potent as symbols and why so many find it easy to identify with them is their humanized image. It is the implicit and explicit projections of human motives on to the behaviour of cetaceans which has given rise to a whole body of cetacean mythology where the metaphor of anthropomorphism plays a major role. (Einarsson 1993: 79)

Mullan and Marvin, after describing the 'Celebration Shamu' show at Sea World in San Diego, wrote: 'The whales have been anthropomorphized ... as a creature which shares and exhibits the same deep emotions, feelings and desires of the human trainers and by implication with the rest of the human observers' (1999: 23).

Although what these authors describe as 'anthropomorphic' are specifically representations of whales, I think there are sound indications that they also reflect how whales are understood. Representations and understandings do not necessarily correspond. We cannot assume that environmentalists, whale-watch guides and Sea World presenters really think of whales as having emotions and purposes simply because they present them in this way, especially given that they have good reasons for doing so – to further their cause or promote their business. But the point is that these representations appear to work. Environmentalists have been immensely successful in generating public sympathy for whales. It is because whales are genuinely understood to be thinking, feeling, conscious beings that so many people object to their being killed (see Milton 2002: 32–3, 46). It might be objected that since most people who support whale conservation have not encountered whales themselves they have no option but to depend on environmentalists' representations to tell them what whales are really like. But when people do encounter whales, as they do at Sea World and on whale-watch trips, their experiences tend to confirm rather than contradict the representations (Peace, this volume).

## What is Wrong with 'Anthropomorphism'?

So what is wrong with describing these representations and the understandings they invoke and to which they refer as 'anthropomorphic'? As I have indicated above, I consider it misleading in three ways. The first of these follows from an observation made by Regan. He pointed out that although 'to anthropomorphize' is taken to mean 'to attribute human characteristics to things not human', what it must logically mean is to 'attribute a characteristic that belongs *only* to humans to things not human' (1988: 6, emphasis in original; cf. Noske 1997: 88; Asquith 1997: 23). This point is easily demonstrated. Human beings generally have two eyes and walk on two legs. If I were to say that an ostrich has two eyes and walks on two legs, this would not normally, within the dualistic cultural tradition in which anthropology and other disciplines have developed, be considered an anthropomorphic statement. The reason is that ostriches self-evidently possess these features, and they are therefore as indicative of ostrich-ness as they are of human-ness.

Why, then, do anthropologists and other scholars take it as anthropomorphic to say that whales, or other non-human animals, have emotions, purposes and personalities? Presumably because these are 'inner' states which are not regarded by analysts as self-evident, so their 'attribution to' non-human animals is seen as an extra step beyond straightforward observation. To understand a non-human animal in terms of inner states is treated as implying an assumption – that they are indeed capable of experiencing such states. Consequently, anthropologists, psychologists and biologists who are wary of assuming too much, feel compelled to describe this kind of understanding as 'anthropomorphic' (see Noske 1997: 88–9). Their caution is misplaced, however, for it simply replaces one assumption with another, possibly more dubious one. In order to describe the way an animal is understood as 'anthropomorphic' we need to assume the opposite of what anthropomorphism itself seems to imply. In other words, we need to assume that the animal concerned is not capable of the inner states supposedly attributed to it, and that these are specifically human characteristics. This assumption is part of the legacy of

Cartesian science, so it may well be part of the frameworks that many anthropologists, psychologists and biologists have brought to their work, but there is no
reason to suppose that it bears any relation to the way most people understand non-
human animals. Descartes is said not to have trusted the evidence of his senses.
Most of us, happily, do not suffer from this handicap.

So my first objection can be summarized as follows. It is only legitimate to
describe people's understandings of non-human animals as anthropomorphic, if
those people believe or assume that the characteristics they are apparently
'attributing' to the animals are, in fact, exclusive to human beings. Not only is
there no evidence, in many cases, to suggest that this is so, but if it were many
instances of so-called anthropomorphism would simply be nonsensical. Although
a whale-watch guide or an environmentalist has clear motives for representing
whales as thinking, feeling beings, most people who understand non-human
animals in this way do not have such motives. The most logical conclusion is that
when people appear to 'attribute' mindedness to dogs and emotions to whales they
are describing what are, for them, self-evident truths. The anthropomorphism is a
product only of the analyst's assumptions. Of course, according to this argument,
anthropomorphism can only ever be a metaphoric device, and never a mechanism
for understanding or describing what non-human animals are thought to be really
like. So another way of phrasing my first objection would be to say that social scientists have assumed that people are using metaphors to describe animals, when in
fact they may be expressing what they see as literal truths (see Asquith 1997).

If people are not anthropomorphizing when they understand non-human
animals as having emotions, purposes and personalities, what are they doing? How
do people come to understand non-human animals in this way? Elaborating an
alternative model will clarify my second and third objections to the term 'anthropomorphism'. I shall suggest, as others have done, that personal experience, rather
than human-ness, is the basis for understanding others, and that understanding is
achieved by *perceiving* characteristics *in* things rather than, as anthropomorphism
implies, *attributing* characteristics *to* things.

## Egomorphism as an Alternative Model

At this point I need to draw attention to an inconsistency in the way the concept of
anthropomorphism is used. Although it is most commonly applied to the way
people understand and represent non-human things, it occasionally, and rather
confusingly, refers to the way we understand other human beings as well. So, for
instance, in the rather specific psychological model that informed the studies of
dog mindedness mentioned above, anthropomorphism is the theory that 'the sole
way in which a person can attribute intentions to another animal (*human or non-
human*) is by an inference from his or her individual case' (Morris *et al.* 2000: 151,

emphasis added). This is akin to what Lockwood called 'applied anthropomorphism', which means using 'our own personal perspective on what it is like to be a living being, to suggest ideas on what it is like to be some other being *of either our own* or some other species' (Lockwood 1983: 7, paraphrased in Mullan and Marvin 1999: 14, emphasis added).

It is this use of personal experience to understand others that I suggest is taking place when people appear to 'attribute' emotions, purposes and personalities to non-human animals, as well as to human ones. But to call this 'anthropomorphism', and to lump it together with the attribution of human (rather than personal) characteristics to non-human things, is inappropriate. I suggest 'egomorphism' as a more suitable term. It implies that I understand my cat, or a humpback whale, or my human friends, on the basis of my perception that they are 'like me' rather than 'human-like'. As Mary Midgley expressed it: 'The barrier does not fall between us and the dog. It falls between you and me' (1983: 130).

In order to suggest how egomorphism works, I draw on the work of two psychologists, James Gibson and Ulrich Neisser, and a neuroscientist, Antonio Damasio. If our understanding of others does indeed depend on how we understand ourselves, then this is the point at which we need to begin, and these three authors have each had something significant to say about the perception of self.

Gibson and Neisser both treated perception as a process of information pickup, through which we discover what the world is 'really like' (Neisser 1976: 9). Gibson (1979), arguing against traditional psychological models of perception, suggested that it is not just the sense organs that pick up information from the environment, but the whole individual. For him, awareness is not located at some centre within the nervous system, it pervades the whole organism (ibid.: 246). He seemed to contradict this, however, by denying mental processes a role in perception: 'the theory of information pickup does not need memory' (ibid.: 254). Consequently, his accounts of perception do not describe how people come to know about their environment. Instead they describe the information present in the environment which he assumes is picked up by individuals living in and moving through that environment. Whatever the shortcomings of his model of perception, Gibson made an important observation: that our perception of ourselves takes place simultaneously with, and is inseparable from, our perception of our environment (ibid.: 240). As we move through our environment we receive information, not only on what surrounds us but also on ourselves as physical bodies located in time and space, and as agents – beings whose actions have effects on our surroundings.

Neisser, who was a student of Gibson's, took this further by exploring how we come to know ourselves. This meant developing a model of perception which explicitly incorporated mental processes. He described perception as a cyclical process which involves anticipation and memory as well as information pickup.

The information we receive from our environment generates knowledge which we use to anticipate further information. New information modifies our knowledge and affects future anticipations (Neisser 1976: 20ff.). For instance, a child learning to crawl and walk will gradually explore more and more of their parents' house, picking up information as they do so. They remember the location of the furniture and other objects and use these memories to guide future explorations. If someone moves the furniture, the child's anticipations are challenged and modified, and their knowledge of their home is gradually refined. Through repeated explorations they become ever-more skilled perceivers of their environment.

Our knowledge of ourselves is generated in the same way. As we move through our environment we come to know ourselves in relation to the things around us; we learn their effects on us and our effects on them. In this way, Neisser suggested, we become aware of an 'ecological self', a self that is formed or specified in relation to its environment (Neisser 1988: 37–41). He also identified an 'interpersonal self' which, he argued, is formed or specified through interaction with other persons (that is, with other selves). We come to know ourselves as persons only in relation to others, through the creation, in our interactions, of 'intersubjectivity'. Neisser described intersubjectivity as a 'mutuality of behaviour', which occurs when 'the nature, direction, timing, and intensity of one person's actions mesh appropriately with the nature/direction/timing/intensity of the other's' (ibid.: 41). This intersubjectivity is perceived directly by the participants, a point which Neisser demonstrated with reference to observations of interaction between mothers and infants (Murray and Trevarthen 1985). Mothers and their babies, in separate rooms, interacted through closed-circuit television. The film of the mother's responses was then rewound and played back on the baby's screen. When the baby tried to interact with the filmed image of its mother, the responses it received were inappropriate, intersubjectivity failed to be established, and, not surprisingly, the baby became distressed (Neisser 1988: 43). This clearly shows that intersubjectivity is perceived not only by the participants but also by third parties. The experimenters, as non-participating observers, were able to tell when it was present and when it was not.

Neisser appeared to assume that intersubjectivity can only be achieved through intra-species interactions. He acknowledged that we can perceive it in the interactions of non-human animals (ibid.: 42), for instance when stags engage each other in battle or when chimpanzees groom one another, but he assumed that human beings generate intersubjectivity only when interacting with other human beings. He did not seek to explain this, other than by recourse to evolution, arguing that we are 'genetically programmed' to take 'the expressions and gestures and vocalizations of other people as evidence of an ongoing intersubjectivity' (ibid.: 41–2). This implies that our 'interpersonal selves', our knowledge of ourselves as persons, can develop only through interaction with other humans and is therefore dependent on their presence.

I suggest that Neisser's understanding of how we come to know ourselves as persons is unnecessarily limited. Intersubjectivity can be achieved in interaction with non-human beings as well as human ones. Perhaps the most striking evidence for this comes from those rare cases of human children who have lost their human families and been brought up by non-human animals.[2] As far as I know, the only detailed observations of such a child interacting with members of his non-human community were made by Jean-Claude Armen (1976), who discovered a boy living with a herd of gazelles in the north-western Sahara in the early 1960s. His description leaves no doubt that the boy and the gazelles who had adopted him interacted with mutual understanding. The boy had learned, within the limits imposed by his human physique, to communicate with the gazelles, to the extent that he occupied a place in their hierarchy (Armen 1976: 85; see also Noske 1997: 164–6). Armen himself had to adopt gazelle postures and gestures in order to be accepted by the child and the herd.

Evidence that intersubjectivity is generated with non-human beings also comes from countless everyday experiences of interactions with pets, livestock animals, wild animals, working animals and sport animals, and, no doubt (though they are not my concern here), gods and spirits. One thinks, for example, of a shepherd's interaction with their sheepdog, or a rider's interaction with their horse. This is not to suggest that such interactions are experienced in the same way by all human beings – ethnographic evidence suggests that this area of human experience, like others, is immensely variable, both culturally and individually. But it is undoubtedly the case that, for some people, some of the time, interaction with non-human animals is experienced as interpersonal. Stroking a cat, taking a dog for a walk, even stalking a prey animal (Tanner 1979), can all generate an experience of mutual understanding. Whether the non-human animals 'really' share that understanding is not relevant; it is enough that they appear to do so, reinforcing our sense both of our own personhood and of theirs.

To summarize the argument so far, I am suggesting that our understanding of non-human animals as persons – that is, as beings with emotions, purposes and personalities – is based on our perceptions of them as 'like me', as distinct from 'like us', or human-like. These perceptions arise in our interactions with them, and in our observations of their interactions with each other, in which intersubjectivity is self-evidently generated. They are no different, in essence, from our perceptions of our fellow human beings as persons, which also depend, as Neisser argued, on information about intersubjectivity.

## Emotions, Feelings and Self-perception

We can develop the argument further by suggesting, as Damasio (1999) has done, that our knowledge of ourselves as persons, our sense of our own selfhood, is generated by our perceptions not only of things going on around us, and between us and our environment, but also of processes going on within our own bodies. Damasio developed a model of the role of emotions and feelings in the emergence of self-consciousness which is worth describing here. His model has three stages. First, external or internal stimuli create bodily changes which Damasio calls 'emotions'; second, we perceive these emotions, and these perceptions of emotion are experienced as feelings; third, we perceive the feelings and thereby we become aware of ourselves as individual 'feeling' beings – in other words, as persons.

Thus Damasio divided what we commonsensically think of as emotion into two distinct phases or parts. In doing so he followed the lead of William James (1884), whose model of emotion has been influential in psychology and is attracting attention from other disciplines. James suggested that an emotion has two components. There is a physical change or process, such as a glandular secretion, a quickening of the heart rate, or the production of tears, and there is a subjective experience, or feeling, of excitement, fear, sadness, or whatever. James argued that, contrary to the popular understanding of emotion, the physical change precedes the feeling. In other words, we cry, and then we feel sad, we tremble and then we feel afraid (James 1890: 449). This reverses the popular understanding that we cry because we feel sad and tremble because we feel afraid.

Damasio used the term 'emotion' to refer only to the physical changes (1999: 42) and, like James, used the term 'feeling' to refer to the subjective experiences, or perceptions, of those changes. What Damasio called 'emotions' can be observed by others. Some, such as changes in brain chemistry and glandular secretions, may be observable only with specialized equipment, but some of the outward effects of these changes can be observed quite easily. We can tell when someone is crying, or blushing, or agitated. Feelings, on the other hand, are entirely private, but because we know what crying, or blushing, or agitation feel like to us we can infer other people's feelings from their appearance and behaviour. Damasio assumed that while most, if not all, animals have emotions, only some are equipped to perceive their emotions – in other words, to have feelings. This ability was an evolutionary development, one which conferred ecological advantage. Organisms that experience feelings are better able to respond to things going on around them. An animal that feels afraid will hide, or prepare to flee, or turn and fight.

But the ability to have feelings is not, according to Damasio, enough to generate self-consciousness. He argued that in order to be fully conscious it is not sufficient merely to have feelings; we need to know that we have them. In other words we need to perceive feelings in ourselves, as distinct from, and in addition to, perceiving the emotions that generate those feelings. This is a difficult argument to grasp because it implies that we can have feelings without knowing it, but Damasio pointed out that we often become aware quite suddenly of what we are feeling; we suddenly realize that we are feeling sad, or depressed, or calm, or elated. And the feeling does not start at the instant we become aware of it; it is present prior to that moment (1999: 36). Self-consciousness, according to Damasio, is constituted not in the feeling of fear, or anger, or joy, but in the awareness that it is *I* who am experiencing these feelings. Self-consciousness confers further ecological advantage. Animals who know that they have feelings are able to plan their activities more effectively than those who do not. We can actively seek pleasure and avoid fear and anger (ibid.: 285). And even when we cannot avoid unpleasant feelings, we can enter situations knowing what we shall feel and having already decided how to respond.

If, as Damasio suggests, emotions and feelings play a central role in our perception of ourselves as persons, it would not be surprising if they are also important in our perception of others as persons. When we perceive the outward signs of emotion we immediately infer an inner world of feeling, and we know from our own experience which signs indicate which feelings. Of course, we might not always get it right – outward signs can sometimes be ambiguous and feelings can often be faked – but we cannot avoid perceiving directly, or believing that we perceive directly, what other people feel. We make the same inferences when observing non-human animals. When we see an antelope stiffen its legs, tense its whole body, and prepare to flee, we infer that it is feeling afraid, and when we hear a dog growling we infer a feeling of anger. We do this by picking up directly information on the animal's mood, just as we pick up information about each other's moods, based on an understanding of how our own moods are related to what our bodies do.

Of course, when observing non-human animals the potential for error is greater because different species have different emotional responses. According to experienced observers of their behaviour, chimpanzees grin when they are afraid or unsettled, but this can be mistaken by human observers as a smile, a sign of enjoyment (Lockwood 1983: 6). But whether or not we make mistakes, we still treat the inner world of non-human animals as available and perceivable, just as we treat each other's moods as available and perceivable. When we see a mother whale supporting her calf to the surface to breathe, we see direct evidence of purpose and emotion – we see caring. Environmentalists and whale-watch guides simply draw our attention to it and reinforce what is, for some of us, as self-evident as the two eyes and two legs of an ostrich.

## Anthropomorphism as a Distancing Concept

I trust that the difference between anthropomorphism and egomorphism is clear from this discussion. If not, it might help to point out that, in order to think anthropomorphically, we need to think in terms of categories. 'Human' is a conceptual category, one in which we place all members of our own species and from which we exclude all non-members. So in order to think anthropomorphically, to understand a non-human animal as having human characteristics, we have to compare one category of beings with another. I have no wish to deny the role of categories in shaping our understanding of the world (Douglas 1966), but I suggest that a great deal of interaction between human and non-human animals is more immediate than this. When I interact with a dog and interpret its behaviour towards me as friendly, hostile, or whatever, I do not necessarily relate the dog's behaviour to human behaviour in general. I simply respond to the interpersonal context in which I am engaged, and seek to establish mutual understanding. If I fail to do this, I might begin to think in more abstract terms about the differences between dog-ness and human-ness, and what dogs and humans mean by particular sounds and gestures; but this is usually unnecessary. Servais captures this point well in her account of human–dolphin interaction (this volume). She points out that 'people succeed in interpreting the dolphin's behaviour as responses to their own behaviour, feelings or emotions', creating a social bond (Bateson 1936). What people experience in such encounters is not so much a sense that dolphins in general are like humans in general (though this will probably emerge on reflection), but a feeling of being understood, here and now, by this particular dolphin.

Following from this, I would contest Einarsson's assertion that anthropomorphizing metaphors reduce the emotional distance between humans and non-human animals (1993: 78–9). Instead, I would agree with Alger and Alger that, 'anthropomorphism is best understood as a distancing concept intended to obscure the real intersubjectivity that exists between human and non-human animals' (1999: 203). By referring to people's understanding of non-human animals as 'anthropomorphic', we are implying that it is not based on the direct experience of mutual understanding, as we assume much interpersonal interaction among humans is, but that it requires a detour into metaphoric thought. As Alger and Alger point out, the distancing of non-human from human animals in this way serves powerful interests, at least in Western cultures. It helps to sustain the myth that non-human animals are not 'real' persons but only metaphoric ones. As a consequence, we can use them in many ways without being impeded by moral sensibilities; we can experiment on them, eat them and use them for our entertainment, and exploit them in countless other ways that industrial economies, sanctioned by Cartesian science, have devised (Alger and Alger 1999: 203–4; cf. Milton 2002: 53).

## Direct Perception and Cultural Construction

I observed, at the beginning of this chapter, that the distinction between perceiving characteristics *in* non-human animals (and other things) and attributing characteristics *to* them, has implications for the debate about the relationship between direct perception and cultural construction. As Ingold (1992) pointed out, the constructionist approach in anthropology has tended to suggest that people understand the world by attributing characteristics *to* things, thereby imposing sets of culturally formulated categories upon what would otherwise be a meaningless array of phenomena. This is probably most explicit in the work of Douglas (1966, 1970). Direct perception, on the other hand, implies that people discover meanings in their environment. Because these two positions appear to be diametrically opposed, there has been a tendency to assume that constructionism is incompatible with a direct perception approach. For instance, Rye suggested that if we apply Ingold's ideas (Ingold being the main advocate of the direct perception model in anthropology) 'we cannot, as it were, any longer be "thinking through cultures" ... about the environment' (2000: 106).

But this assumption is based on a misunderstanding. The implication of Ingold's argument is not that people understand the world through direct perception *instead of* through cultural construction, but that cultural construction cannot take place without direct perception. The logical flaw in the constructionist approach is its implication that the world is meaningless unless and until it is culturally constructed. Cultural models of the world have to be constructed out of something; they cannot be fashioned out of meaninglessness (see Ingold 1992). Direct perception, through which we pick up information about our environment, provides the necessary raw material. So direct perception and cultural construction are complementary processes, not conflicting ones. The crucial difference is that direct perception, on its own, generates a degree of understanding of the world, whereas cultural construction cannot take place at all without perception. At the very least, in order to take on our own culture's constructions as accurate models of the world, we need to perceive the media through which they are communicated to us – namely, other people and their products – as sources of information. And if we can pick up information directly from these sources, there is no reason to suppose that we cannot do so from non-human sources as well (see Milton 2002). In this way, direct perception lays the foundations for cultural construction. Without it there would be no cultural ideas through which to think about the environment or anything else.

There is a further misunderstanding of the direct perception approach. The beauty of constructionism is the ease with which it has enabled anthropologists to address the fact of cultural diversity. The question of why different social groups understand the same world in different ways is answered, in general terms, with the proposition that they each generate and perpetuate their own cultural constructions. As long as knowledge of the world is assumed to be constructed, it is relatively easy to see why the knowledge held by one group should be different from the knowledge held by another. However, if at least some of the knowledge that constitutes any cultural construction is acquired through direct perception of the world, this diversity becomes more puzzling. If meanings are perceived in the world, rather than being imposed upon it, why do we not all perceive the same meanings? Why don't we all perceive non-human animals as intentional, emotional beings? Why do only some of us perceive their personhood, while others perceive their potential as food, or as wealth, in the form of ivory or skins?

Ingold's answer was that perception takes place in the course of practical engagement with the world. We do not simply gaze upon the world, we act within it, and it is the nature of our activities that shapes the kind of information picked up through direct perception. Any particular object might hold a number of different meanings. A cave might afford shelter to someone caught in a storm, or a hiding place to someone fleeing from an enemy; the meaning perceived depends on what kind of activity is being engaged in. A logical consequence of this argument is that people who engage in similar kinds of practical activities will reach similar understandings of the world (Rye 2000: 107), and we can see this consequence emerging in the kinds of generalizations made by anthropologists about, for instance, hunter-gatherers' or cultivators' perspectives on nature (Ingold 1996; Bird-David 1992).

This model accords well with Neisser's understanding of perception as a learned skill. In the course of learning how to engage with their environment in ways necessary for their survival, prosperity or enjoyment, people learn to perceive different characteristics in it. So, for instance, people will perceive different properties in trees, depending on whether they use them primarily as sources of fuel, of food or of building materials, or encounter them as obstacles blocking their path. Cultural diversity in environmental perception is produced by diversity in human practice.

But to place the emphasis entirely on the nature of human activity tends to present the environment as a passive partner in the relationship. Perceptions emerge, not only out of what we do with and towards objects in our environment but also out of what they do to us. I would not wish to say that this is particularly so in the case of non-human animals, for there are many other natural agents which have the power actively to shape our understanding – storms, volcanoes, earthquakes, rivers, trees, even stones (Bird-David 1999). But the point is easily made with regard to non-human animals. A hunter might develop a particularly acute understanding of an animal's agility or cleverness if it repeatedly succeeds in evading his attempts to catch it, while those who give themselves up easily might be perceived as stupid. Whales, if only they knew it, have considerable influence over how we perceive them. They can perform for our cameras by waving their tail flukes, frustrate our efforts to get close, or gently shepherd their offspring to within our admiring gaze. They could, presumably, try to pitch the boatload of whale-watchers into the sea. As a result, we come to know them as aloof, or playful, gentle or aggressive. Such labels can, of course, be used as anthropomorphic metaphors, but for the most part they simply describe the perceptions of one apparently emotional, intelligent being by another.

## Acknowledgements

I am grateful to participants in workshops and seminars at the 2000 EASA conference in Kraków, at the University of Oslo, at Goldsmiths College, University of London, at the University of Lancaster, and at Queen's University Belfast, for comments on earlier drafts of this chapter. I am also grateful to John Knight and Berg's anonymous reader for their suggestions.

## Notes

1. The use of psychological studies to illustrate this point is, I acknowledge, slightly problematic because 'anthropomorphism' has a rather precise meaning in psychology (Morris *et al.* 2000: 151–2), which covers instances that I would wish to call 'egomorphism' as well as those to which I think 'anthropomorphism' properly applies. This point is discussed later in the chapter (see pp. 260–1).
2. I appreciate that a degree of sensationalism often surrounds such cases and that their use as 'evidence' might therefore be regarded as dubious. However, there seem to be no grounds for doubting that Armen's observations, described here, are accurate.

## References

Alger, J. M. and S. F. Alger (1999), 'Cat Culture, Human Culture: An Ethnographic Study of a Cat Culture'. *Society and Animals* 7(3): 199–218.

Armen, J.-C. (1976), *Gazelle-boy*. London: Picador.

Asquith, P. J. (1997) 'Why Anthropomorphism is *Not* Metaphor: Crossing Concepts and Cultures in Animal Behaviour Studies', in R. W. Mitchell, N. S. Thompson and H. L. Miles (eds), *Anthropomorphism, Anecdotes and Animals*. New York: State University of New York Press.

Bateson, G. (1936), *Naven: A Survey of the Problems Suggested by a Composite Picture of the Culture of a New Guinea Tribe Drawn from Three Points of View*. Cambridge: Cambridge University Press.

Beirnes, P. (1994), 'The Law is an Ass: Reading E. P. Evans' *The Medieval Prosecution and Capital Punishment of Animals*'. *Society and Animals* 2(1): 27–46.

Belk, R. W. (1996), 'Metaphoric Relationships with Pets'. *Society and Animals* 4(2): 121–45.

Bird-David, N. (1992), 'Beyond "the Original Affluent Society": A Culturalist Reformulation'. *Current Anthropology* 33(1): 25–47.

Bird-David, N. (1999), '"Animism" Revisited: Personhood, Environment and Relational Epistemology'. *Current Anthropology* 40 (Supplement), February: 67–91.

Damasio, A. R. (1999), *The Feeling of What Happens: Body and Emotion in the Making of Consciousness*. London: Heinemann.

Douglas, M. (1957), 'Animals in Lele Religious Symbolism'. *Africa* 27: 46–58.

Douglas, M. (1966), *Purity and Danger: An Analysis of Concepts of Pollution and Taboo*. London: Routledge and Kegan Paul.

Douglas, M. (1970), *Natural Symbols*. London: Cresset.

Einarsson, N. (1993), 'All Animals are Equal but Some are Cetaceans', in K. Milton (ed.), *Environmentalism: The View from Anthropology*. London and New York: Routledge.

Evans, E. P. ([1906]1987) *The Criminal Prosecution and Capital Punishment of Animals*. London: Faber and Faber.

Gibson, J. J. (1979), *The Ecological Approach to Visual Perception*. Boston: Houghton Mifflin.

Guthrie, S. (1993), *Faces in the Clouds: A New Theory of Religion*. Oxford: Oxford University Press.

Ingold, T. (1992), 'Culture and the Perception of the Environment', in E. Croll and D. Parkin (eds), *Bush Base: Forest Farm*. London: Routledge.

Ingold, T. (1996), 'Hunting and Gathering as Ways of Perceiving the Environment', in R. Ellen and K. Fukui (eds), *Rethinking Nature and Culture: Ecology, Cognition and Domestication*. London and New York: Berg.

James, W. (1884), 'What is an Emotion?' *Mind* 9: 188–205.

James, W. (1890), *Principles of Psychology*. New York: Holt.

Leach, E. (1964), 'Anthropological Aspects of Language: Animal Categories and Verbal Abuse', in E. H. Lenneberg (ed.), *New Directions in the Study of Language*. Cambridge, MA: MIT Press.

Lockwood, R. (1983), 'Anthropomorphism is Not a Four-letter Word'. Unpublished manuscript (cited in Mullan and Marvin 1999).

Midgley, M. (1983), *Animals and Why They Matter*. Athens: University of Georgia Press.

Milton, K. (2002), *Loving Nature: Towards an Ecology of Emotion*. London and New York: Routledge.

Morris, P., M. Fidler and A. Costall (2000), 'Beyond Anecdotes: An Empirical Study of "Anthropomorphism"'. *Society and Animals* 8(2): 151–65.

Mullan, B. and G. Marvin (1999), *Zoo Culture*. Urbana and Chicago: University of Illinois Press.

Murray, L. and C. Trevarthen (1985), 'Emotional Regulation of Interactions between Two-month-olds and Their Mothers', in T. M. Field and N. A. Fox (eds), *Social Perception in Infants*. Norwood, NJ: Ablex.

Neisser, U. (1976), *Cognition and Reality: Principles and Implications of Cognitive Psychology*. San Francisco: W. H. Freeman and Co.

Neisser, U. (1988), 'Five Kinds of Self-knowledge'. *Philosophical Psychology* 1(1): 35–59.

Noske, B. (1997), *Beyond Boundaries: Humans and Animals*. Montreal: Black Rose Books.

Rasmussen, J. L. and D. W. Rajecki (1995), 'Differences and Similarities in Human Perception of the Thinking and Feeling of a Dog and a Boy'. *Society and Animals* 3(2): 117–37.

Regan, T. (1988), *The Case for Animal Rights*. London: Routledge and Kegan Paul.

Richards, P. (1993), 'Natural Symbols and Natural History: Chimpanzees, Elephants and Experiments in Mende Thought', in K. Milton (ed.), *Environmentalism: The View from Anthropology*. London and New York: Routledge.

Rye, S. (2000), 'Wild pigs, "Pig-men" and Transmigrants in the Rainforest of Sumatra', in J. Knight (ed.), *Natural Enemies: People–Wildlife Conflicts in Anthropological Perspective*. London and New York: Routledge.

Tanner, A. (1979), *Bringing Home Animals: Religious Ideology and Mode of Production of the Mistassini Cree Hunters*. St John's, Newfoundland: Institute of Social and Economic Research, Memorial University of Newfoundland.

Willis, R. (1975), *Man and Beast*. St Albans: Paladin.

Willis, R. (ed.) (1990), *Signifying Animals*. London: Routledge.

# Index